College and Career Readiness Anchor Standards for Language

Standard	Chapter Coverage
Conventions of Standard English	
1. Demonstrate command of the conventions of standard English grammar and usage when writing or speaking.	Chapter 3, Part I & Part II; Chapter 4, Parts II & III; Chapter 5, Parts II & III; Chapter 6, Parts I & II; Chapter 7, Parts I, II, & III; Chapter 8, Parts I, II, & III; Chapter 9, Parts I & II; Chapter 10, Part I
2. Demonstrate command of the conventions of standard English capitalization, punctuation, and spelling when writing.	Chapter 3, Part I; Chapter 4, Parts I & III; Chapter 5, Part III; Chapter 6, Parts I & II; Chapter 7, Parts I & III; Chapter 8, Parts I, II, & III; Chapter 10, Part I
Knowledge of Language	
3. Apply knowledge of language to understand how language functions in different contexts, to make effective choices for meaning or style, and to comprehend more fully when reading or listening.	Chapter 3, Parts II & III; Chapter 4, Parts I, II, & III; Chapter 5, Parts II & III; Chapter 6, Parts I & II; Chapter 7, Part III; Chapter 8, Parts I, II, & III
Vocabulary Acquisition and Use	
4. Determine or clarify the meaning of unknown and multiple-meaning words and phrases by using context clues, analyzing meaningful word parts, and consulting general and specialized reference materials, as appropriate.	Chapter 3, Part III; Chapter 4, Parts I & II; Chapter 5, Part II; Chapter 6, Part I; Chapter 7, Parts I & II; Chapter 8, Parts I, II, & III
5. Demonstrate understanding of word relationships and nuances in word meanings.	Chapter 4, Parts I, II, & III; Chapter 5, Part II; Chapter 8, Parts I, II, & III
6. Acquire and use accurately a range of general academic and domain-specific words and phrases sufficient for reading, writing, speaking, and listening at the college and career readiness level; demonstrate independence in gathering vocabulary knowledge when encountering an unknown term important to comprehension or expression.	Chapter 3, Part III; Chapter 4, Parts I, II, & III; Chapter 5, Parts II & III; Chapter 6, Parts I & II; Chapter 7, Parts I, II, & III; Chapter 8, Parts I, II, & III; Chapter 10, Part I

(Continued inside the back cover.)

College and Career Readiness Anchor Standards for Language

Standard	Chapter Coverage
Conventions of Standard English	
1. Demonstrate command of the conventions of standard English grammar and usage when writing or speaking.	Chapter 3, Part I & Part II; Chapter 4, Parts II & III; Chapter 5, Parts II & III; Chapter 6, Parts I & II; Chapter 7, Parts I, II, & III; Chapter 8, Parts I, II, & III; Chapter 9, Parts I & II; Chapter 10, Part I
2. Demonstrate command of the conventions of standard English capitalization, punctuation, and spelling when writing.	Chapter 3, Part I; Chapter 4, Parts I & III; Chapter 5, Part III; Chapter 6, Parts I & III; Chapter 7, Parts I, II, & III; Chapter 8, Parts I, II, & III; Chapter 10, Part I
Knowledge of Language	
3. Apply knowledge of language to understand how language functions in different contexts, to make effective choices for meaning or style, and to comprehend more fully when reading or listening.	Chapter 3, Parts II & III; Chapter 4, Parts I, II, & III; Chapter 5, Parts II & III; Chapter 6, Parts I & II; Chapter 7, Part III; Chapter 8, Parts I, II, & III
Vocabulary Acquisition and Use	
4. Determine or clarify the meaning of unknown and multiple-meaning words and phrases by using context clues, analyzing meaningful word parts, and consulting general and specialized reference materials, as appropriate.	Chapter 3, Part III; Chapter 4, Parts I & II; Chapter 5, Part II; Chapter 6, Part I; Chapter 7, Parts I & III; Chapter 8, Parts I, II, & III
5. Demonstrate understanding of word relationships and nuances in word meanings.	
6. Acquire and use accurately a range of general academic and domain-specific words and phrases sufficient for reading, writing, speaking, and listening at the college and career readiness level; demonstrate independence in gathering vocabulary knowledge when encountering an unknown term important to comprehension or expression.	Chapter 2, Parts II, & III; Chapter 5, Part II, Chapter 8, Parts I, II, & III; Chapter 4, Part III; Chapter 5, Parts I, II, & III; Chapter 5, Parts II & III; Chapter 6, Parts I & II; Chapter 7, Parts I, II, & III; Chapter 8, Parts I, II, & III; Chapter 10, Part I

(Continued inside the back cover.)

Teaching Writing Grades 7–12 in an Era of Assessment: Passion and Practice

Teaching Writing Grades 7–12 in an Era of Assessment: Passion and Practice

Mary L. Warner

San José State University

Jonathan H. Lovell

San José State University

PEARSON

Boston   Columbus   Indianapolis   New York   San Francisco   Upper Saddle River
Amsterdam   Cape Town   Dubai   London   Madrid   Milan   Munich   Paris   Montréal   Toronto
Delhi   Mexico City   São Paulo   Sydney   Hong Kong   Seoul   Singapore   Taipei   Tokyo

Vice President, Editor-in-Chief: Aurora Martínez Ramos
Associate Sponsoring Editor: Barbara Strickland
Editorial Assistant: Laura Marenghi
Marketing Manager: Christine Gatchell
Production Editor: Mary Beth Finch
Editorial Production Service: S4Carlisle Publishing Services
Manufacturing Buyer: Linda Sager
Electronic Composition: S4Carlisle Publishing Services
Cover Designer: Diane Lorenzo

Library of Congress Cataloging-in-Publication Data

Warner, Mary L.
  Teaching writing grades 7–12 in an era of assessment: passion and practice/ Mary L. Warner,
San José State University, Jonathan H. Lovell, San José State University. –First edition.
      pages cm
  ISBN-13: 978-0-13-313635-7
  ISBN-10: 0-13-313635-3
 1. English language–Composition and exercises–Study and teaching (Middle school) 2. English
language–Composition and exercises–Study and teaching (Secondary) 3. English language–Composition
and exercises–Evaluation. I. Title.
  LB1631W335 2014
  428.0071'2–dc23
                                                                                    2013010301

4

ISBN 10:   0-13-313635-3
ISBN 13: 978-0-13-313635-7

To Bennett, Cora, and Rory; Allison, Sophie, Gavin,
and Richard, and all future writing students who will learn
from and with readers of this book.

About the Authors

Mary Warner has been teaching English for 37 years—nine years in middle and high school and 28 years in post-secondary. Mary is a Professor of English at San José State University, where she also is the Director of the English Credential Program and serves as Co-Director of the San José Area Writing Project. As Director of the English Credential Program, she routinely networks with middle and high school teachers in the 33 school districts in Santa Clara County.

Her special teaching interests include Literature for Young Adults and the Bible as Literature. Warner is the editor and author of two chapters in *Winning Ways of Coaching Writing: A Practical Guide for Teaching Writing Grades 7-12* (Allyn and Bacon, 2001) and author of *Adolescents in the Search for Meaning: Tapping the Powerful Resource of Story* (Scarecrow Press, 2006). She has also published numerous reviews for ALAN Picks and serves as a reviewer for *The ALAN Review*.

Mary is a member of the School Sisters of Notre Dame, an international congregation of women religious dedicated primarily to the education of women and youth.

Jonathan Lovell taught English and Composition for 7 years at the high school and college levels before "discovering" the field of English Education in 1977 with a position at Teachers College. He is a Professor of English at San José State University, where he serves as the Director of the San José Area Writing Project and the Co-Director of the English Credential Program. In the former role he co-directs the project's invitational summer institute, where each of the authors represented in this book began to envision themselves as both teachers and authors.

His academic interests include the relation of brain research to the teaching of writing, models of professional development for K–12 teachers, and the "carry-forward" effect of participants' summer institute experience in their school year classrooms. He maintains a blog on these and related issues entitled "jonathan's edutalk." His articles have appeared in *California English, Language Arts,* and *The National Writing Project Quarterly,* and he is the co-editor, with Bonnie Sunstein, of *The Portfolio Standard: How Students Can Show Us What They Know and Are Able to Do* (Heinemann, 2000).

Carolyn Anzia has enjoyed teaching Language Arts at the middle-school level for fourteen years. During that time, she has worked with other teachers in her district and in neighboring districts to align writing instruction and to develop meaningful writing assessments. She served as a department chair for five years and currently leads an inter-district English articulation committee. Carolyn attended Stanford University, where she received her B.A. in English, M.A. in Education, and teaching credential. Since 1999, she has taught 7th and 8th grade Language Arts at Crittenden Middle School in Mountain View, California.

Brandy Appling-Jenson loves her job as a 7th grade Language Arts teacher at Crittenden Middle School in Mountain View, CA! Brandy has been teaching for 8 years and has served as Department Chair of her English Department for 2 years. She received her undergraduate degree in literature from San José State University in 2004, and her teaching credential from the same institution in 2006. In addition to teaching, Brandy is an active participant in the activities of the San José Area Writing Project both as a student and as a presenter, and she has worked as a mentor teacher for credential students through SJSU. When Brandy is not talking about books and writing at school, she is home with her husband enjoying playtime with her two daughters.

Martin Brandt earned a bachelor's degree in English at San José State University in 1988. In 1991 he began his teaching career at Independence High School in San José. There he made the discovery that teaching writing is hard. It took him more than a decade to recover from this epiphany. He joined the San José Area Writing Project in 2003 and has spent the decade since reveling in the professional problem of how to teach writing. In 2011 he earned a master's degree in composition from San Francisco State University.

Maria Clinton has taught at the secondary level for 22 years; she has taught the entire range of English courses, from remedial reading, to English as a Second Language, to Advanced Placement, in addition to presenting at local and state conferences. A winner of the Dorothy Wright Outstanding Teaching Award, Clinton holds degrees in English and Educational Leadership from San José State University, and she taught in San José, California, for 18 years. She and her family moved to the Denver area in 2008, where she now teaches English and works with the freshman transition program at Northglenn High School, in Northglenn, Colorado.

Kathleen Danzey Cohen has taught third grade through twelfth and adult ed and been a teacher mentor. Soon after participating in the Invitational Summer Institute of the San José Area Writing Project. She found a special professional niche–teaching writing across the curriculum. Kathleen has participated in both the California Social Studies Project and the San José Area Writing Project. She also represented her school as the California League of Middle Schools Educator of the Year nominee. She was honored to be the Cupertino Union School District Teacher of the Year. Kathleen attended Gonzaga University and graduated from the University of San Francisco where she also received her teaching credential. She holds a resource specialist credential from UC Santa Cruz.

Brenna Dimas worked in multiple educational roles from a very young age. In 2006, she combined her passion for education and literature, becoming a language arts teacher at Rancho Milpitas Middle School in Milpitas, California. Since joining the Rancho staff she has taught 7th and 8th grade Language Arts, as well as reading intervention and English Language Development classes. Being a firm believer in the power of collaboration, Brenna served as a cross-curricular team leader at her site for 3 years, and she currently heads Rancho's language arts department. She is also privileged to participate in exciting collaboration work as a

Teacher Consultant for the San José Area Writing Project, presenting on the subjects of reading and writing at district, local, state, and national conferences. Brenna earned her B.A. in English and Comparative Literature and English single subject teaching credential from San José State University and her M.A. in Education from Santa Clara University.

Kathleen Ann González started her career as a teacher but has come to discover that she is a writer and dancer as well. While she spends most of her time trying to infect teenagers with her great enthusiasm for literature and writing, she makes time to write about her work and her travels. Her first book, *Free Gondola Ride,* is about the gondoliers of Venice, while her second book, *A Small Candle,* includes interviews with participants in the Camp Everytown Program. She is currently working on a book about Giacomo Casanova. González has worked with the San José Area Writing Project since 1996 as a participant and Teacher Consultant. She earned her National Board teaching credential in 2000. Her first twenty years of teaching were in public high schools in San José, California; she was chosen district Teacher of the Year in 1998. Gonzalez is currently teaching at the Woodside Priory in Portola Valley, California.

Marie Milner loves to teach, loves to write, and loves to teach about writing. She has taught for over twenty years in the East Side Union High School District in San José, California, and is currently teaching at Andrew P. Hill High School where she has been for over 17 years. Marie has been an associate director of the San José Area Writing Project for six years where she facilitates a Professional Learning Community for secondary school English teachers. She received her degree and teaching credential from San José State University and has been a classroom mentor, workshop presenter, and 6-time winner of the Dorothy Wright English Teacher Award through SJSU.

Suzanne Murphy, a native Californian, thinks she has the best job in the world. For 18 years, she has taught writing and literature in a middle school setting within the Diocese of San José. She holds both B.S. and Masters degrees from Santa Clara University, and she received her teaching credential in 1994. Her passion for the teaching of writing has led her to exciting collaborative work both with teachers in her district as well her esteemed colleagues in the San José Area Writing Project.

Jay Richards has been teaching English to 8th graders since 1996 and credits his experience in the 1997 Invitational Summer Institute at the San José Area Writing Project with positively impacting his views on writing about literature. National Board Certified in 2001, Jay has written for the National Council of Teachers of English (NCTE) journals: *English Journal* and *Voices from the Middle;* he has also had one of his articles excerpted in Kylene Beers' *When Kids Can't Read, What Teachers Can Do.* A frequent presenter on reading and writing strategies at the SJAWP, Jay lives and works in San Carlos, California, with his wife of 22 years who is an elementary school teacher, and his three children.

Amy Thompson is passionate about teaching. For over twenty years she has been a classroom teacher, a mentor to new teachers, and a presenter at state and local conferences. She received two Striving for Excellence Awards and twice represented her school as the California League of Middle Schools Educator of the Year nominee. Amy has also been nominated by students, staff, and parents for the Disney Teacher of the Year Award. She received her degree from the State University of New York, College at New Paltz and her credential from the California State University at Chico. Amy currently teaches at Union Middle School in San José, California.

Brook Wallace has enjoyed teaching at Westmont High School in Campbell, CA since 2003. In addition to sharing her love of nonfiction, interdisciplinary connections, literature, and writing with her students, she has served as English department chair and as a mentor teacher for student teachers from Stanford and San José State Universities. She has been a trainer for the California State University's (CSU) Expository Reading and Writing Course (ERWC) since 2006 and has written ERWC modules for San José State's Upward Bound and Early Start programs. She also enjoys presenting to and collaborating with colleagues through the San José Area Writing Project. Brook earned her B.A., M.A. and teaching credential from Stanford University and M.A. in Educational Leadership from San José State University.

Table of Contents

List of Tables and Figures

10   *Keeping Heart: Dealing with the Realities of the Paper Load While Providing Authentic Response by Kathleen González and Maria Clinton*

Foreword

by Jayne Marlink, Executive Director, California Writing Project

When I read the title of this book, the first thought I had was of a compliment Sheridan Blau, the former Director of the South Coast Writing Project at UC Santa Barbara, often pays to teacher-leaders of California or National Writing Project sites. "Writing project teachers are alchemists," he says. "They turn (insert any classroom dilemma or educational bad circumstance here) to gold." The teacher-authors of this book are all teacher-leaders with the San José Area Writing Project, and they prove Sheridan Blau right. Only a group of teacher-alchemists would describe the first decade of the 21st century as an era of assessment; however, they would only do so because they turned a time that was (for most) focused on testing and accountability into teaching and assessment gold.

Since 2001, after the passage of No Child Left Behind, I have visited countless low-performing, high-needs schools, all labeled so because they had not made Adequate Yearly Progress as determined by their students' scores on California's standardized achievement test. Very few teachers at those schools speak of the last decade as an era of assessment. When pressed, they have described instead how their teaching of writing has had very little to do with student writing and everything to do with preparing students for state tests. Consider the following anecdotes.

In response to a workshop on how to help students learn to write "My Turn" essays, the type of essays made recognizable by *Newsweek*, a group of middle school teachers remained well into what was supposed to be a break for lunch to discuss the implications for their teaching. I joined them when I heard one of them vent, "We can't teach anything we've just learned about. Not one thing." Mistakenly thinking that she was saying the way the essay was organized was too difficult to teach or perhaps the task was irrelevant for their students, I asked her to explain what she meant. She sighed. "We want to teach it all. We are sure the project will motivate our students. But our principal says if we can't connect each day's instruction to a single California Standards Test question, we can't teach it. We can't figure out a way to break down what we just learned to fit the CST test-prep way we have to teach writing and reading."

Also consider this anecdote: During a faculty meeting at a high school designated as being in its fourth year of Program Improvement, the principal shocked his teachers by telling them that they were no longer going to teach writing or even use short-answer writing in any of their end-of-unit tests. When that was met with disbelief, he went on to say that student writing just doesn't count enough on the state tests that determine if the school has met its achievement targets and where it ranks against schools across the state. For that reason, all tests and as many assignments as possible would need to be completed on a Scantron form. Students needed daily practice bubbling in answers to multiple-choice questions in every subject. The administration would be collecting the Scantron results to make sure all teachers were in compliance with the new policy.

I wish I could say that these two anecdotes are the exception, but I can't. After 2001, as increasing numbers of California schools were designated as being in Program Improvement and the only way to shed that status was meeting achievement targets based on test scores, I observed more and more similar test-prep practices displacing the teaching of writing. Schools chose to use programs that focused on students writing in response to brief excerpted literature passages and bland informational paragraphs, or focus on the types of writing tested by the California Standards Test and the California High School Exit Exam. Many districts narrowed the curriculum even more by creating pacing guides that again included only what would be tested and detailed what every teacher would teach, some even to the point of linking what is taught to a fixed calendar. In far too many high-needs schools and districts, writing instruction—beyond the fill-in-the-blank or formulaic three- to five-paragraph varieties—has been given short shrift or completely ignored.

Now reconsider alchemy. As you read the teacher-authored chapters in this book, remember the constraints on teaching writing that have handcuffed many of their teaching colleagues, and then watch and listen to the alchemists at work. Most of these teacher-authors also teach in schools designated as being in Program Improvement; however, as you read what they have to say, you will notice immediately the truth of this book's title, *Teaching Writing Grades 7–12 in an Era of Assessment: Passion and Practice.*

Teaching writing—These teachers teach writing and grapple with what that means for the particular student writers they teach. They develop writing projects that draw on their students' cultures, interests, experiences, and prior knowledge. They work with each other to create writing assignments and instructional sequences that help students learn written genres that are integral to their success in school, college, and the work world.

Assessment—Assessing writing, not testing it, is central to their teaching of writing. Assessment informs their day-to-day teaching and the instructional adjustments they make to address students' needs, the conversations they have with their students as they are working through a writing assignment or project, and their feedback to students about a completed piece of writing. Assessment informs their individual and collaborative hard work to improve their teaching and their students' learning and writing.

Passion—These teachers are passionate about writing and teaching writing. They are even more passionate about the promise and potential of their student writers.

Practice—Writing itself is a practice discipline, and these teachers are engaging their students in the writing discipline, challenging them to practice new strategies and explore varied genres for communicating their ideas. As their students are practicing, these writing teachers interrogate and improve their own teaching practices, and they do so in a professional community of like-minded practitioners. Through this book, the teachers are going public with their teaching practices—their struggles, breakthroughs, and successes.

In a recent publication, researcher Ann Lieberman (2006) notes, "Teachers come to the writing project most often as individuals who are isolated in their schools and essentially struggling alone with the inevitable dilemmas of teaching" (190). In the writing project they become members "of a supportive professional community." In the San José Area Writing Project supportive professional community, as these teacher-authors worked with their teaching colleagues to improve and write about their teaching and assessment of writing, they became a community of teacher-alchemists.

Works Cited

Lieberman, Ann. "The National Writing Project: Commitment and Competence." In Ray Bachetti et al., eds., *Reconnecting Education and Foundations: Turning Good Intentions into Education Capital* (San Francisco, CA: Jossey-Bass, 2006): 185–207.

Preface

Teaching Writing Grades 7–12 in an Era of Assessment: Passion and Practice is a book for teachers by teachers. It is a book about teaching writing, arguably one of the most difficult academic areas to teach, yet one of the most essential. Further, the teacher-writers of the book assert that writing, especially if it is authentic, must be taught comprehensively. It cannot be segmented into distinct measurable skills, despite the arguments of many proponents of outcomes-based assessment. The book emerges from over five years of discussing, drafting, writing, revising, and more revising—our process mirrors the writing process and "walks the walk" we expect of our students.

Each of the more than 30 teachers who have contributed to this book in some form or another has been a participant in the Invitational Summer Institute, a five-week intensive program that is the staple of the National Writing Project (NWP). During the Summer Institute, 20 teachers from kindergarten through college spend the mornings demonstrating their best practices for teaching writing and their afternoons doing their own writing. Graduates of the Summer Institute become teacher-consultants (TCs) who can offer professional development in the teaching of writing.

The TCs who have created this book are teacher-leaders in their schools and districts; they continue to hone their practice because they are driven by the belief that writing is not simply a skill or competency that can be measured or charted by a single test. This book does not purport to be a guide for testing; rather, each writer emphasizes ways to replicate the key idea of Dr. Seuss's *Hooray for Diffendoofer Day!*—writing should focus on teaching our students to think. The authors have a passion for writing; they believe in their students' potential; they want their students to succeed; and they know that their students are more than a "test score." In an era when funding for education is cripplingly limited and public policy is stuck in simplifying the complex issues affecting adolescent literacy, teachers find themselves in the eye of the storm. Those teachers who have not had any coursework preparing them to teach writing are even more vulnerable because they have not had the benefit of instruction in the teaching of writing, yet they are expected to get their students to "produce."

Teaching Writing Grades 7–12 in an Era of Assessment: Passion and Practice should serve as a guide and source of inspiration, particularly for those who have not had access to professional development in the teaching of writing. In a time when the Internet has become a primary source of information and when websites with lesson plans abound, the specific value of *Teaching Writing Grades 7–12 in an Era of Assessment: Passion and*

Practice is that the teachers are "real people teaching real students." While it could be argued that the "virtual" has become the new norm, we argue that English teachers want to begin with the "actual"—hearing from teachers who have the credibility and knowledge about teaching writing and the "evidence" of success shown in their students' writing.

Among the features unique to this book are the middle and high school teachers who share their best practice and provide samples of student writing that confirms the value of their pedagogy. Aligning curriculum across grade levels is an ideal not easily attained. Chapters 4, 5, 6, 7, and 9 of *Teaching Writing Grades 7–12 in an Era of Assessment: Passion and Practice* each begin with a middle school teacher or teachers giving detailed descriptions of pedagogy appropriate for seventh and eighth graders; the other half of these chapters offers applications of the topic for high school students. Chapters 3 to 10 each address the range of writers we teach including English language learners and reluctant writers and readers. The authors demonstrate that their pedagogy, their strategies for teaching writing that is authentic and comprehensive, incorporates the Common Core State Standards.

Teaching Writing Grades 7–12 in an Era of Assessment: Passion and Practice begins with two chapters that directly address teachers as writers and as teachers of writing, highlighting two essentials for teachers: confidence in our own writing and a sense of the broader context of composition studies that emphasize writing as process rather than product. Jonathan Lovell in Chapter 1, "Passion and Practice: Personalizing the Theoretical," shares the rich heritage of leaders in composition studies from James Britton onwards—passionate educators who have profoundly influenced the work of the National Writing Project and professional development in the teaching of writing. Mary Warner in Chapter 2, "Promoting the Passion: Teachers as Writers, Teachers as Collaborators," discusses the importance of teachers' perceptions of themselves as writers because these perceptions affect how we approach this all too often daunting task in this era of assessment. Chapter 2 further explores collaboration and partnerships among all the "players" in the complex world of teaching writing because no teacher should feel alone and unsupported, particularly when class sizes increase, the paper load becomes overwhelming, and the numerous publics we serve ask why writing is not improving.

In Chapter 3, "Building on the Formulaic: Into, Through, and Beyond," Maria Clinton, Martin Brandt, and Brook Wallace address the complex issue of formulaic writing—acknowledging the need for structure while evoking stronger, more fluent, and articulate writing. Maria Clinton opens the chapter with ideas for reaching reluctant, formula-reliant, and personal writers. Martin Brandt then offers a discussion of sentence patterns that can promote facility with language. Brook Wallace concludes the chapter with a discussion of the power of nonfiction analysis to help student writers move through and beyond the formulaic. While Maria, Martin, and Brook are all high school teachers, their strategies can easily be adapted for middle school students.

Chapter 4, "Creative Reading in Support of Writing: Developing Meaningful Response to Literature," emphasizes the complementarity of reading and writing. Middle school teachers Jay Richards and Brenna Dimas examine ways to respond more comprehensively to literature. Jay Richards discusses how being a better teacher of reading can help one become a better teacher of writing; his framework can again be applied to high school students as well as middle school students. In Part III, Marie Milner describes the strategies she implements to evoke a range of writing in response to independent reading. In Part IV, Mary Warner explores the power of the Book Pass to build a passion for reading.

Chapter 5, "Finding Your Writing Voice," follows the chapter on creative reading. It again includes perspectives of middle and high school teachers, as Mary Warner, Kathleen Cohen, and Marie Milner present ways to use readers' theatre, personal narrative, and mentor texts to develop voice. Voice is an elusive quality that is vital to authentic writing. Teachers of writing need to help students hear the voices in the text, hopefully connect to these voices, and then move to developing their own.

Chapter 6, "Bringing Passion to the Research Process: The I-Search Paper," continues to explore the importance of voice in authentic writing. Middle school teachers Brandy Appling-Jenson and Carolyn Anzia, as well as high school teacher Kathleen González, build on Ken Macrorie's seminal work on the I-Search paper. Particularly in the era of assessment when teachers may feel they haven't time to teach research, the I-Search paper fulfills the Common Core State Standards while engaging students where they live.

Multigenre writing, the topic of Chapter 7, "Expanding the Boundaries: The Uncharted Territory of Multigenre Writing," provides a natural progression from the I-Search paper. Multigenre products allow students to engage in several levels of response that create an entire image. Suzanne Murphy launches this chapter with a scaffolded process of multigenre writing with middle school students. Maria Clinton and Marie Milner, both high school teachers, implement some of the dimensions of multigenre writing explained by Suzanne to vary research and a study of *Romeo and Juliet*: Maria describes how she uses multigenre writing in the Museum Exhibit. Marie Milner, in Part III, demonstrates the variety of genre she uses to enhance her students' responses to *Romeo and Juliet*.

In Chapter 8, "Empowering English Language Learners: Moving Toward Competency as Speakers, Readers, and Writers," Marie Milner offers extensive ways to help English language learners in particular, but all writers in general, become confident and fluent writers by lowering the affective filter that produces fear in those acquiring a new language. Marie's numerous strategies for empowering ELLs can easily be adapted for middle grade students, especially since facility with written communication develops more slowly than oral communication.

In Chapter 9, "Practical Guidelines for Portfolios: Promoting Qualitative Assessment in a Test-Prep Climate," middle school teachers Amy Thompson and Suzanne Murphy, and high school teacher Kathleen González, highlight the ways portfolios can and do specifically answer the demands of assessment, providing qualitative, substantive, and essential evidence of the ways our students can learn the comprehensive literacy of writing. While the concept of portfolio keeping has been well established, in this era of assessment many teachers find their time and energy diverted to managing test preparation; this chapter offers new perspectives on the power of portfolios to help students become active participants in their own learning.

The book ends with Chapter 10, "Keeping Heart: Dealing with the Realities of the Paper Load While Providing Authentic Response," on the topic of grading. Knowing that our students DO need to write and that their writing deserves response, the writers of this chapter, Kathleen González and Maria Clinton, address the question of how we can maintain a passion for writing, evoke this passion in our students, and find the time to provide feedback.

Acknowledgements

In addition to the 12 middle and high school teachers who wrote chapters or parts of chapters for *Teaching Writing Grades 7–12 in an Era of Assessment: Passion and Practice*, we thank the following teachers who attended Advanced Institute sessions, joined in discussions of the book's content, provided feedback to writers, and shared their best practices: Brooke Bailey, Carla Dunavan, Jane Gilmore, Jan Goodspeed, Tara Holcomb, Jordan Huizing, Mara Milazzo, Debra Navratil, Tommy Ochoa, Marissa Potts, Todd Seal, Dara Smith, Lindsey Stewart, Anna Shortt Thomas, Margaret Tomita, Jennifer Touchton, Sandy Trotch, Erika Vaughan, and Karen Winchester. Nancy Zuercher, former Director of the Dakota Writing Project, reviewed chapters and provided feedback.

Our thanks also to the reviewers of the manuscript: Daniel E. Boster, Ralston High School (Ralston, NE); Kristina J. Doubet, James Madison University; Doris Ann French, New Mexico State University–Alamogordo; Erin Gatfield, Compass Honors High School (Meridan, ID); Melissa Ann Geiselhofer, Northern Arizona University; Bryan Gillis, Kennesaw State University; Phyllis M. Hakeem, American International University; Susan Hampton, Virginia Middle School (Bristol, VA); Rebecca Harper, Augusta State University; Daphne Hubbard, Kennesaw State University; Melanie Hundley, Vanderbilt University; Jeff Kass, Pioneer High School (Ann Arbor, MI); Lynette Miller, Licking Heights Local School District; Barbara Morgan-Fleming, Texas Tech University; Peggy Semingson, University of Texas at Arlington; Guy Trainin, University of Nebraska; Tracey B. Ward, Olentangy Liberty High School (Powell, OH)

We also thank the many students whose writing enlivens so many of our chapters, and whose dedication to the difficult task of improving their writing gives us great hope for the future.

We thank Professor John Engell and the Department of English and Comparative Literature at San José State University for his support and for providing the meeting place for so many of our writing and revising sessions over the past five years. Most importantly, we thank the late Jim Gray for "inventing" the Writing Project, initially sited at the UC Berkeley campus, as well as Mary Ann Smith and Jayne Marlink for continuing Jim's legacy as successive Executive Directors of the California Writing Project.

Passion and Practice: Personalizing the Theoretical*

by Jonathan Lovell

Introduction

In introducing *Teaching Writing Grades 7–12 in an Era of Assessment: Passion and Practice* with attention to the theorists and theorist-practitioners who served as pioneering founders, my goals are twofold. The first is to demonstrate the practical but profound influence of these founders on our practices as teachers of writing today, especially in light of the emphasis on writing found in the Common Core State Standards. The second is to put some flesh on the bones of these seminal thinkers, showing how what they wrote was deeply enmeshed in what they did as practitioners themselves. As Malcolm Gladwell (*Outliers: The Story of Success*, 2008) and Howard Gardner (*The Disciplined Mind: What All Students Should Understand*, 1999) have helped us to understand, excellence in performing any activity is dependent on a willingness to perform this activity over and over again. The question for the authors discussed in this opening chapter is the question all teachers confront, however much they believe in the essential nature of repeated practice in relation to performance excellence: why might my students *wish* to engage in the performative activity of writing? And why might they wish to engage in this practice with not just dogged persistence, but with genuine passion?

For readers of this book not fortunate enough to be familiar with the work of these founders, my hope is that my accounts will serve as a direct and memorable avenue to understanding them. It is especially important that this act of tough-minded homage be done during this "era of assessment," since the broad, comprehensive, and inspiriting view of language growth espoused by these founders is presently in danger of being marginalized or simply forgotten. While each account is embedded in a personal narrative, the events

1

I relate are similar to those experienced by any teacher who confronts challenges in his or her teaching, but is fortunate enough to be introduced to new perspectives that transform his or her understanding of what students can accomplish in their writing. While the teacher-authors represented in this book reflect the direct influence of these theorists only occasionally, these seminal thinkers contributed significantly to my own shaping of the San Jose Area Writing Project's Invitational Summer Institutes. It is these summer programs, in turn, that provided such fertile ground for the rethinking of practices in the teaching of writing that you will reading about in the chapters that follow.

James Britten and the Value of "Expressive" Language

In 1969, in my second and final year of study at Oxford University, I happened to find a recently published paperback entitled *Language, the Learner and the School* by Douglas Barnes, James Britton, and Harold Rosen, all of the London Institute of Education. What help might this publication provide, I wondered, for a position I'd soon be assuming teaching English to 10th and 12th graders at an independent day school in Wilmington, Delaware?

The perspective these researchers brought to their study was intriguing. What happens, they asked, when students move from being taught by a single primary grade teacher to the six or seven different teachers of their subject-centered secondary classrooms? In asking this question, these researchers brought to their observations a point of view that sounds strikingly contemporary: how do students at the middle and high school levels come to understand the often quite different "academic languages" used by their different subject area teachers? And how does the language these different teachers use to describe and explain their different subject areas compare and contrast to the language the students themselves might use to explain what they already know and what they are in the process of learning?

What gave particular resonance to the work of this group, however, in contrast to the focus today on having teachers gradually lead their students to an increasing sense of command of the academic language of their respective disciples, was the respect they had for how students expressed themselves when they met in small groups to discuss what they were learning, independent of a teacher's guidance. I was sufficiently intrigued by the contrasts between the "expressive" language the seventh grade students in the study used to convey their understanding of what they had learned and the academic language used by their secondary level teachers that I vowed to conduct my own small classroom experiment when I began my teaching. Rather than tell students what I thought they should notice about the short stories we were reading for our 10th grade curricula, I would take out my notepad and write down what they said. And I was prepared to wait quite a long time, in silence, before I said anything myself. Otherwise, so I reasoned, I could not be sure if what I was listening to was my students' own "expressive" language or their desire to sound as much as possible like their teacher.

It turned out that my students did have to endure quite long spells of silence in those first few weeks of my teaching, and I'm not certain that I made very productive or beneficial use of the student-centered language that I learned as a result. What I did learn was that the majority of the students I taught were simply not very interested in talking about short works of fiction that had been "pre-packaged" by a publisher who cared little about what interested them, and who marched them doggedly through groups of stories according to what these works of fiction revealed about the salient characteristics of the short story genre. In other words, it did not matter if I did not say a thing, since the organization and academic focus of the anthology we were using spoke volumes "on my behalf." While I gradually abandoned my experimental role as an observer and recorder of my students' responses to the short stories they were reading, I did not forget the impact that reading those initial research studies had had on me as an eager and expectant young English teacher.

When I returned eight years later to the work of this group of researchers, their writing had become much better known, both in England and the United States. In response to the influential teaching and writing of James Britton, author of *Language and Learning* (1970), the world of English Education that I re-entered in the fall of 1977 was abuzz with discussions of "expressive writing," writing-across-the-curriculum, and the development of writing abilities from the early to the later teenage years.

In my position at Columbia University's Teachers College for which I'd been hired, my job was to organize an MA program in English Education for prospective secondary level teachers and create new EdD and PhD programs in the teaching of reading and writing.

I was qualified, however, for neither of these roles, having managed to get through my interview by doing some quick research in the field of composition studies and somehow managing to persuade my interviewers that I knew what I was talking about. When the spring semester came around, however, I was in deep trouble. I was responsible for teaching a course entitled Composition for Teachers of English, with my audience composed of the dozen or so MA students I had begun to work with that fall as well as about 30 New York City high school English teachers who were taking the course to move up a notch on their salary scales.

What made teaching this course especially troubling for me, however, was my own writing. I was trying to complete the second chapter of my dissertation—a study of the work of the Pre-Raphaelite poet and painter Dante Gabriel Rossetti—but what I was in fact doing was crossing out sentences and paragraphs I'd written months earlier and feeling like I was sinking slowly and inexorably into an ever-deepening verbal morass. What I really needed to do, I remember thinking, was re-title my course De-composition for Teachers of English. That was a subject I knew something about.

I managed to make it through the first few Monday evening classes. Following the graduate school model with which I was most recently familiar, I lectured to the class on the research by Douglas Barnes, James Britton, and Harold Rosen that I described previously. As this research evolved in the late 1960s and early 1970s, it paid increasing attention to the disconnect between the "expressive language" students might use to convey their initial responses to what they read, and the overly dry, academic language they were required to use in their writing, especially as they moved from 7th to 12th grades.

Peter Elbow and the Value of Respectful Listeners

While this research was indeed quite important, the lecture-discussion style in which I presented it to my class was a disaster: a modeling of just the sort of dry academic language that Britton, Barnes, and Rosen were arguing against. Just how disastrous was revealed to me by a note my chair left on my desk a few weeks into the semester. "I thought I'd better pass along this letter written to President Cremin of Teachers College," it read. "I wouldn't take it too seriously, but it does suggest problems that might be worth addressing." A student in my class who was teaching at the innovative private day school to which President Cremin had sent his own children wrote the letter. In the letter, she referred to a lecture that Cremin had recently given on the need to bring a greater sense of professionalism to teachers at the K–12 level. An excellent way to start in this direction, she suggested, would be to fire a recently hired assistant professor teaching a course entitled Composition for Teachers of English.

As I was sitting disconsolately at my desk, expecting to find my belongings unceremoniously dumped onto the street at any moment, two of my graduate students walked into my office. "We heard you were having some trouble with that course in the teaching of writing," they told me. "We thought you might find this book helpful. We use it in our CUNY basic writing courses and find the practices it recommends work very well."

The book was *Writing Without Teachers* (1973) by Peter Elbow. I figured at that point I had nothing to lose, so I began reading. What immediately drew me in was Elbow's account of himself as a writer. He'd had more and more trouble with his own writing as he progressed from college to graduate school and had become hopelessly stuck in the writing of his own dissertation. Since his inability to write disqualified him from any potential job he might get teaching English Literature at the college level, the only job he was qualified for, ironically, was as an instructor of freshman composition.

Elbow did more than write about his own travails as a writer, however. More usefully, he outlined a program for addressing the deep-seated doubts and failures of nerve and confidence that he suggested we all face as writers, no matter our age or grade level. Try writing in short bursts, Elbow suggested, not letting your "editorial mind" prematurely censure what you've written. Try writing these short bursts at unusual times of day or in inconvenient places. I came to call this approach "Writing in difficult circumstances," and often practiced it by writing before I'd had my morning coffee or on the New York City subway as it lurched its way from station to station.

The most distinctive and important component of Elbow's approach, however, is his insight into the importance of getting response to one's writing. Just as the internal editor in our mind tends to censure our work prematurely, so do those who respond to our writing. And yet getting response is crucial to discovering what we have to say. Therefore, Elbow suggested that rather than reading a writer's initial drafts silently, authors should read their writing aloud to a small group of listeners: once through a first time so listeners gain a sense of the content of the writing, then a second time so they gain a sense of its emerging shape. Elbow further argued, quite surprisingly and innovatively, that rather than having listeners suggest revisions to the writer, they should describe the effect of hearing the author's words read aloud.

Listeners would begin by recalling words and phrases they'd remembered from the piece, then they would summarize the piece as a whole, and finally they would tell the author what hearing the piece read aloud led them to think about as they were listening to it. These "showing," "telling," and "generative" responses should be written out by the listeners, Elbow suggested, then read aloud and handed to the authors who had their pieces responded to in this objective fashion. In this way, authors themselves could decide how to revise their writing so that it produced the desired effects on listeners, or effects that they admired in other pieces they'd heard in their small groups of writers and listeners.

I was fascinated. I decided to put Elbow's approach to the test, producing a "composition manifesto," as my students came to call it, for the next class. "We will write each week," I announced, "including your instructor." And I went on to explain that we would form small groups of five or six, read our pieces of writing aloud to one another, respond in the ways I'd just learned from reading this compelling new book, and document what happened to us and to our writing as we went through this process.

And for those in the class that chose to stick it out, our writing—and more importantly, our appetite for producing and revising our writing—did indeed improve: steadily, obviously, and often quite dramatically. I later came to see that what Elbow was proposing was the creation of a community of respectful and skilled listener-readers as much as confident and competent writers. That's what these elaborate rituals of response were all about: gaining steady and consistent practice in learning to become attentive and respectful listeners. And in the process of becoming these listener-readers, writing is "brought out" of us that responds directly to, and is in a sense the creation of, this new community of writers and listeners. One of Elbow's most enduring legacies is that most 21st century K–12 teachers have come through college composition classes where peer response groups are the norm.

Lucy Calkins and the Value of Writer's Workshop

Four years later, in response to a position my wife was offered at UC Berkeley, I left my tenure track position at Columbia and assumed a one-year renewable position at UC Davis teaching freshman composition.

At Davis, I was one of 40-odd composition instructors. Some were graduate students in English, some were Davis residents, and a few like me were PhDs in English looking for full-time tenure track positions elsewhere. Everyone taught the same course, using a session-by-session instruction manual based on Frederick Crews' *Random House Handbook of Rhetoric and Composition*.

My students at Davis were quite different from those I'd taught at Columbia. Products of California's affluent and protected suburbs, they treated composition instructors as service providers whose main purpose was to ensure that they, the service recipients, maintained their 4.0 GPAs. "What must we do on this comparison/contrast paper to get an A?" they would ask. Or "Could you tell us *exactly* what you want on this descriptive writing assignment?"

They'd arrive at my office door, graded papers in hand, asking me to show them which words, phrases, and commas they should change to upgrade their paper from a B − to an A. Soon, they were coming up to me as I walked into class, asking me with an edge to their voices if I might "make the next assignment clearer," so they would "know what I wanted" and could "give it to me."

I knew exactly what I wanted. I wanted to shake my students by their shoulders until their collective teeth rattled, saying to them: "Write about something that *matters* to you, or I will go completely bonkers!"

I recall driving to Davis one morning, numb with apprehension, with a pile of 30 "classification" papers sitting expectantly on the passenger seat beside me. In these papers my students had been asked to "select a generic group of things and describe the features that distinguish the sub-categories that make up this group." Although I'd skimmed these papers the night before, I now had to re-read and grade them before my first morning class. As I sat at the table of the lab classroom I'd been assigned, working doggedly to complete this task, it seemed to me that every single paper described the bicycles ridden on the Davis campus and the various sub-categories into which these bicycles might be classified.

"What should we do, Professor, to get an A on this paper?"

"Write about something that matters to *me*," I wanted to shout, "or I assure you I will start swinging from the trees outside our classroom windows and loping across campus on my legs and forepaws."

I was in the middle of my first semester, my desk at home littered with piles of composition assignments I could not bear to look at, when I received a call from my former department chair at Teachers College. Because our decision to move to California was made quite late in the prior semester, my chair had decided to leave my position vacant for a year so that a departmental committee could conduct a proper search for my replacement.

"We have an interesting candidate for your English Education position," my chairman said. "I wonder if you could help us out." He explained that while the candidate's research had been in the general field of English Education, she'd focused her studies on upper elementary level students. "But it's first-rate stuff," my chairman said, "really first rate. Could you give this candidate a call, perhaps have her send you her current work-in-progress, and write an evaluation to the search committee of her appropriateness for the position?"

"Glad to," I replied, trying to sound more confident than I felt. "Do you want me to be an advocate for the position as well? I would suspect she's being courted by other universities." My chairman replied that he'd be pleased if I would, describing the candidate as a "rare find."

I called her the following weekend, and when she asked if Columbia usually called candidates as parts of their searches, I told her that hers was an unusual case.

"'Unusual' good or 'unusual' bad?" she asked me.

"'Unusual' good," I said, mentioning my chair's reference to her as a "rare find."

"How would he know? What's he read of mine he likes so much?"

This is more difficult than I'd anticipated, I thought to myself. I wonder what she has written? So I asked her about her research.

The manuscript arrived a week later: 300 pages wrapped in brown paper. I started reading immediately. The content drew me in at once. Here were third and fourth graders writing exactly as I wanted my college freshmen to write: choosing topics of consequence to them; experimenting with different modes of writing—narrative, poetry, drama—and getting thoughtful and respectful feedback on their pieces from their teachers and fellow classmates. And the writing that the students in these classrooms produced was absolutely stunning. Several years later, I used the book that emerged from this dissertation, *Lessons From a Child* (1983), as one of the textbooks for a college level writing course I was teaching. One of my students in that course came into my office shortly after the class had begun, asking anxiously, "You don't expect us to write as well as the kids in this book, do you?"

The author of that small but seminal volume, *Lessons From a Child*, is Lucy Calkins. I wrote an enthusiastic review of her candidacy for my former department, which I first showed to my then middle school-aged daughter. "It's well written, Dad," she remarked, "but this person *does* walk on the ground like the rest of us, doesn't she?" As it turned out, she was selected for the position at Teachers College, where she is still teaching. Having written, among many other publications, the highly successful K-2 and 3-5 *Units of Study* for the teaching of writing and *Pathways to the Common Core: Accelerating Achievement* (2012), and having directed the influential Teachers College Reading and Writing Project over many years, it's now clear that she *does* indeed walk on the ground like the rest of us, only more sure-footedly and quite a bit faster.

Donald Graves and the Value of Learning From Our Youngest Writers

In the spring of 1982, however, the University of New Hampshire group through which Lucy Calkins was introduced to the field of composition research was just starting to gain wide attention. Its leader, Donald Graves, was known at the time primarily through his authorship of the Ford Foundation monograph *Balance the Basics: Let Them Write* (1978). In this powerful study, Graves pointed out that for every dollar spent on the teaching of writing, one hundred dollars are spent on the teaching of reading. Even more tellingly, he noted that for every dollar spent for research on the teaching of writing, one thousand are spent for research on the teaching of reading. His conclusion was that by not taking advantage of a child's initial urge to write rather than to read, we significantly underestimate the power of the "output languages" of writing and speaking in favor of the "input languages" of reading and listening.

This monograph, along with the fact that Graves was receiving the David H. Russell Research Award for authoring this study and concurrently publishing his seminal work *Writing: Teachers and Children at Work* (1983), was creating quite a stir in the hallways and sessions of the 1982 NCTE Annual Convention in Washington, DC. As a rather wide-eyed attendee at this conference, I was greatly impressed with the energetic and dedicated cadre of young scholars that Don Graves had drawn into his orbit: Lucy Calkins of Teachers College (discussed earlier in this chapter), Nancie Atwell of Boothbay Harbor, Maine (soon to publish *In the Middle: Writing, Reading, and Learning with Adolescents* in 1987), Mary Ellen Giacobbe of Atkinson, New Hampshire (later to publish *Talking, Drawing, Writing: Lessons for Our Youngest Writers* in 2007), Linda Rief of Durham, New Hampshire (later to publish *Seeking Diversity: Language Arts with Adolescents* in 1992), and Tom Romano of Edgewood High School in Trenton, Ohio (soon to publish *Clearing the Way: Working with Teenage Writers* in 1987). But I was also impressed with the fundamentally important perception about language growth on which much of the research and practice of this University of New Hampshire group was based.

This perception might be expressed by observing that while most parents would never dream of putting their hands over their children's mouths if they uttered the words "mama" or "papa," telling them instead not to speak until they could say the words "mother" or "father," something analogous was happening quite routinely in the teaching of writing in our nation's elementary school classrooms. Rather than recognizing and honoring children's desire to write, as well as their confidence that they had something important to say, and rather than learning the predictable patterns of "invented spelling" that young children routinely use when they begin to write, teachers were closing the door on these nascent efforts at written communication, focusing their attention instead on handwriting, spelling, and the basic punctuation conventions of simple sentences. By imposing this adult perception of the "fundamentals" of written communication prematurely, teachers were unwittingly creating a nation of students who either hated to write or were convinced that they were "horrible writers." It was just as if parents had indeed put their hands over their children's mouths when they began to speak, with the analogous result that we were raising a nation of children who were being essentially chastened into silence.

That's effectively what we'd done in our practices in the teaching of writing, specifically in this era of ever-increasing high-profile assessments. Rather than capitalize on the simplicity and depth of Graves' innovative understanding of how students might grow as writers and how we might assist them more humanely and productively in our practices as teachers, we have been increasingly focused on testing that segments writing into component parts, and in the process largely destroys our students' urge or desire to write.

James Gray and the Value of Writing Teachers Collaborating Across All Grade Levels

A few months after meeting Don Graves and his impressive cadre of young teacher-researchers, I assumed a position in English Education at the Reno campus of the University of Nevada. One of my new position's job requirements was that I collaborate with a group of K–12 teachers who formed a professional development community known as the Northern Nevada Writing Project. While I had some familiarity with the Writing Project through my collaboration with Sondra Perl and Richard Sterling, the New York City Writing Project Directors, during my time at Teachers College, my experience was still quite limited. As part of my new position however, I was fortunate enough to be asked by the two co-directors of the Northern Nevada Writing Project (both high school teachers) to apply to the Bay Area Writing Project's Invitational Summer Institute.

I spent over four-and-a-half weeks during the summer of 1984 in the company of 25 other K–college teachers on the UC Berkeley campus, under the direction of Jim Gray, founder of the Writing Project. Having now served as a director or co-director of 28 subsequent invitational summer institutes, it seems clear to me that there is a compelling connection between the inspiration for attending to younger students' beginning writing development among the researchers at the University of New Hampshire and the concurrent founding of the Bay Area Writing Project at the University of California at Berkeley in the mid-1970s.

Both the University of New Hampshire program under Don Graves and the University of California Berkeley/Bay Area Writing Project program under Jim Gray began with the perception that there were talents and abilities among their target populations that had gone largely unnoticed because these quite different populations had not been given the opportunity to "see" the emergence of their own abilities in a concrete and convincing manner. In the case of young children, this was largely because most teachers believed that several small "steps" needed to be mastered before younger writers could "walk" with confidence as mature writers. In the case of practicing teachers, the worker-supervisor model under which the field of public school teaching continues to function today made it all but certain that administrators would fail to see their "teacher-workers" as valuable and insightful sources of knowledge. Looked at from this perspective, neither the young writers in Don Graves' initial studies of elementary school children in Atkinson, New Hampshire, nor the mostly middle and high school teachers who made up the Bay Area Writing Project's initial 1974 Invitational Summer Institute were accustomed to being heard or listened to with the idea that they had something important to say, something important to teach the rest of us.

In the University of New Hampshire research studies, what gives young writers the confidence they have something to say is the time and the patience their teachers provide for them to think through, draft, and revise their writing. In the Writing Project Summer Institutes, what builds this confidence in having something worthwhile to say is the evenly allocated time that every participant is given to present a workshop demonstration of a "best practice" in the teaching of writing to the other participants in the institute. Both practices accomplish similar goals. They begin with individuals who are uncertain or deeply skeptical that their "words" are worth listening to, and they provide these individuals with an attentive and respectful audience that helps to bring forth the very "words of consequence" that the young writers or selected teachers are half-convinced they do not possess.

It is no accident that both programs came around to a belief in the fundamental importance of teachers as writers. The forerunner to the Writing Project, as Jim Gray explains in *Teachers at the Center* (2000), led to the somewhat accidental creation of "afternoon writing groups" in which small groups of teachers write and get response to their writing. This now-standard feature of all Writing Project Summer Institutes was an unanticipated outcome (one which evolved during the pre-1974 years when Gray's summer programs were located on the UC Davis campus and were NDEA funded) of several high school teachers' desire to "try out" some of the practices in the teaching of writing that had been presented during the morning sessions. Similarly, it was only in his later writings that Don Graves began to understand the importance of teachers consistently bringing their own experience as writers to their conferences and mini-lessons with their students. A major legacy then of Don Graves and Jim Gray is this focus on teachers as writers.

Don Murray and the Value of Attending to the Practice of Professional Writers

I read Don Murray's *A Writer Teaches Writing: A Practical Method of Teaching Composition* (1968), along with Janet Emig's *The Composing Processes of Twelfth Graders* (1971), in preparation for my interview for the English Education position at Teachers College. What struck me in Murray's accounts of his own practices as a writer was how authentic and (not infrequently) moving they sounded. His words fairly leapt off the page, and it was clear to me that the urgency and vitality of what he had to say were directly related to the honesty with which he described, and often dissected, his own practices as he moved slowly

Todd Rafalovich

Jonathan Lovell

and often painfully from initial draft to final product. The "lesson" conveyed by Murray's book is twofold: writing is far more messy and labor-intensive than had been generally acknowledged by traditional approaches to the teaching of writing, and the most convincing and heartfelt instruction in this field of endeavor would come from someone who was himself or herself a passionate practitioner.

It was Murray's call to arms in this respect that led me to insist, in my "composition manifesto" to my Teachers College students, that we would all write, "including your instructor," and that we would reflect on what we'd learned about our own writing in relation to our teaching of writing, as we progressed from draft to draft on our various pieces of writing. And it's Murray's message that reverberates in my mind today as I ask the participants in our San José Area Writing Project Summer Institutes to use their end-of-institute evaluations to describe their experiences with their afternoon writing response groups and to reflect on what they will take from these experiences to their classrooms in the coming year. Two of the participants' responses from our 2011 summer institute indicate the power of the connection that teachers begin to make once they see themselves as *writers* teaching writing:

> After we settled down and got a chance to get to know one another, we got along great. We discussed how we wanted feedback. Some wanted 50% positive / 50% constructive; another wanted it "ruthless"; another only wanted us to tell her she was a good writer. So we settled on 50/50 and nothing mean. It was healthy to compromise. After we read one another's work aloud, passed it around, commented, made changes, brought it back—rinse, wash, repeat—we were all so much closer. We saw improvements and wonderful work come from places we didn't even know existed. It was amazing.
>
> I hope to create and foster the use of writing groups in my own classes this coming year because I feel it was such a valuable experience for finding out that I was a writer. Correction—that I **am** a writer. I have rekindled something long shoved off as youthful pretentiousness. I believe that if I can create a safe enough space within small groups, I can create a safer space in the whole classroom.
>
> — *Melissa M, 11th–12th Grade Teacher*

My experience with my afternoon writing group was very cathartic. We would meet after each morning session and debrief everything. Most of our afternoons were spent talking and reminiscing. After writing and reading so much, but having little time to comment . . . most of us were bursting at the seams to share . . . anything and everything. We found ourselves sharing stories, life experiences, quotes, comments, concerns, etc. We would jot down ideas, etc. then parade home with "homework" and writing assignments. It turned out that this was what led to the majority of the creative spark for me. I would take most of this home, let it percolate, and then start my actual writing around 10 pm or so.

I think the biggest experiences I will take to my classroom for this coming year are the options that were provided by our Afternoon Writing Group facilitator and the fact that, sometimes, you just have to talk about things before you write. Sometimes I assign things without talking through them. I think it would help to allow students to sit in writing groups of about 3 or 4 to bounce ideas off one another before they start writing. This could help get their creative spark lit.

—*Katie N, 9th–10th Grade Teacher*

Both of these responses demonstrate the significance of Don Murray's insistence that teachers of writing not only "talk the talk" but also "walk the walk." As we face the predictable onslaught of "hard-wired" approaches to the teaching of writing in our public school classrooms in the name of aligning our curricula to the Common Core State Standards, it is helpful to remember Don Murray's frequent admonition that creating writing worth reading involves a process that is by nature messy, unpredictable, and idiosyncratic.

Ken Macrorie and the Value of Bringing Voice to Research

If Don Murray represents the typical New Englander in his dedication to a strong work ethic shading toward dogged persistence, Ken Macrorie represents the irreverence of the typical westerner. He never met a grammar rule he didn't like . . . to break. Born in the Mississippi River town of Moline, Illinois, Macrorie frequently evokes, both in his stance toward writing and in his own writing voice, the spirit and voice of Mark Twain: "Persons attempting to find a motive in this narrative will be prosecuted; persons attempting to find a moral in it will be banished; persons attempting to find a plot in it will be shot. By Order of the Author" (preface to *The Adventures of Huckleberry Finn*). It therefore comes as something of a surprise that Macrorie was a good deal more involved than Murray, five years his junior, in working within traditional organizations in the field of English Education. He was a Professor of English at Western Michigan University from 1961 to 1978, where his focus was on teacher training (or "re-educating teachers trapped in unproductive teaching methods," as he put it). He served as editor of NCTE's professional journal, *College Composition and Communication*, from 1962 to 1964, when it was regarded as the leader of the assault on the "current traditional" paradigm in writing instruction. And finally, he served for 13 years, both before and after his retirement from WMU, at the Bread Loaf Graduate School of English, a summer master's program conducted under the auspices of Vermont's Middlebury College, where he taught practicing high school teachers to become writers and to take that knowledge back to their classrooms.

In terms of this chapter, however, it is Macrorie's re-conceptualizing of the writing of the traditional research paper that will illuminate his many contributions to the field of writing instruction. The book that introduced many to Macrorie's boldly original reconsideration of research writing was *Searching Writing* (1980), or as the book was more helpfully re-titled in 1988, *The I-Search Paper*. In Chapter 6 of this book, you will read how middle school teachers Brandy Appling-Jenson and Carolyn Anzia, as well as high school teacher Kathleen González, have adapted Macrorie's *I-Search Paper* strategies for their own classrooms. In this chapter, however, I focus on the impact Macrorie's original text had on my teaching of freshman composition classes at San José State University.

Like most college level freshman composition programs, San José State requires the completion of a "research paper" as part of every student's introductory level writing requirements. On the one hand, I understood the rationale for this requirement, since such "academic" writing would be routinely required of students as they moved to higher-level university classes. On the other hand, I was all too aware of the pull my students would feel toward simply "lifting" their material from previously published sources. I was not unsympathetic to this pull. It's one we have all felt to one degree or another, after all, and it's especially understandable when beginning level college writers are placed in academic environments where they have very little notion of what constitutes authentically compelling academic writing.

This is where Macrorie's understanding of what it means to search, whether for an obscure bit of evidence that might illuminate a larger academic argument or for something as relatively mundane as the best price on a car stereo system, comes to the fore. I can't recall if Macrorie also suggested a gallery walk to heighten interest in these initial searches, but that's what I did with my San José State freshman classes. Everyone wrote down his or her research question on a large piece of poster paper (with one nervy freshman writing in his, "What is the meaning of life?") and then everyone in the class did a gallery walk past these posters, writing graffiti-like comments on these easel sheets if one knew something about the content of the search or if one had a suggestion for the author about how he or she might pursue the search.

The next steps were to "research one's topic" and to keep a running record of the steps one took to move closer to discovering answers to his or her research question. At least one interview with one informant was required for the search, and I customarily prepared for these by setting a question for the class as a whole and then bringing in an informant that the class could collectively interview. A further requirement was for a "saturation report," where the researcher would describe a setting that had come to be significant in his or her search. As with the whole-class interviews, I would generally take the class on a short "field trip" around the building in which the class was being held. Then I would ask everyone to select a setting they found memorable and describe that setting in a way the rest of the class might recognize.

The culmination of the I-Search paper was for students to write a narration of their pursuit of their question. They would start with what they knew or didn't know about their topic, follow this with an "argument" that explained to their readers why the question they were pursuing was important to them, document the steps they took to learn the answer(s) to their question, and conclude with a summary of what they had learned by the time "the whistle blew" and they had to end their search. Needless to say, issues with plagiarism were simply non-existent with such a rich and compelling experience of "researching" a question of one's own choosing. What surprised me, however, was the vibrancy and liveliness of my students' voices in the papers they submitted.

I sent a batch of these papers to Macrorie himself, then living in retirement in Las Cruces, New Mexico. He wrote back a few months later, explaining that it took him some time to read through what I'd sent him and asking me to please send less next time. While he complained that he could not fully understand how my students managed to survive my "barrage" of instructions (a "running syllabus" I provided for my students, made up of single-spaced narratives describing each successive class), the papers they wrote clearly demonstrated that I must be doing something right. "They are a delight," he wrote. "So loose in the saddle, so lively, so uncluttered with the usual hogwash of freshman compositions." I could hardly have asked for a more satisfying recognition of my students' writing abilities, nor a more compelling argument for the value of re-conceiving the research paper as an authentic quest, placing the student writer at its center.

James Moffett and the Value of the "Ladder of Abstraction"

In focusing on James Moffett's contributions to the field of composition instruction, I return to my early days teaching 10th grade in Wilmington, Delaware, then fast-forward to my final two years teaching Composition for Teachers of English at Teachers College. My purpose in doing so is to illustrate the profound influence that the theorists discussed in this chapter have had, and continue to have, on the practice of writing at all levels, and also to illustrate how these theories might be practically applied in actual, concrete teaching situations.

In my teaching in Wilmington, I enjoyed and was stimulated by teaching my 12th graders, but it was my 10th graders I truly loved. They were at such a volatile and important stage in their intellectual and emotional development, and I came to believe that if I taught wisely I could make a significant difference in their lives. What was at issue, to my mind, was whether or not I could persuade my 10th graders to entertain more than one point of view on a given subject.

What frustrated me in trying to come up with teaching practices that would serve to jostle my 10th graders from their often quite strong allegiance to a predetermined position was the pervasive influence of the five-paragraph theme. As described by Janet Emig in *The Composing Processes of Twelfth Graders* (1971), the "Fifty-Star Theme," as Emig nicknamed the five-paragraph theme, was both frustratingly persistent in the secondary level English language arts curriculum and wholly unrelated to any real purpose or practice in the larger world:

> Why is the Fifty-Star Theme so tightly lodged in the American composition curriculum? The reason teachers often give is that this essentially redundant form, devoid of content in at least two of its five parts, exists outside their classrooms, and in very high places—freshman English classes, business communication, and in the "best practices" of the "best writers." This fantasy is easy to disprove. If one takes a collection of writers who current critical judgment would agree are among our best, can one find a single example of any variation of the Fifty-Star Theme? The answer is no. (97)

I found I could persuade my 10th graders to "inhabit" a point of view different from their own by engaging them in dramatic re-enactments; however, when my 10th graders wrote an argumentative paper, all the intellectual and emotional suppleness they displayed in their dramatic re-enactments went out the window. Was Friar Lawrence to blame for Romeo and Juliet's tragic deaths? He certainly was, argued any number of my 10th graders. To prove it I will devote my first paragraph to a thesis stating that he was guilty, then will write three body paragraphs in which I will locate details from the play that support my thesis, and will finish with a concluding paragraph that reminds you that Friar Lawrence was indeed guilty of the tragic deaths of Romeo and Juliet. While I found myself, not too surprisingly, assigning more and more dramatic re-enactments and fewer and fewer "opinion papers" for my 10th graders as I progressed from my first to my third year of teaching, I never found a satisfactory way of addressing the deeper question of how to persuade my students, at least in their writing, to unleash themselves from the safety and security of their predetermined positions.

Eight years later, at Teachers College, when I began teaching my Composition for Teachers of English course for a third time, I faced a similar but more vexing version of this same mind-set. My writing course now used both Peter Elbow's *Writing Without Teachers* (1973) and James Moffett's *Teaching the Universe of Discourse* (1968) as its primary texts, and had become well enough known and highly enough regarded to attract a small but vocal population of graduate students in the Teaching of English to Speakers of Other Languages Program at Teachers College. "This business of a student-centered approach to writing development is perhaps a defensible strategy for English speakers," they argued, "but it simply will not work with our ESL adult populations." These TESOL teachers were quite clear that what *their* students needed were clearly structured lessons with a strong focus on grammar and conventions. "How are they going to avoid making mistakes in their writing unless we, as their teachers, point these out to them?" they would ask. "And if we were to put this Elbow nonsense to use in our classrooms, all we'd observe would be the blind leading the blind."

While I did not agree with these strongly held opinions about the writing development of adult ESL students, I could not challenge them effectively as a practitioner since my own experience was limited to a single summer's teaching, many years earlier, in Hong Kong. How might I introduce points of view that gently questioned these quite plausible pedagogical certainties? How might I do so without claiming more than I could reasonably claim on the basis of my own quite limited teaching experience with adult ESL learners?

Appropriately enough, the answer came right from Moffett's *Teaching the Universe of Discourse*. "Start by understanding how difficult it is," Moffett might be imagined as saying, "to theorize about best practices in the teaching of writing to ESL adults." To do so convincingly, according to the theory set forth in Moffett's book, involves not only imagining a large general audience of readers, but also the writer's ability to hypothesize "what *could* happen" in many future ESL classrooms beyond those in which one has actually taught.

These imagined admonitions come from a theory of discourse that Moffett had been developing since his early years teaching English to high school students in New Hampshire. As presented in the collection of articles that formed the basis of his book, this theory posits that all acts of written communication can be understood as occurring at one point or another on a "ladder" of increasing abstraction regarding the "distance" between the author and his or her subject on the one hand, or between the author and his or her reader on the other. A writer writing notes to himself or herself about an object or event that is close at hand—"what is happening"—would be engaged in writing that represents the closest possible "distance" between author and subject. Conversely, a writer presenting a theory about "what might happen" in a periodical designed for a general readership would be engaged in writing that represents the greatest possible "distance" between both subject and audience. It did not take me long to realize, given this perspective on writing argumentatively, that I was asking my Teachers College TESOL students to write persuasively from something akin to the farthest points "out" on both sides of Moffett's abstraction ladder. I was asking them, that is, to tell "what happens" in adult ESL classes while addressing a wholly imagined audience of general readers.

Assisted by a sequence of mimeographed writing assignments then circulating among those familiar with Moffett's work (later published as *Active Voice: A Writing Program Across the Curriculum,* 1981), I began to design a sequence of writing assignments along the lines suggested by Moffett's "ladder of abstraction." My primary purpose was to present a practical application of Moffett's theory of discourse so that everyone in the class could experience this rather complex theory firsthand. I also hoped, however, that I might unsettle some of the fixed notions of conventional, grammar-oriented writing instruction that were held by my TESOL students.

I started by asking my students to write from the perspective of a speaker on a soapbox in Central Park advocating practices in the teaching of writing that were the opposite of those presently held by the author. What would such a speaker say to defend his or her position? What arguments and examples would such a speaker use to convince his or her listeners of the compelling nature of his or her point of view?

Next, I asked my students to write out a dialogue between this strident soapbox speaker and themselves, toning down the stridency of the speaker's stance so that the conversation might be civilized and even-tempered.

Third, I asked my students to imagine that the speaker moved upstate so that face-to-face conversation was no longer possible. I advised that the conversation be continued, but this time as an exchange of medium length letters (I suggested four; most students wrote six to eight).

Finally, as this sequence of writing assignments evolved as I taught it for my fourth and final year at Teachers College, I asked my students to step back and imagine they had just discovered this exchange of letters and had decided to edit them for publication. They would provide a preface in which they told readers something about the backgrounds of the two writers, insofar as they had been able to "unearth" these personal backgrounds in their "research." They would also say something about the importance of the topic these two letter writers were addressing—a level of importance that led them to decide to publish this consequential exchange of views.

As it turned out, I never did add the final step I had originally envisioned for this sequence—transforming this final "edited exchange of letters" into a formal argumentative essay. I think what we all realized by the time we became "editors" of these two correspondents' exchange of letters is that the forcefulness of one or another of their opening points of view was far less interesting than what motivated them to adopt their initially antagonistic stances and what led them to engage in extended correspondence with one another. What I do know is that I stopped hearing about the indispensability of a grammar-based approach to the teaching of writing to adult ESL students, or to non-ESL high school students in New York City public schools for that matter, and I did hear a great deal about the "characters" that my students had brought into being as a result of the seriousness with which they assumed their roles as editors.

What I would say today is that this particular sequence of writing assignments utilized my 10th grade students' ability to "inhabit" the role of someone other than themselves, putting this talent in the service of helping us all to view those holding opinions diametrically opposite to our own with greater understanding and sympathy. And isn't that what "teaching toward adulthood" is all about? This is the contribution that Moffett helped us realize: we were all teaching writing in a wider "universe of discourse" where our roles were to help our students and ourselves come into greater awareness of our capacities not only as writers but also as more fully developed human beings.

Lessons Learned From the Founders of Passion and Practice

The chapters of *Teaching Writing Grades 7–12 in an Era of Assessment: Passion and Practice* that follow introduce a wide range of teaching practices that have been refined and modified over the years by middle and high school teachers committed, as were the founders I've just discussed, to the centrality of writing in their English Language Arts curricula and to the potential of each of their students as writers. While the last 12 years, with their emphasis on educational policy focusing exclusively on "accountability" as measured by test scores, have unquestionably been difficult and frustrating times for these teachers, the teacher writers in this book have each found ways to "make their writing curriculum work for them," to borrow Tim Gunn's mantra from *Project Runway*. Since each of these teachers is also a writer, as well as a colleague with whom I've worked directly in one or another of the Invitational Summer Institutes of the San José Area Writing Project, they also represent a group about which I'm especially proud. Not only have they found a way to bring their passion for writing and the teaching of writing to their students, they have also found the time, energy, and commitment to bring what they have learned to the wider audience of this book's readers.

References and Resources

Atwell, Nancie. *In the Middle: Writing, Reading, and Learning with Adolescents.* Portsmouth, NH: Boynton/Cook, 1987.

Barnes, Douglas, James Britton, and Harold Rosen. *Language, the Learner and the School.* Harmondsworth, England: Penguin Books, 1969.

Britton, James. *Language and Learning.* Harmondsworth, England: Penguin Books, 1970.

Calkins, Lucy. *Lessons From a Child.* Portsmouth, NH: Heinemann, 1983.

_____ . *Units of Study for Primary Writing: A Yearlong Curriculum.* Portsmouth, NH: Heinemann, 2003.

_____ . *Units of Study for Teaching Writing, Grades 3–5*. Portsmouth, NH: Heinemann, 2007.

Calkins, Lucy, Mary Ehrenworth, and Christopher Lehman. *Pathways to the Common Core: Accelerating Achievement*. Portsmouth, NH: Heinemann, 2012.

College Composition and Communication. Journal of the National Council of Teachers of English. Urbana, IL.

Elbow, Peter. *Writing Without Teachers*. New York: Oxford University Press, 1973.

Emig, Janet. *The Composing Processes of Twelfth Graders*. Urbana, IL: National Council of Teachers of English, 1971.

Gardner, Howard. *The Disciplined Mind: What All Students Should Understand*. New York: Simon & Schuster, 1999.

Giacobbe, Mary Ellen. *Talking, Drawing, Writing: Lessons for Our Youngest Writers*. Portland, ME: Stenhouse Publishers, 2007.

Gladwell, Malcolm. *Outliers: The Story of Success*. Boston, MA: Little, Brown and Company, 2008.

Graves, Donald H. *Balance the Basics: Let Them Write*. Ford Foundation, Papers on Reseach About Learning, 1978.

_____ . *Writing: Teachers and Children at Work*. Portsmouth, NH: Heinemann, 1983.

Gray, James. *Teachers at the Center: A Memoir of the Early Years of the National Writing Project*. National Writing Project, 2000.

Macrorie, Ken. *Searching Writing*. New Jersey: Haydon Book Company, 1980.

_____. *The I-Search Paper: Revised Edition of Searching Writing*. Portsmouth, NH: Boynton/Cook, 1988.

Moffett, James. *Teaching the Universe of Discourse*. Boston, MA: Houghton Mifflin, 1968.

_____. *Active Voice: A Writing Program Across the Curriculum*. Portsmouth, NH: Boynton/Cook, 1981.

Murray, Donald. *A Writer Teaches Writing: A Practical Method of Teaching Composition*. Boston, MA: Houghton Mifflin, 1968.

Rief, Linda. *Seeking Diversity: Language Arts with Adolescents*. Portsmouth, NH: Heinemann, 1992.

Romano, Tom. *Clearing the Way: Working with Teenage Writers*. Portsmouth, NH: Heinemann, 1987.

* Portions of this chapter appeared in different form in the Winter 1996 and Summer 1999 issues of *California English*.

2

Promoting the Passion:
Teachers as Writers,
Teachers as Collaborators

by Mary Warner

Introduction

What is your perception of yourself as a writer? How do you see yourself in relation to teaching writing? Do you enjoy writing? These questions are critical for us as teachers of writing. If we are passionate about a topic, a book, or any area of learning, we can more easily engage our students. This chapter precedes the pedagogical chapters directed toward student writers because we cannot teach well what we don't know or what we find intimidating. Furthermore, our perceptions of ourselves as writers and teachers of writing and our attitudes about teaching writing affect how we approach this often daunting task in this era of assessment. Above all, no teacher should feel alone and unsupported, particularly when class sizes increase, the paper load becomes overwhelming, and the numerous publics we serve ask why writing is not improving.

Consider the following scenarios and what they indicate about the range of situations we find ourselves in regarding the teaching of writing.

Scenario 1

The [North Carolina] Writing Test is coming up soon, so my students are preparing. It is really hard to teach someone how to write. I can do workshops, conferences, practice, and editing all day long, but these kids don't even know how to get started. I find myself making sentences up with them, and even hoping that they are quick enough to write down exactly what I'm saying rather than nothing at all. I hope that at least I'm demonstrating the thinking process for them, and it will pay off in the end. There's no time for grammar, and I just wish I could tell if I was actually teaching them how to interpret reading. It isn't something I've successfully learned how to gauge.

These words come from a then initially licensed teacher in her second year of teaching middle school language arts. In her undergraduate preparation for a BSEd in English Education, April had a course in the Teaching of Writing as well as coursework in creative writing. She clearly enjoys writing. As her academic supervisor when she student taught, I observed the many creative activities she used to engage her students. Her email identifies several key issues for writing teachers: facing state-mandated writing tests and feeling compelled to "teach to the test"; the difficulty of "teaching" anyone to write; students' preparedness and motivation or lack of motivation for writing; how to integrate grammar; and the relationship between thinking and writing—even how to teach thinking. Above all, in a more personal note not included in the previous excerpt, she expressed the loneliness that is all too common among new teachers—she wants advice and the opportunity to dialogue about the many complex challenges in teaching writing; she wants support from seasoned teachers; she wants to know that she is not alone—but she isn't sure to whom she can go for advice or guidance or with whom she can dialogue.

Because it's been five years since I began drafting this chapter and it's gone through several revisions, I recently contacted April again to share what I had written. Her response to this chapter shows her growth as a teacher of writing; it also identifies some essential issues for all teachers of writing:

> *I read over my quote . . . and amazingly enough, I still, for the most part, feel that way about writing. It is still extremely challenging to take students who have no concept of organization, style, voice, and what makes sense in a sentence and turn them into great writers, or even mediocre ones. It is even more challenging to get a student who doesn't care about writing and sees no value in it to practice the grammar skills necessary to be able to write sentences with logical and sensible structure. . . . I [now] have a stronger appreciation of the practice of modeling writing for my students, and am more aware of how I verbally address a student's particular weaknesses in writing. By participating in the writing process with my students, just as I was doing 7 years ago, I can show my enthusiasm. I can show how fun and creative that all types of writing can be, even essays. I have been able to plant that seed of passion, excitement and opportunity into a large fraction of my students, so that they want to take their own ideas and run with them.*
>
> *Once they have that desire, they are much more willing to do the editing and revisions because they want their work to be the best it can be. Then there is a trickle down effect because they want to share their work with everyone else, and once others see that a child their own age is producing great work, sometimes it inspires them to want it a little more. . . . With students who are struggling, I have found that words of encouragement along with re-teaching are always more effective than the dreaded red marks covering the paper they've been working on for an hour. Taking the time to let them know that even though they can improve, they've got great ideas; this lets them know the problem isn't impossible to solve.*
>
> *And making the time to build individual relationships with all of the students is by far the most important thing I do as a teacher because whether it comes to writing or just making it through the day . . . they will move mountains to make you proud of them . . . most*

of my students want to see that tear that falls down my face when I hear them share a piece of writing. . . . That's something they love to work towards, and is something that even the weakest of writers can do.

Scenario 2

The following quotes come from a veteran high school teacher whom I "met" when she emailed asking for teaching ideas for a ninth grade English course using the novel *Forgotten Fire* by Adam Bagdasarian. During an online search, Sylvia had found my syllabus for Children's Literature where I taught the novel. I willingly shared a number of ideas with her. She responded with the following: *"What a kind, considerate, helpful note! As I sit here wiping away the tears of frustration after a day and a half of in-service on assessment in standards-based education, I needed that collegial assistance!"* In a follow-up email, I commiserated with her about "assessment in standards-based education" and professional development sessions like these that sap our passion for teaching instead of energizing us. What is more debilitating in trying to motivate students to write and to see the intrinsic value of writing than tying it solely to assessment?

A tangential comment—when I take an inventory of reading interests in my university courses, Literature for Young Adults or Children's Literature or The Bible as Literature, my students often talk about "losing interest in reading" once they reach middle or high school, even though they loved reading when they were younger. An even less frequent occurrence is when they comment on any writing they do or have done, particularly writing that they do outside of required coursework. They seem to have little sense that writing could be an activity as fulfilling as reading. Furthermore, as various data show the decline in reading among adolescents, there is even more of a decline in writing or seeing any interest in writing for anything beyond school assignments. Sylvia's frustrations about the emphasis on assessment-based education demonstrate another obstacle to fostering any passion for writing—when students and teachers face the barrage of assessment, there is even less possibility for any enjoyment from or desire to do writing.

Once I'd faxed Sylvia a helpful author's interview, from my edition of *Forgotten Fire*, I received this response:

I got your fax before leaving last night—what a bright spot in a depressing day! If you do presentations to teachers, I will wager that you avoid the pitfall of using a degrading tone and message: "You are DOWN here and need to come UP here to the vision (meaning her vision since we haven't invested in its urgency) with me." That lack of recognition of the validity of where we are and the clear picture of the rationale for moving elsewhere strands me on an island of frustration. I want to do what's best for the learning environment and the students and I want to be in compliance with my employer. I wish they'd practice what they preach.

The particularly poignant phrases in this email are "the lack of recognition of the validity of where we are" and Sylvia's feelings of being "strand[ed] on an island of frustration." Her words substantiate a central aim of this chapter: to explore ways that teachers of English/ teachers of writing on all levels can validate each other through collegiality. Such collegiality might be an antidote to the "UP here/DOWN there" dichotomy so easily created in the standards-based educational environment. Additionally, when teachers are trapped into the contexts of "on-demand" writing and writing "to the test," the possibility of making writing appealing or of tapping student interest decreases exponentially.

Sylvia's specific reference to presenters—particularly university instructors working with public school teachers or administrators delivering in-service—avoiding the use of degrading tones and messages creates another direct link to the focus of this chapter. In my positions in English Education at three different universities, I've had a number of opportunities for collaboration with public school teachers: being a participant in the Dakota Writing Project (DWP) Summer Institute in 1995 and in the San Jose Area Writing Project (SJAWP) Summer Institute in 2006; directing a summer course for teachers grades 7 to college called A Dialogue About Reading, Writing and Thinking; being a member of the 10th Grade Writing Assessment Committee in North Carolina; facilitating the Advanced Institute: Writing Your Best Practice with middle and high school teachers; team-teaching English Methods courses with high school teachers; and coordinating writing partnerships between my students (pre-service teachers) in a college course on teaching composition to middle and high school students.

These opportunities and ongoing experiences with the California Writing Project (CWP), the San Jose Area Writing Project (SJAWP), and the National Council of Teachers of English (NCTE) have shown me again and again what collaboration can do for teacher morale and how the collaborative community of writers model creates the most successful professional development. These positive experiences of professional development are the antithesis of those Sylvia experienced. These collaborations make clear that no one level—university, secondary, middle, or elementary—has teachers who are "better than" teachers on another level or have more authority or knowledge. The key is tapping into the expertise on any level and sharing what applies to learners on other levels. The power of teachers teaching teachers—a foundational National Writing Project (NWP) philosophy—and the community of writers that is established in Writing Project institutes are primary ways to pass on the passion for writing.

Scenario 3

In another context, at a meeting of supervisors for the student teachers in our English Credential Program, several supervisors who are retired high school English teachers commented that our student teachers really need help in how to teach writing. The co-editor of this book, Jonathan, and I simply nodded our empathy and awareness of the void. We had only recently (first offered in Fall 2006) created a course, Writing and the Young Writer, addressing that need; to this point, however, we had not had a teaching of writing course. Ironically, the retired high school English teachers probably had never "officially" been taught to teach writing either, but they had learned to integrate writing as they progressed through their careers. Courses in the teaching of writing in teacher preparation programs are also a fairly recent addition. The current "era of assessment," however, demands that teachers deliver explicit writing instruction that surpasses merely integrating writing assignments within literature courses. Few teachers have been prepared for such instruction.

Scenario 4

Paula Stacey, developmental editor of books in K–12 education and long-time English teacher, in her September 2011 article "Let's Stop Teaching Writing," describes watching and participating in the evolving writing curriculum since her first teaching job 30 years ago. She notes that students, in the name of writing instruction, are being asked to jump through an "ever-expanding and increasingly byzantine set of hoops," but less and less are actually being asked to write. In reflecting on her own education Stacey realizes that the writing she was asked to do, [mostly] ". . . explaining my thinking about the subjects I was studying, created an authentic engagement with ideas and content that was blissfully uncomplicated by format and process or half-baked notions about writing for a made-up audience." Stacey's "modest proposal" then suggests that we ask students questions, read their answers, and ask more questions; these exchanges allow for real thinking and real writing.

The teachers and prospective teachers of the previous scenarios and the issues described are representative of the multiple reasons for developing a passion for writing as well as indicative of why the passion for writing has waned. Our understanding of the many challenges related to teaching writing and our desire to collaborate as peers and partners in the struggle are central purposes of this book. The book may be most beneficial for those teachers of English, whether they are pre-service or in-service, who have never had a course in teaching of writing. These teachers are at an even greater disadvantage in the era of assessment because they face the expectations of "producing" passing scores on the various state writing tests, while not having the preparation. They may well like to write, as is true of many English majors who go on to be teachers of English, and been successful writers themselves; as we all know though, being able to do something yourself is far different from being able to teach others to do it.

Where, then, do teachers in any one or more of the scenarios described find the engagement with writing that provides the impetus for lifelong writing, for "beyond the test writing," for going beyond formulaic writing? How do they find the desire to write themselves and thus to impart the appeal and passion for writing to their students? Building on my own journey and experiences with those who fostered and continue to support my writing—since I, too, am a teacher of writing who never had a formal course in the teaching of writing—this chapter identifies several ways to develop and promote a passion for writing.

- You as Writer; You as Teacher of Writing
- "Hang Together"
- "Writing Your Best Practice"
- Find a Mentor/Be a Mentor
- Collaborate/Be a Collaborator—Form Partnerships
- Search Out Professional Communities That Challenge and Support

You as Writer; You as Teacher of Writing

Patricia Belanoff and Peter Elbow's book, *A Community of Writers* (1999), contains an Inventory for Writers that includes questions about how often students write and whether they enjoy writing. Three questions in the "Attitudes Toward Writing" segment are especially pertinent regarding motivation:

1. Do you enjoy writing?
2. In general, do you trust yourself as a person who can find good words and ideas and perceptions?
3. Do you think of yourself as a writer?

For many years as I taught composition courses, I asked my students to fill out the inventory. Recently, I've wondered how I would fill out this survey, realizing I should have done what I asked my students to do. Writing is not easy for me; the collection of "rejections" for journal articles I've submitted and the editors' calls for revision of chapters and books are daunting. All too often I've experienced some of the sentiments expressed by Liesel Meminger in *The Book Thief* by Markus Zusak (2005). Liesel has been given a notebook and is told by the mayor's wife, from whom Liesel has been stealing books, that she should write. Liesel reflects "but there would be punishment and pain, and there would be happiness, too. That was writing" (524–525). Liesel also comments "words are so heavy" and in the final line of the novel sums up her feelings about writing: "I have hated the words and I have loved them, and I hope I have made them right" (528). I, too, have hated and loved the words. Yet in planning this book and particularly in writing this chapter, I'm revising my perspectives about writing, about why the passion for the language I hold for reading and literature should be no different than the passion for writing.

Consider taking stock of the writing you do in a week. Such an inventory of you as a writer can lend a new appreciation to what we ask of our students. If some of the writing you do is onerous and prosaic, consider how your students might find some of the writing you require. If you note how pressured you are to meet deadlines for some of the writing tasks, remember the time pressures of your students. In reviewing the writing I have done, I quickly identified a wide range. Even in the age of emails, I still love writing letters, birthday cards, and cards for special events, seasons, and days. In my teaching position, I'm constantly writing to students and for students—responses to their written work, letters of recommendation, and emails answering a variety of concerns, as well as creating writing prompts, essay topics, and exams. As a supervisor of student teachers, I write observation reports, formative and summative evaluations, and even more letters of recommendation. As a university professor, I write grants, statements of purpose to accompany tenure and promotion requests, proposals for conference presentations, journal articles, reviews, books, and more tedious items such as the English Program Approval document for the State Commission on Teacher Credentialing.

Once you have your inventory, consider the following questions: How many of these writing events are enjoyable? Which are pleasurable? What is the appeal of writing? Or maybe better questions are: How is it that we are able to do all these kinds of writing? What are we learning as we write? In what ways are we "not alone" because we write? Reading provides rich contact with language and the written word that feeds the writer's soul. Experiencing the wonder and pleasure of good writing certainly motivates me and can motivate our students. Any self-reflection on why we write must take into account the richness of what has been written and the terrible poverty we'd experience in so many contexts without the written word. Lily, the 14-year-old protagonist of Sue Monk Kidd's *The Secret Life of Bees* (2003), constantly writes to make sense of the harsh world of prejudice and abandonment that threatens to destroy her. Our students, and we as teachers of writing, can have a passion for writing if we write and surround ourselves with living examples of writing that leads us to a deeper sense of humanity.

A creation of J. K. Rowling, "the pensieve," which first appears in *Harry Potter and the Goblet of Fire* (2000), presents the perfect image for how writing can aid the complex and frequently harried lives that our students (and their teachers) live. Dumbledore, in his typical wisdom, explains to Harry, "I sometimes find, and I am sure you know the feeling, that I simply have too many thoughts and memories crammed into my mind" (597). He demonstrates as he "siphons the excess thoughts from [his] mind, pours them into the basin, and examines them at [his] leisure" (597) that the pensieve is a repository for these excess thoughts. Once the excess thoughts are in the pensieve, "it becomes easier to spot patterns and links" (597). The essential gift of writing is its power as a pensieve, for getting our thoughts on paper (or "on screen" as is more likely in our technological world) and giving us space to examine and make sense of our thoughts and, consequently, of our lives. Could there be any greater appeal for writing than to find and make meaning?

"Hang Together"

In *A Wind in the Door* by Madeleine L'Engle (1973), Meg Murry is in conversation with the high school principal, Mr. Jenkins. At this point in the novel, Meg's youngest brother, Charles Wallace, is critically ill and needs to be in harmony with the universe in order to survive. Meg reminds Mr. Jenkins: "Remember, Mr. Jenkins, you're great on Benjamin Franklin's saying, 'We must all hang together, or assuredly we will all hang separately.' That's how it is with human beings and mitochondria and farandolae and our planet, too, . . . We have to live together in—in harmony, or we can't live at all" (147). Franklin's admonition, quoted by Mr. Jenkins and Meg, is pessimistic, yet realistic. English teachers on all levels from elementary through post-secondary need to "hang together" in the face of standards-based education and mandated state writing tests; they need to collaborate on curriculum that scaffolds the writing process; and they need to avoid the "blame game" attitudes of "Why don't these students know (fill in the blank)?" or "Why weren't they taught (fill in the blank)?"

My first experiences with high stakes writing tests—one of the most insidious causes of the "blame game"—were in North Carolina. I began teaching at Western Carolina University about the same time as the NC Standard Course of Study established World Literature, non-British and non-American, as the subject matter for 10th grade and the State Department of Public Instruction required a 10th grade writing assessment. Almost immediately, since I was teaching Fundamentals of Teaching Composition, I needed to become familiar with that 10th grade writing assessment and the field of World Literature. Additionally, for the pre-service teachers in my course who were going to teach in elementary and middle schools, the State required writing assessments in fourth and seventh grades—a major stretch since my own teaching and subsequent work in English Education had been primarily in high school. My route to acquiring knowledge of the content and specifics of these various assessments took several paths—all of which included networking.

I listened to and learned from the cooperating/host teachers with whom I had student teachers, traveling throughout western North Carolina to meet with English teachers at their schools, on "their turf." All too often university faculty expect the teachers to come to "us"; instead, in a concerted effort to be collaborative and more credible, I went to their school settings. Unknowingly, I was operating on one of the assumptions of the NWP expressed by Jim Gray, the founder of the Bay Area, California, and National Writing Projects:

> Universities and schools can work together as partners in a cooperative effort to solve the writing problems common to both levels. New collegial and nonhierarchical relationships among professors, instructors, and teachers are essential; the top-down tradition of past

university/school programs is no longer useful as a staff development model. (Gray qtd. in Olson, 1997, xi)

The high school teachers I met with, these practitioners, knew the "real world of teaching English" and were making their way in the new frontier of assessment demands. As they shared their concerns about giving "their" students over to student teachers who didn't have the experience, I realized the importance of working with these veteran teachers to know the mandates and state curriculum.

To assure I grasped the issues related to End-of-Course (EOC) and End-of-Grade (EOG) tests, I responded when invited by K–12 Language Arts consultants and personnel from the NC State Department of Public Instruction to be on the 10th Grade Writing Assessment Committee. After I became a Certified Trainer, I attended the training sessions to help the pre-service 10th grade teachers go into the field with as much expertise as possible and to try to assuage some of the cooperating teachers' anxiety about "turning over" their students to novice teachers.

A part of "hanging together" is linking with state language arts consultants—to learn the "rules" of the game and possibly to find ways to infuse passion into writing to the tests, or better, to teach "writing to learn"—the kind of writing that moves out of formulaic boundaries. Even more fundamentally, networking with language arts consultants or curriculum specialists opens channels of dialogue—those in state and district offices need practicing teachers to test and challenge the designs and standards; practicing teachers likewise need to voice concerns and provide input. Neither group can afford to antagonize the other or be adversarial. Given the budget constraints for education, those in State Departments of Public Instruction are more likely to have funding or better access to funds than individual teachers, schools, or districts.

In A Dialogue About Reading, Writing, and Thinking, a summer institute I designed for teachers in North Carolina, the major premise was to foster dialogue among middle and high school teachers, university English faculty, and professionals from the business world about partnerships in literacy. The impetus for this institute came from hearing—all too often—my university colleagues bemoan the lack of writing skills of first year college writers; high school teachers talk about what seemed not to have been taught to their students in middle grades; and people in professional writing contexts and numerous politicians berate the lack of writing skills they see. The primary text for the institute was Regie Routman's *Literacy at the Crossroads: Crucial Talk About Reading, Writing, and Other Teaching Dilemmas* (1996). In her introduction Routman explains she never saw herself as a political person, but the current educational climate calls her, and all teachers of English language arts, to a new responsibility.

But we can no longer keep our doors closed and be passive. We can no longer be naïve or silent. We must speak out because our silence speaks volumes. Today, the political climate is against us in many places. Make no mistake. There is a backlash in education that demands our attention. We need to get smart, vocal, and politically savvy, and we need to do it now. (xvi)

Building from Routman's commentary on the effects of the backlash, particularly directed at reading and writing, the participants in the institute began with explaining their teaching contexts. My university English department colleagues really had little knowledge about English language arts taught in middle and high schools and were quite unaware of the pressures of high stakes testing. More specifically, without knowledge of the effects of assessment-driven teaching on the teaching of writing in middle and high schools, my university colleagues hadn't understood why so many first year university students retain the formulaic writing patterns and lack integration of the conventions of writing. Some of the high school English teachers participating did not know what was being taught in the middle grades. The institute allowed for a sharing of expectations and realities; professional business people explained the kind of writing demanded in the workplace. Professional writers—some graduates of the university where the institute was held—talked about the importance of writing in obtaining jobs. From the knowledge shared, participants designed writing strategies to use in their teaching contexts, but fundamentally, the institute fostered an understanding of the complexity of teaching writing.

"Writing Your Best Practice"

Nearly a year after I first began drafting this chapter, I created an Advanced Institute for middle and high school teacher-consultants of the SJAWP called Writing Your Best Practice. Teacher-consultants are the "graduates" of the Writing Project's five-week Invitational Summer Institute (ISI); having had an extended time of partnering to demonstrate their best teaching ideas, they learn from each other about the teaching of writing and doing their own writing. They are some of the best examples of teachers "hanging together."

When I got what seemed like "an inspiration" for the Writing Your Best Practice institute, I had no idea of what it could become. I was "stuck," facing writer's block as I anticipated writing this book. Admittedly my English Education position at a large university demands more hours than I have and seriously limits time for research and writing, but even more, I've come to realize, I cannot write this book alone. I'm not "right there, right now" in middle and high school English classrooms; the realities I knew in my years of teaching middle and high school English have changed; I *need* these teacher-consultants, these reflective practitioners who are totally dedicated to becoming better writers and helping their students become better writers. And the process of collaborating with this core group of middle and high school teachers actually replicates the best of the writing process. Each time we met, we continued to build a community of teachers who were writing and learning.

The words of the TCs who participated speak for themselves about what these teachers have experienced and continue to experience through writing communities like the Advanced Institute. In response to evaluation questions about what worked in the July 2007 Institute, middle school teacher Carla Dunavan commented

- time to discuss our best practices with a diverse group of teachers (diverse meaning from different schools, grade levels, classroom clientele, etc.)
- focus questions that got us thinking about the day's task, chapter to work on, etc.
- time to talk and time to write—communication (people came when they could and were kept up to date via email/scribe notes, etc., when they couldn't attend)
- being with a group of compassionate and passionate teachers who clearly loved what they were doing

Amy Thompson, another middle school teacher, commented, "I can't say enough about the group. I love being part of a club where the people are intelligent, well read, want what's best for kids, are open to improving their craft. It's been great."

During the 2008 Institute days, we were able to polish chapters and continue the process. Again, the evaluative commentary expresses the essence of this chapter—of how teachers can develop and sustain a passion for writing. Kathy González and Maria Clinton, high school English teachers, clearly articulate the strongest values of collaboration. Kathy González likens the work we did together to the goals of National Board Certification in that we reflect on our practice and continually improve it. Kathy also highlighted, as so many of the other participants did, the "fabulous by-product of gleaning new ideas from colleagues."

Maria Clinton shared ". . . the hours I spent there were like an oasis of calm amid the sea of activity and stress that is my life right now . . . I got to hear some great writing from my colleagues, I 'harvested' more good teaching ideas for next year, and it motivated me to keep writing." Maria also identified how the writing and revising we do in the Advanced Institute mirrors the writing process we do with our students: "Doing that writing and sharing it with my colleagues reminded me again about how risky writing can be for our students, but also how fulfilling it can be when one is surrounded by supportive peers."

Additionally Maria articulates how the Writing Project's approach to professional development can really bring "heart" to the teaching of writing:

> Their attitude is so different from many staff developers who come to our schools. . . . Many professional staff developers have the attitude of possessing the "secret of success" for students, which makes the rest of us feel really stupid for having taught all these years without figuring it out. Writing Project consultants, on the other hand, just share what works for them, and they invariably do it with great humility and humor. They are open and eager to hear adaptations we might make to their ideas, and they are the first to tell you that they "harvested" their ideas from other sources. . . . I can picture Writing Project consultants in their classrooms with their students, and I wish I could be there to learn from them.

Note in each participant's comments the recurring themes of validation, collaboration, the development of a writing community, the importance of time and an immediate goal for writing, the practice of the writing process, and insight into our students' writing process. Lindsey Stewart, a middle school language arts teacher, participated in the Advanced Institute for the first time in June 2008; as a "newcomer" to the Institute, her response is most "telling":

> For me this was an amazing time of meeting with other teachers around the Bay Area and discussing different writing strategies we use in the classroom. I had the opportunity to discuss topics and strategies that will be included in the book . . . to read over a couple chapters of the book and critique/edit the piece. In doing so, I not only offered suggestions, but I also jotted down useful ideas/teaching strategies that I plan to incorporate into my own classroom! It's amazing how much I can learn in just one day when I'm networking with other talented teachers.

Find a Mentor/Be a Mentor

My first post-doctoral teaching position in English Education brought me in contact with a wonderful mentor, Stewart Bellman, at Black Hills State University. Stewart had taught Methods of Teaching English and Composition for the English Teacher—courses I was teaching for the first time. He directed me to *Practical Ideas for Teaching Writing as a*

Process (1997), a publication created by the California Writing Project (CWP), which for the first time in my then 20 years of teaching gave me the theory for my practice, for what I had intuited, and helped me realize why some of my methodology hadn't succeeded. Carol Booth Olson, University of California Irvine, later divided the book into two volumes: one devoted to elementary and middle grades and another for high school and college. These became my primary texts at my next institution where the Teaching of Composition course called for me to guide K–college teachers of writing.

Practical Ideas for Teaching Writing as a Process introduces the philosophy and purposes of the National Writing Project (NWP)—an organization that truly mentors teachers of writing. The NWP is also the only federally funded writing program, with continuous funding provided for over 25 years. While the NWP and its various state sites are not the only possibilities for teachers of writing, they are the most established and best organized. Grasping NWP's philosophy and purposes may be one of the best ways to become a mentor.

First, writing is a process, a recursive process that requires far more than a single "shot" for any writing assignment. I can never fault my students who don't really think about revising writing because I remember how seldom I did any more than a single draft of papers in high school or undergraduate work. Maybe I had some natural ability as a writer simply because I've always been a reader and "absorbed" language, but this relatively obvious concept about writing as a process with all that entails was quite revolutionary for me. Clearly revising is about more than simply "correcting" or copying text over; it's "re-vision" or seeing anew or thinking anew. And passionate writers know the importance of reflecting on or thinking about ways to communicate more precisely. The "era of assessment" with so many calls for on-demand writing further militates against a sense of writing as process; yet if we are to teach writing in a context of lifelong learning, the central premise of writing as recursive is essential.

Carol Booth Olson explains that part of the California Writing Project's (CWP) and subsequently the NWP's philosophy about writing is the understanding that "there [has been] a shift in emphasis from learning to read and write, to reading and writing to learn and to our emerging sense that literacy is not the possession of minimal competency or basic skills but the development of a richer, deeper, and more integrated base of understanding and knowledge" (*Practical Ideas for Teaching Writing as a Process,* vii). Teachers of writing need to understand this shift in emphasis and implement it in their "writing" lives before they can guide student writers in comprehending such a crucial emphasis.

In *Shadowlands*, Lewis is meeting individually with one of his students. As the student, a young man who has been an enigma for Lewis, is explaining why "he reads," he quotes his own father who said, "We read to know we're not alone" (Fleischer, 115). The essence of integrating reading and writing to help our students and us as writers and teachers of writing suggests we both read and <u>write</u> "to know we are not alone." We do these important acts to be more fully human. Especially in my first semesters of teaching teachers to teach writing, I needed to understand this shift in emphasis; now I see the reading and writing to learn as one of the most powerful appeals of language.

A second focus of the Writing Project is on thinking about learning and helping our students to know "*how* to solve problems and make their own meaning from what they learn" (Olson, vii). This focus may also have been intuitively obvious to me; however, without a mentor to guide me to a work like *Practical Ideas for Teaching Writing as a Process*, the work that framed the emphases and substantiated what I was practicing,

Todd Rafalovich

Mary Warner

I would not be the teacher I am. Ironically, another 10 years or more have passed since my first contact with the ideas and philosophy of teaching writing compiled in *Practical Ideas for Teaching Writing as a Process*, and only now in courses like Children's Literature and Literature for Young Adults have I implemented a strategy that I realize focuses on students "[making] meaning from what they learn."

Students in my Children's Literature course were writing literary analysis essays in response to five core novels, and were struggling to move beyond summary to analysis and even to formulate a claim to prove. After they submitted the first two or three papers and I tried to provide feedback that would bring some clarity to their writing, I gave the students the opportunity to do an in-class essay where they could explain what they'd intended to do in their essays. This "essay on their essays," a type of metacognition, provided the students with an opportunity to articulate what they understood they were writing and what they had learned about writing literary analysis. This example demonstrates another piece of wisdom I learned from Stewart and his Writing Project background: the importance of reflection on your pedagogy—in a sense, being a lifelong learner in how to teach.

In the intervening years since these "aha" moments on the significance of conceiving of writing as a process and of integrating reading, writing, and thinking, standards-based education—with its insistence on measurable outcomes—has caused a kind of regression, particularly for those new to teaching and who have not been introduced to the richness of writing as a process. Textbook companies, eager to provide the ultimate solution to raising test scores, market lock-step materials designed so that any teacher who simply follows each direction can successfully teach writing, at least the kind of writing that is "on-demand" and completed in a single sitting. Administrators driven to have student test scores high enough to earn merit pay and to avoid the stigma of being "program improvement schools" dictate the strategies and the professional development so teachers have little say, thereby frequently lacking any validation for their own expertise.

The prescriptive teaching materials can aid novice teachers and give beginning writers a basic structure; however, they often lack a sense of "life." The formulaic processes frequently isolate rather than integrate, and what is not integrated in this case is the creative, imaginative, playful sense of language and the act of writing—the passion. In such constrained settings is it likely that teachers or students "are having fun yet?" When writing is linked only to product and products that have to be measurable—and measurable in predictable ways—fun or enjoyment is unlikely; student interest, motivation, or desire to write is even less likely. And teachers of writing who are mandated to use whatever will bring results are stifled by these restrictive methodologies.

Stewart had been a director of the Dakota Writing Project and readily modeled the Writing Project philosophy of "teachers helping teachers." He tapped the talents of middle and high school teachers who had honed their expertise in writing instruction and quickly convinced me of the importance of enlisting Writing Project TCs to help pre-service teachers prepare to teach writing. Since my own teaching of writing in middle and high school was, at that time, about 10 years in the past, and my methods had not integrated writing as a process, it was crucial to identify in-service English teachers who were the best consultants, those who were entirely credible because they were refining their practices and had student samples to demonstrate what worked for various writing projects and in different learning contexts. Once I'd "shared" my classroom with teacher practitioners, learning along with my pre-service teachers, I knew I could never go back nor did I want to go back to "solo teaching," especially if I wanted to provide the best learning context for future teachers.

Stewart also modeled the importance of "cross-teaching levels" collaboration. First on the university level, he coordinated a tri-state grant for Faculty Development in such topics as cooperative learning, critical thinking, and response to student writing. On the middle through high school teaching level, he taught me about the writing groups, which are a component of the Writing Project Summer Institutes. From the idea of these writing response groups, I developed writing partnerships between my pre-service teachers and the students of the middle or high schools they would teach. The partnerships served many purposes, not the least of which was giving the pre-service teachers, now years "removed" from the writing of their future students, direct contact with what and how seventh or ninth grade students, for example, wrote.

In one unforgettable partnership, the pre-service teacher found that her seventh grade partner could correct the grammar she was using in papers for college courses, which she, the "teacher-to-be," hadn't understood. And the writing her seventh grade partner shared with her wasn't "beneath her"—he was writing a novel! These writing partnerships also created opportunities for pre-service teachers to practice the "language of response" and to see the challenges of describing writing assignments for students. In the journal accounts my students wrote, describing their writing partner sessions, they incorporated reflection on writing and learning—that all-important second focus for why we write.

Possibly the most important type of "cross teaching levels" that Stewart taught me about was the level of learning with and from your students. In Chapter 13 of *Winning Ways of Coaching Writing: A Practical Guide for Teaching Writing Grades 7–12*, edited by Mary Warner (2001), he describes several strategies for writing with your students, specifically trying to write in the style and voice of students—your middle and high school students, for example. The cliché of "walking a mile in another's shoes" takes on a whole new meaning when we try to "write in another's [shoes] voice." Stewart died in November of 2003 from a brain tumor; fortunately, many of his wise and time-tested teaching strategies are recorded in *Winning Ways of Coaching Writing*; he is a seminal example of a mentor, teacher, and lifelong learner who promoted the passion for writing.

As I've learned through the emails with Sylvia, from countless former students who are now teachers, and through online resources created by NCTE and various Writing Projects, opportunities to be mentors and to be mentored abound. If you have questions or concerns about writing, or if your passion is waning, try locating a mentor or consider becoming a mentor. Maria Clinton, cited earlier in this chapter, shared her perspective on being a mentor during the Writing Your Best Practice Institute: "Every time I supervise a student teacher or mentor a new teacher, I steal not only their teaching ideas, but also their enthusiasm and fresh, positive attitudes. They [beginning teachers] tend to inspire me and keep me from getting complacent or cynical."

Collaborate/Be a Collaborator—Form Partnerships

As shown from the previous examples, opportunities abound for you as a teacher of writing to collaborate and find support. In addition to the numerous possibilities connected with the NWP, NCTE also provides innumerable resources and contexts for collaboration. One specific professional development aspect of NCTE is CoLEARN: "Research-Based Professional Development Resources from the Experts."

Whatever your position in English language arts, you do not need to struggle alone. If you're a university instructor, connect your pre-service students with "real world" writing situations and students through writing partnerships; team-teach methods courses with middle and high school teachers of writing; meet with them to find out the realities of their teaching worlds; be cognizant of the writing assessments and state tests.

If you're an in-service teacher, connect with universities in your area and inform English preparation programs about what you want to see in your new colleagues, what you need to help you survive the "era of assessment," and how you can do more than just "teach to the test"; participate in local, state, and national English teacher associations like the NWP and NCTE; share your successful teaching strategies; support your newer colleagues—take a student teacher; try doing collegial journals; participate in a study or inquiry group; start a book club—read about writing and the best pedagogies; and be proactive about the professional development in your school or district.

If you are a pre-service teacher, ask your professors about NWP, NCTE, and the necessary resources to support you in the challenges of teaching writing, particularly in the current climate of assessment; seek out "real world" writing experiences; partner with teachers in grade levels where you will teach; and read, write, and develop the habit of being a lifelong learner.

Search Out Professional Communities That Challenge and Support

Building from the notions of "hanging together," being partners in literacy, and participating in collaborative opportunities like the Advanced Institute, a concrete way to sustain a passion for writing is to participate in workshops and professional development. The extensive presence of the NWP, with writing projects in every state in the nation—many states have several writing projects, most often connected with state universities—provides powerful and sustaining professional development. Writing projects host invitational summer institutes, bringing together teachers who have developed successful writing practices. These teachers share their pedagogies and theories, participate in writing response groups, and strengthen themselves as writers. The "graduates" of invitational summer institutes become the teacher-consultants offering writing project sponsored in-service and professional development throughout the school year.

If you are feeling the "assault" of teaching writing "to the test," of struggling to motivate student writers, of simply not knowing how to teach writing, locate a writing project near you. Go to the NWP online: http://www.nwp.org/. Once you explore what the NWP has to offer, ask your administrators, curriculum specialists, or professional development personnel to provide the kind of in-service the NWP espouses and is committed to. Some of the tenets describing effective professional development include

- ongoing and systematic programs that make it possible for teachers to come together regularly throughout their careers to evaluate the best practices of other teachers
- programs to improve student writing [involving] teachers at all grade levels and in all content areas
- programs that use writing as a means of discovery and a way of learning (Jim Gray, cited in Olson, xi)

In the time I've been a co-director of the SJAWP, I've had opportunities to hear so many teacher-consultants "testify" about the transforming and renewing experiences of invitational summer institutes and of ongoing professional development that is life-giving rather than energy-draining. I have been amazed at teachers' desire and initiative to seek out the kind of intellectual and professional communities created by writing projects. One example is TC Pamela Cheng of the SJAWP, who has co-directed the Invitational Summer Institute and initiated the SJAWP's Young Writers Camp. She moved from New York, where she had experienced a rich and supportive context in her language arts teacher preparation. When Pam moved to the Bay Area, she actively sought out a professional intellectual community here before she had even obtained a teaching position. And though her initial experience was with a group geared much more to university level teaching, she was led to the SJAWP. After being a participant in the ISI, Pam became the co-director of the summer institute. A highly effective and creative elementary teacher, she is a model of the lifelong learner and practitioner the writing project supports and fosters. Pam currently holds a district-level position, enabling her to encourage many more ELA teachers to infuse their writing instruction with passion.

Consider again the key points of this chapter from the perspective of some reflective question:

- When you reflect on yourself as a writer and as a teacher of writing, what reading is feeding your writing soul? What are you and your students writing that is leading you to a deeper sense of humanity?
- In what ways have you been able to support a colleague or someone teaching in middle school if you're a high school teacher or vice versa? Have you had an opportunity to "hang together" so as not to "hang separately"?

- Would you consider writing and sharing your best practice? How might articulating your rationale for writing practices help you find value in what you do?
- Is there someone who is a mentor for you in the teaching of writing? Are you that mentor for colleagues? Could you become a mentor?
- When have you had opportunities to collaborate? Have you considered partnering with peers across grade levels?
- What professional communities might you join?

As Dumbledore explained to Harry, we do indeed "have too many thoughts and memories crammed into [our] minds." Use the essential gift of writing in its power as pensieve to give you, and by consequence your students, the space to examine and make sense of your thoughts and lives.

References and Resources

Belanoff, Patricia, and Peter Elbow. *A Community of Writers*, third edition. McGraw-Hill, 1999.

CoLEARN: "Research-Based Professional Development Resources from the Experts." http://www.ncte.org/profdev/online/108671.htm

Drake, April. Emails to Mary Warner. January 2006, December 2011.

English Companion Ning. Jim Burke, moderator. Englishcompanion.ning.com

Fleischer, Leonore. *Shadowlands*, based on the screenplay by William Nicholson. New York: Signet Books, 1993.

Kidd, Sue Monk. *The Secret Life of Bees*. Penguin, 2003.

Koester, Sylvia J. Emails to Mary Warner. August 2005.

L'Engle, Madeleine. *A Wind in the Door*. New York: Dell Publishing, 1973.

NCTE: National Council of Teachers of English. http://www.ncte.org

NWP: The National Writing Project. http://www.nwp.org/

Olson, Carol Booth, ed. *Practical Ideas for Teaching Writing as a Process at the High School and College Level*, Revised Edition. Sacramento, CA: California Department of Education, 1997.

Routman, Regie. *Literacy at the Crossroads: Crucial Talk About Reading, Writing, and Other Teaching Dilemmas*. Portsmouth, NH: Heinemann, 1996.

Rowling, J. K. *Harry Potter and the Goblet of Fire*. New York: Scholastic Press, 2000.

Stacey, Paula. "Let's Stop Teaching Writing." *Education Week*. Web. 28 September 2011. http://www.edweek.org/ew/articles/2011/09/21/04stacey.h31.html

Warner, Mary L., ed. *Winning Ways of Coaching Writing: A Practical Guide for Teaching Writing Grades 7–12*. Boston: Allyn & Bacon, 2001.

Zusak, Markus. *The Book Thief*. New York: Alfred A. Knopf, 2005.

3

Building on the Formulaic: Into, Through, and Beyond

by Maria Clinton, Martin Brandt, and Brook Wallace

Introduction

As the teacher-authors of this book have met over the last five years, our discussions have often addressed the paradoxes of the formulaic. We acknowledge that, in many areas, structure aids the beginner. Playing out this analogy with middle and high school students, we can point out that when you begin to drive a car, you strictly follow many basic steps: adjusting all mirrors before you put the car in drive; coming to a complete stop—with the speedometer registering zero—at stop signs; and checking mirrors as well as looking over your shoulder when making lane changes. Once you become more experienced, you do most of these actions instinctively, subconsciously. It's the same with the formulas used to guide writers—developmentally, such structures provide needed scaffolding. The challenge is to avoid getting stuck in the formula.

The authors of this chapter provide helpful processes for teachers to use to guide developing writers as they struggle to master and then move beyond formulaic writing. Maria Clinton opens with ideas for evoking stronger writing from reluctant, formula-reliant, and personal writers. Martin Brandt then offers a discussion of sentence patterns that can provide the basis for more fluent and articulate writing. Brook Wallace concludes the chapter with a discussion of the power of nonfiction analysis to help student writers move through and beyond the formulaic.

Part I: Moving Students Who Are Reluctant, Formula, or Personal Writers "Into, Through, and Beyond" by Maria Clinton

Introduction

As the moments ticked away before the bell rang, the students busily gathered up their belongings and tucked them away in their backpacks. I looked up from my seat to see Brandon standing in front of me, shifting his weight from his right foot to his left. I smiled at him, and he said, sheepishly, "Uh, Mrs. Clinton, would you like to read my poems?"

"Sure," I replied. "Would you like me to just read them, or would you like some feedback?"

He looked indecisive for a moment, but then, looking quickly around to see if any of his classmates were near, said, "Oh, feedback. Any suggestions you could give would be great."

I had taught Brandon as a freshman and then again as a senior. He was a big, hulking boy, even at 14. He played football, was rather quiet, and seldom spoke to me voluntarily when he was a freshman. As a senior, he only came out of his shell toward the end of the year. Although he had previously confided to me that he wanted to be a writer, I was somewhat surprised that he confided in me that he had begun writing poetry.

I enjoyed his poetry. Typical of adolescent verse, it was somewhat angry, but also artfully understated. I gave him a few specific suggestions and asked him to bring me more if he wanted. All this was done quietly: he obviously didn't want his classmates to know that he was a poet.

When Brandon gave me his poems he was in my Advanced Placement Literature class—a class where we read widely, discussed intensely, and wrote constantly. He had difficulty with the analytical writing required for this class. He struggled with it all year, and when he did write acceptable papers, his style was stilted and awkward. It was obvious that he didn't enjoy or really have any interest in analytical writing. Yet, his poems were carefully crafted, showing great detail with an economy of words.

The Writers We Meet

When I think about the teaching of writing, I visualize Brandon and his classmates. They come to analytical writing with a range of feelings and attitudes:

"Writing is boring."

"Why do we have to write? When will I ever use this writing? Is this writing going to help me get a job? Is it necessary?"

"I'm not smart enough to be a good writer."

"I'll never be able to get a good grade on this writing."

In our classrooms, we have several distinct groups of writers, each with different needs, but all of whom can be guided to write with passion. Three specific groups I've identified in my own classrooms are

- **Reluctant writers:** These students may write when they are assigned to, but they don't really see the relevance of writing to their own lives. Mark was one of these students. He was planning to become a mechanic and had already received training for his future career. As a freshman, he turned in very few assignments and had to make up units in summer school. As a senior, he was determined to do all his assignments, so that he could get his units, earn his diploma, and move into the world of work. He did, indeed, turn in every assignment, but saw no reason to improve his craft, as he saw my assignments as hoops through which he had to jump. Many students, particularly the older ones who have chosen a career path, don't see writing as useful or necessary in their lives. Some, like Mark, will do what they must to graduate. Others will choose not to do assignments, and, as a result, may not pass our classes.
- **Formula writers:** These students have learned the lessons of formulaic writing well. When faced with a writing task, they immediately plan out their five-paragraph essay. They compose a topic sentence, list three main points, find quotes to support their points, and restate those main points in their conclusions. Then they are finished. Their essays are correct; they are also unbelievably boring. Yet, when the teacher assigns such an essay a C, the student is bewildered. "Why didn't I get an A?" Katie asked me several times. She proudly pointed out her transitions. "First," "Second," and "Third" appeared at the beginning of each body paragraph of every essay she wrote for the first three months of school. She always had quotes as support. She always restated her thesis and her main points in the conclusion, and every essay, no matter the topic, sounded the same. Katie was a very conscientious student and wanted to get good grades, but she couldn't figure out why she wasn't earning A's on her papers. She was writing exactly as she had been taught.
- **Personal writers:** These students are passionate when they are writing for their own purposes. They write during their free time, about topics they choose. They write to express their thoughts and feelings; exactly what we want all our students to do. Unfortunately, their interest and passion seldom transfer to their academic writing. They don't see any relationship between their own writing, which they love, and the writing the teacher assigns, which they tolerate. They will work at the craft of their personal writing, revising and asking others—even occasionally their teachers—for feedback. But these passionate writers often rush through their academic assignments so they can get to the writing they really care about. Brandon was one of these students.

Identifying the Needs of These Groups of Writers

- **Reluctant writers** need to be shown how writing can be relevant and useful in their work and personal lives.
- **Formula writers** need to be shown how to move beyond the formula and how to develop their own personal voice.

• **Personal writers** need to be shown that by exercising their "writing muscles" in the classroom, they can learn skills and techniques that will help them in their personal writing as well. We need to do this in a way that doesn't squelch their creativity.

Some writing activities are useful for all three groups of students; others will encourage a particular group, specifically. For example, I use a variety of journaling activities in my classroom. These journals help accomplish several objectives for all three groups of writers. Among these are:

• increasing student writing fluency
• practicing writing to explore what they think and know
• practicing specific writing skills

Family Message Journals

This activity is based on the work of Peter R. Stillman in his *Families Writing* (1989). Stillman talks about writing as a way to build family relationships and pass on family history. In addition, he says that "The truth is that writing is a central means of learning, whether it's academic or personally revelatory. It's as much for finding out as for reporting" (6). I want my students, especially the reluctant and formula writers, to see writing this way. At the beginning of the year, I ask students to purchase a notebook to be used exclusively as a "Family Message Journal." We staple the attached handout to the first page.

September _____, 2012

Dear Family,

This is my message journal notebook. I will be writing in it and bringing it home from English class a couple of times a week. This will be a way for me to practice and improve my writing skills, and also tell you about what I am learning in school.

Please write a short note back to me each time I write to you. It is requested that when you write back to me, you "model" letter format by including the date, a greeting, a body, a closing, and a signature, please. I need to bring my journal back to school each day. If you have any questions, ask me, or contact Mrs. Clinton at Northglenn High School.

Sincerely,

Students choose an adult from their home or personal life to correspond with during the year. I prefer that it be a parent or grandparent, but students can also choose a neighbor, family friend, coach, or minister.

Once a week or so, I end class by asking them to write an entry in their Family Message Journal. Some sample entries are:

- Tell your parent about your first week in high school.
- Reflect on your first six weeks. What went well for you, and what would you like to improve?
- Explain the *Romeo and Juliet* performance project to your parent. Use two of our vocabulary words in your message.
- Ask your parent if he or she ever read *Romeo and Juliet*. If so, ask your parent what he or she remembers about it.
- Ask your parent what he or she knows about the Civil Rights Movement.

The topics tend to focus around what we are doing in class. I originally started doing this assignment to increase communication between the classroom and home, without me having to make multiple phone calls. Since most of the students are writing to their parents, I want to increase that communication without assigning topics that are too threatening or invasive for the students. I tell the students that I will never ask them to write about something that is really quite personal; if they choose to write something like that, they are free to do so, but I don't force them.

Once they have written their entry, their homework is to take their journal home, show it to their parent, and have their parent respond. Some topics simply require the parent to sign, acknowledging that he or she has read the entry; others require the parent to write a short response.

As we organize the logistics of the Family Message Journal, I give students guidance about how long their parent's response should be and how to organize their time at home to make sure they connect with their parents. For example, students and their parents often need to designate a spot to place their journals on the nights that they need a response, so that parents who get home late realize they need to read the journal.

I don't actually collect the journals for grading. I want the students to be accountable for the assignment, but I also don't want to intrude on the conversation between students and their parents. Sometimes, when the topic asks a question about something we are studying, like the Civil Rights movement, for example, we discuss in class some of the responses they got. Always, though, I check their journals and stamp their homework calendars if they got their response. I never take off points for grammar or spelling because I just do a quick journal check at the beginning of class. However, I have discovered that parents will hold their children accountable for writing carefully; they often respond with comments like, "Write neater please. I can't read this," or, "Check your spelling." I never ask parents to do this; it is an added bonus to have a different audience for students' writing.

With this assignment, I am flexible on due dates. Sometimes, parents are out of town or get home late, so students can't get their journals signed. If this occurs often though, I discuss with the student and parent how they can make the assignment run more smoothly.

Differentiation

This assignment is very easy to differentiate. The most important method of differentiation that I utilize is based on language. Because the purpose of the Family Message Journal is to communicate with their chosen audience, the students must write in the language their parent reads. Many students are reluctant to ask about this and may feel unable to do the assignment if no one at home speaks English. Therefore, I always mention that if the student's parent speaks Spanish, then the student should write in Spanish and the parent can answer in Spanish. I have even had some parents dictate their answers to their children because they themselves couldn't write comfortably in any language. What matters is that the student is using writing for communication with an audience that is not the teacher.

I originally began the Family Message Journals simply as a way to increase communication between the classroom and home. However, the benefits of the Family Message Journals have gone far beyond my original intentions. For example, the actual communication that the journals promote is often deeper and more positive than students are used to receiving at school. I expected the journals to be a forum to let parents know what was happening in my class, but what has actually happened is that many parents use the journals to offer encouragement, pass on wisdom, and express their great love for their children.

Example 1:

Dear Mom:

I am working on a project about two criminals, Bonnie and Clyde. Me and my partner learned that they committed 13 murders and kidnappings. I need you to help me get the stuff I need to make it and this will involve a lot of looking. Also this will help me tremendously. I am going to say this now and again later "Thanks for all the help mom."

Dear Tristan:

It will be my pleasure in helping you with your project. I am a big fan of Bonnie and Clyde. This is going to be a great opportunity for us to spend time together. I look forward to it. Know I am always here for you. I love you dearly.

Mom

Example 2:

Dad:

In English this quarter we are reading a book called Of Mice and Men. *This book takes place in the 30s (the Great Depression). The two main characters are Lennie and George. One of these characters has a mental disability but is physically built to do hard labor (Lennie). The other character, George, is very intelligent but is smaller in appearance and takes care of his friend Lennie. So far they work on a ranch to earn money but the bosses son doesn't like Lennie because he is physically built. This is what we are reading in English class for the 2nd quarter. (I will go into further detail later, I couldn't write all the details because my hand would hurt)*

Aspen:

I'm glad you're reading this because I think I missed a lot of the good stuff when we read it in high school. I was distracted very easily. I do remember feeling bad about how Lennie was treated. Well my hand is starting to hurt from all this writing. Good night.

Love ya

I've found that this Family Message Journal helps my three groups of writers in the following ways:

- **Reluctant writers:** Many of the topics ask students to practice particular skills, like proofreading for sentence fragments or using vocabulary words. These are concrete, mechanical skills that transfer to workplace writing. Parents also give very positive feedback for the skill practice. They say things like, "Wow, I didn't know you knew that word. You are learning so much. Keep up the good work." In addition, sometimes these students find that it can be easier to communicate with their parents through this forum, which also helps them realize that writing can be useful for something besides work.
- **Formula writers:** These students also need to learn that good writing requires other qualities besides fulfilling a formula. Journal topics such as "What makes a good marriage?" which ask students and their parents to explore ideas, are exercises in writing to discover, which most students don't see as an essay assignment. They write in more of a stream-of-consciousness or conversational style. Because they have generated text, I can have them go back into their journals during class, asking them to highlight their main ideas or any new ideas that occurred to them as they wrote. In the process, they discover that writing "is a way of thinking, a passage into the mind, where the riddle lies. . . . Writing, in other words, takes us where we might not otherwise venture" (Stillman, 10–11).
- **Personal writers:** These students often find journal writing more interesting and authentic than analytic writing; at the same time, many of the topics foster valuable skills that can be transferred to their personal writing.

Conversation Journals

Conversation Journals capitalize on the fact that students love to write each other notes. Non-writers and formula writers will write copious, creative notes to their friends. They will text message; IM; email; communicate through Facebook, Twitter, or other social media; and write secret and "not so secret" notes during class. Writing as a communication tool is extraordinarily important to them when they are writing notes to their friends. The Conversation Journal puts this interest to work in the classroom.

A Conversation Journal is very similar to a message journal, except that these Conversation Journals are used within the school setting for a dialogue between two students. These journals do not go home. I use Conversation Journals when I have an even number of sections of a class, although they could be used between older students and younger students from different grade levels. Each student is given a partner in a different class section. Each pair shares a journal, which stays in the classroom at all times. Then, as we are reading a particular book, I will assign my students a variety of journal topics. The partner in the first class will write his or her answer to my prompt. When the other partner comes to class, he or she reads his or her partner's response, and then writes his or her own response to both my prompt and his or her partner's comments.

This activity allows students to use writing to have an ongoing exchange of ideas. Topics may include

- Do you believe in love at first sight? Is it true love?
- Does destiny or fate play a role in *Romeo and Juliet*?
- Was George right to kill Lennie at the end of *Of Mice and Men*?
- Will George ever buy the ranch? Why or why not?

As always, I can use this journal to have the students practice other learning skills as well. I may ask the students to see if they can use our vocabulary words or use personification in their entry.

Evaluation

Because of their conversational nature, these journals are very interesting to read. They stay in the classroom, so when I have time to read through them and make comments, I can easily do that. Since students write their journals during class, I give them participation points for the day when we do this assignment. An added benefit is that the journals serve as a formative assessment. Based on the evidence that students cite in their journal entries, I can assess what the students understand in their reading, and can tell if any students are confused. Often, if students are confused, their partners will clarify ideas for them, so that I don't need to address these confusions in class.

Differentiation

Students produce better writing when they get to choose a topic that appeals to them or with which they have a connection. When students are engaged in the topic, my reading of their papers becomes more enjoyable, as I seldom have to read 100 papers on the same topic. After they have written and responded in their journals throughout a unit of instruction, I ask my students to reread their journals to find a topic that appeals to them. Not only do they find possible topics but they also discover they've done prewriting for their papers as well. They already have their own ideas to consider and include in their papers, but they also have their partner's responses to inform their writing.

For the three groups of writers in our classrooms, Conversation Journals also serve an important purpose.

- **Reluctant writers:** As with any journal, I use Conversation Journals to practice skills that these writers may need. Just as important, though, Conversation Journals show reluctant writers that writing for a "real" audience can be engaging and less like an assignment. My students often get into very intense discussions in their journals; they want to spend more time than I am able to give them. Non-writers discover that writing in class, although always somewhat artificial, can be fun and informative. It serves a valuable purpose; it is not just a hoop to jump through.

- **Formula writers:** Like any other teenager, formula writers spend a great deal of time texting their friends and writing each other notes. They know that informal note writing is enjoyable and can also be a way to communicate their feelings. The Conversation Journals show them that writing for school can also be a fun and informative way to exchange ideas. Since they are writing to a peer, these journal entries are not structured in a formulaic way. They write about issues that are raised in our discussions, supporting their ideas (often at their writing partner's insistence) with examples. Conversation Journals demonstrate to formula writers that writing doesn't have to be formulaic to be persuasive and powerful.
- **Personal writers:** Just like the formula writers, the personal writers find this activity a more engaging way to respond to literature. They are able to express themselves creatively, but the structure of the topics forces them to use their writing skills to address academic topics.

Reading Histories

My Reading History project is adapted from the book *Speaking of Reading* by Nadine Rosenthal (1995). I was concerned about my non-reading students, and as I explored ways to share the importance of reading not just adequately, but also well, I discovered this book. Rosenthal tells about her own reading history, which progressed very slowly through her childhood, until as an adult she became friends with an avid reader, who became her "reading mentor." As Rosenthal's interest in reading grew, she eventually became a literacy teacher. Rosenthal says, "Those of us who read successfully find that reading gives us pleasure and enriches our lives immeasurably, and it gives us options, control over our lives, and the ability to make informed decisions" (xiv). For *Speaking of Reading,* Rosenthal interviewed a wide variety of people, from the famous—Kareem Abdul-Jabbar and Isabel Allende—to the not-so-famous, categorizing them as different kinds of readers: from "Voracious Readers" to "Adults Learning How to Read." Each chapter conveys the "Reading History" of the person interviewed. In the Reading Histories, the subjects explore their attitudes toward reading, their good and bad experiences with reading, and the role and importance of reading in their work and personal lives. I like the metacognition that is clear in these essays; many are tools for the subjects' discovery of facets of their own personalities. Joan Didion says, "I write entirely to find out what I am thinking." I want my students to understand their own attitudes toward reading and writing, and using the Reading History is a good way to find out.

At the beginning of the year before we set our reading and writing goals, I assign a Reading History. I share a few of the Reading Histories from the book, usually selecting different kinds of readers: a Voracious Reader, a Frustrated Reader, and an Adult Who Is Learning How to Read. The students read these essays, which leads to a class discussion of the importance of reading. I present statistics about the number of functionally illiterate Americans, the percentage of prison inmates who are illiterate, and earnings predictions based on various education levels. We also examine the variety of ways in which the speakers organized their Reading Histories.

Then, I ask students to complete the following:

Reading History

As we start our outside reading for this year, we have looked at and discussed the role of reading in the lives of several adults. This assignment asks you to examine the role reading plays in your own life.

Write your own Reading History. This paper may be organized in a few different ways.

It may be written chronologically, beginning with your childhood reading experiences, and ending with the present.

On the other hand, it could be organized by topic, with paragraphs describing how you learned to read, whether you enjoy reading and why, and the role reading plays in your life. You will need to choose the best organization based on what you have to say.

As you plan your writing, consider these topics:

* Who taught you to read? Was it fun? Easy? Difficult?
* Do you like to read? Why or why not?
* Is reading easy or difficult for you?
* Do you like others to read to you? Who read to you when you were little?
* How does reading make you feel? Why?
* Where do you like to read?
* Do you read for fun? Do you read for school or work?
* What do you like to read? What don't you like to read?
* What does reading mean to you? How important is reading to you?

This should be an essay, not a list of answers to the questions. Make sure you use specific examples so that the reader can understand why you feel the way you do. Talk to your parents if you don't remember learning how to read. They may be able to help you get ideas.

DUE: _____

Before they write, I have the students interview their parents and other family members about their early reading and writing experiences. I tell them to go through old schoolwork their parents may have saved to spark their early memories of learning. We brainstorm about favorite bedtime stories. I share with them my reading and writing history. (I am a Voracious Reader). Sometimes, I ask other teachers and the principal to come in and talk about their Reading Histories; I specifically encourage teachers from subject areas other than Language Arts. After the students have done this "research" and we have talked about it in class, they brainstorm their ideas and write their papers. Excerpts from two student samples follow:

Raquel:
In addition, reading is almost always difficult for me, because I have bad comprehension. Having bad comprehension hurts me, because I could read a whole book, and not know what I just read. Sometimes, I will catch myself having an I-have-no-idea-what-is-happening-right-now, look. So I eventually get bored with a book, and have to put it down, because I have no clue what is happening. Also, having bad comprehension makes me angry sometimes, because

having homework means reading, and when I try to read instructions, I don't get what they are asking or saying. This means it is hard for me to do homework, because I don't know if it will be wrong or right. Therefore, I have to have other people read them for me, so they can put it into their own words so I can understand it better.

Michelle:
It wasn't until middle school, that I felt true hatred towards reading. That's right, mythology. I didn't have a class based solely on mythology, but my geography and history classes looked into it a bit. It was only for a week, two at the most, but mythology was terribly confusing and more boring than anything I had ever read in my life. I may not like reading, but if I had to pick one subject to read, it would be non-fiction. My reasoning is that non-fiction is easy to picture and easy to understand because it really happened and chances are, I remember it happening.

In conclusion, just because someone is good at reading, doesn't mean they enjoy it.

Evaluation

Even though the Reading History is the students' first essay of the year, I am pretty gentle when I grade it, just giving points for having a complete essay. After we do this essay, the students write their reading and writing goals for the year, so they go back over the essay quite carefully to evaluate their strengths and weaknesses. In addition, I find that students put significant effort into the essay because they are telling me about themselves. Most of the essays give me an accurate view of the students as readers and writers and provide information that I need from the beginning of the year.

Differentiation

The way I differentiate depends on the class and the particular skills I want to highlight. Most of my honors freshmen, for example, are very capable "formula writers." They don't want to turn in a paper that doesn't feel like an "essay," particularly at the very beginning of high school. With these classes, we often talk about alternative ways of organizing their papers. Instead of writing a thesis and three main points, I show the students that they can write their papers chronologically, and that if they do this, they may end up with more than five paragraphs! I will provide these students with a reading timeline to complete to help them organize their papers.

With an on-level or remedial class, I generally have them do lots of "research" first. They do interviews with their parents, peers, and other adults, and then write to explore, without a great deal of attention paid to organization at first. Depending on the skill level of the class and their need for further input, I then have them peer revise for organization. I have included some sample interview sheets.

Because the students reveal a great deal about themselves and their attitudes toward literacy, these papers help me get to know my students as learners and as individuals. When I read about a student who felt humiliated by a teacher when he was trying to learn to read,

Sample A

Reading Survey   Name _____

Instructions: Survey at least three people (20 or more years older than you) about the following questions. Write down their answers and be prepared to discuss these in class on Thursday!

Name _____, Age _____, Relationship to you _____

- **How do you use reading in your everyday life?**

- **How has reading improved your life?**

Sample B

English 9   Name _____
Reading Interview

Instructions: Survey your parents and siblings about your Reading History. Ask them the following questions:

- Who read to me when I was little? Did I have a favorite book?
- How old was I when I learned to read? Was it easy? Difficult?
- What were my favorite things to read when I was little?
- Is reading important in your life? How do you use reading in your life?
- Does reading give you power? In what ways?

I know to be gentle, particularly when I ask him or her to read aloud. When I learn that a student is a voracious reader, I know I will need to challenge him or her. I don't have to guess what kind of readers my students are because they discover it for themselves and tell me. This helps me plan more effectively.

These papers also reveal students' writing skills. Students tend to put a great deal of effort into this assignment and actually write quite extensively because they like writing about their lives. This helps me identify the strengths and weaknesses of individual students. In addition to assisting my planning, these Reading Histories meet the needs of the three different types of writers in the following ways:

- **Reluctant writers:** These students know that they don't like to read and write, and they don't think they write well, but they don't really know why. This assignment helps them discover something about themselves, often something significant they never knew about themselves and their lives. Writing in this case is a tool for discovery; it helps them think and learn about themselves.
- **Formula writers:** Like the reluctant writers, many of these students don't necessarily like to write. They have learned the formula, and since they don't really see writing as anything beyond a formula, they don't realize that writing can be passionate and emotional. For these students, too, just like the non-writers, the experience of the Reading History shows them that writing can help them do more than fulfill an assignment. These writers often write more than five paragraphs and are surprised that this is possible.
- **Personal writers:** These writers are generally most comfortable with this assignment, as they are writing about themselves and their feelings. Their writing is often rich in examples. At the same time, though, I have the opportunity to teach them some organizational skills with this assignment. The Reading History shows them that it is possible to write an essay that conveys some feelings, rather than just meaningless information.

Standards

Each of these assignments meets important Common Core State Standards see http://www.corestandards.org

Writing (Grades 9–12)

Assignment	Anchor Standard for Writing
Family Message Journals and Reading Histories	Write narratives to develop real or imagined experiences or events using effective techniques, well-chosen details, and well-structured event sequences
Conversation Journals	Write arguments to support claims in an analysis of substantive topics or texts, using valid reasoning and relevant and sufficient evidence
Family Message Journals, Conversation Journals, and Reading Histories	Produce clear and coherent writing in which the development, organization, and style are appropriate to the task, purpose, and audience

This is a listing of the minimum standards these assignments meet. However, since I often require students to practice specific mechanical and vocabulary skills within the journal assignments, the students are actually practicing other standards as well.

The three groups of writers I've just described appear in middle school and high school classrooms, and the suggested activities are applicable to middle and high school students. Investing in "intro" activities that encourage all three groups of writers should help them all move more easily and confidently beyond the formulaic.

Part II: Chunks, Scaffolds, and Names:
A Pedagogy of Sentence-Level Instruction
by Martin Brandt

About six or seven years into my teaching career, I found myself hunkered down in a miserable sort of non-aggression pact with my most challenging classes. Every year I got at least two such classes. The students in these classes struck me as uneducable: cynical, recalcitrant, vulgar. They fought at lunchtime and came back boasting of their exploits; they showed up at class stoned or drunk, grinning proudly when the fact was recognized by their classmates or teacher; they punctuated their sentences with every conceivable grammatical application of the F-word and giggled with delight when I took offense. They had little chance of graduating high school: "I am loser, hear me roar," seemed to be in their every word and gesture, and I felt utterly hopeless in my inability to teach them.

It hadn't started this way. I had wanted to be that teacher from the movies—the quirky outsider who comes in and, through his or her unorthodox but brilliant teaching methods, manages to tap into the latent genius of the students and liberate them from the thrall of their ignorance, passing them all on to Ivy League colleges. But it didn't work. It failed miserably. These students were as distinctly unimpressed by friendly, quirky, unorthodox teaching methods as they were by the rest of school. They saved their best work and their best face not for big, beautiful, eternal abstract questions, but for vocabulary lists and worksheets.

Ergo my non-aggression pact.

OK, you want worksheets, I'll give you worksheets. If busywork is the only way to make you behave halfway decently, then busywork you shall have. I won't try to teach you anything of value, and you won't do anything to drive me crazy. Vocabulary pre-test on Monday: *affect* versus *effect, there, they're,* and *their, here* and *hear;* Tuesday: worksheet on problematic words; Wednesday: worksheet on finding the verbs; Thursday: worksheet— gleaned from *Warriner's Grammar*—on comma placement; Friday vocabulary post-test, worth double the pre-test. Grade and correct your tests, enter your scores. Everybody still alive? No fights, pregnancies, or public drunkenness? Good.

Recalling the above sentiments years later, I am of course deeply ashamed. I make these admissions now in the spirit of guilt and confession. If I had looked harder, or viewed my students in a less condescending manner, or been more disposed to listen to them, I might have seen earlier that they have in fact a deep linguistic facility, regardless of whether or not they're termed "remedial." I would have noticed the cleverness latent in the vulgar banter that I so often objected to, and I might have asked questions about their perspective rather than hastening to dismiss it. In so doing, I might have placed myself in a position to build a healthy teaching relationship that acknowledged their "incipient excellence" (to borrow from Mina Shaughenessy, 1976). Instead, caught in my stance of "remediator," I could only see their failures.

But there is always hope, and if like doctors, teachers should "first, do no harm," then I was at least doing my students no great or lasting harm. The worksheets, the vocabulary lists—were all garbage, but none of it toxic. But my garbage pedagogy seemed better than not being able to teach.

And I did want to teach—to teach *well* and not simply endure a series of miserable non-aggression pacts for the rest of my career. I wondered *why* I could not get these students to write anything of any real interest. I wistfully enjoyed the work of writers I admired and asked myself if I could get my students to write like my heroes.

One day, reading a back issue of *Outside* magazine, I came across Jon Krakauer's account of the 1998 Mt. Everest disaster, which he had witnessed firsthand. Krakauer's article would become the basis for his page-turning best seller, *Into Thin Air* (1998). Reading the article, I found this opening sentence, pulling me like a rip current into the depths of his tale:

> "Straddling the top of the world, one foot in Tibet and one in Nepal, I chipped the ice from my oxygen mask, hunched a shoulder against the wind, and stared absently at the vast sweep of earth below."

Now that's some fine writing. *That's* the kind of sentence I like to read: dynamic, elastic, fluid—but none of my students (and not just the toughs) seemed capable of writing that way. I couldn't really tell what it was about that sentence that made it swing and strut the way it did. What would it take to get my students to write even *one* sentence like that? In a moment that I now see as a turning point in my career, I came up with the idea of breaking the sentence into chunks and having my students imitate its phrasing. Divided thus, the sentence took on the appearance of a poem:

> *Straddling the top of the world,*
> *one foot in Tibet and one in Nepal,*
> *I*
> *chipped the ice from my oxygen mask,*
> *hunched a shoulder against the wind,*
> *and stared absently at the vast sweep of earth below.*

I provided space between the lines so that my students would write beneath each one, and showed up one midweek morning with my new, nameless creation.

"Mr. B., what's this? We gonna read a poem today? Since when do we read poems?"

"It's not a poem. It's a sentence."

"That's a sentence?"

"Sure it is. Read it."

We read it. Grammatically speaking, I had no idea what to call the different chunks, so I improvised: "See how that first part starts with an '-ing' verb? See if you can do that. Write a phrase that starts with an 'ing' verb."

They did.

"See how that second line has one foot in one place and another foot somewhere else? See if you can do that with a different detail. Write about your hands if you want."

They did.

"See how the third line has just one word, 'I'? That's the subject of our sentence. You can use the same subject if you want, or put another name there."

They did.

"OK, so how many things does that 'I' *do* in this sentence? Three, right? They're in the remaining three lines. Now make *your* 'I' do three things, one action per line."

They did.

"OK, now I'm going to come around and check and provide whatever help you might need."

Most of the sentences needed work, inappropriately merging lines, confusing different grammatical parts, or leaving out portions of phrasing that I considered necessary. They were thin on detail, using one to three words where Krakauer would have used six or seven. But they were getting there. Then, in a moment of true courage, one student brought me the sentence he had been laboring over quietly in the back corner. "Hey Brandt, how about this? Whaddya think?"

> "Sitting in my bedroom, one hand on a cold 40-ounce Old English and the other holding my bong, I took a hit, inhaled deeply, and leaned back on my bed, ready to get high."

"This is where I was supposed to tell my student, 'This is not appropriate subject matter for class, young man.'" But I couldn't. He had successfully negotiated the grammatical challenges of imitating Krakauer's sentence. Sure, it was inappropriate subject matter for school, but a lot of truly great writing is inappropriate subject matter for school. Plus he had done it entirely on his own and in my years of teaching, I had not seen a better sentence from any student—nerd or thug—and I wanted to read more like it. "Good job," I said. "That's what I'm talking about! Listen to this one, everybody!" And I read the sentence aloud to the class, so they could hear that one of their "thug" classmates had written a sentence worthy of the greatest nerd.

I now know that the sentence modeling I had just done was a widely used and respected practice—especially as a component of a comprehensive sentence-level pedagogy. For the time being, I was happy to use sentence modeling in whatever cobbled-together fashion I could, and began scouring back issues of *Outside* magazine and contemporary journalism for more sentences, sometimes using several sentences from one article, to give the students practice in pacing:

> *The great white shark*
> *slowly cruising outside the flimsy submerged cage*
> *in which I'd imprisoned myself*
> *was probably only 12 or 13 feet long*
> *and weighed, at a guess, 2,000 pounds.*
> *It seemed quite docile,*
> *menacing only in its profound grace.*
> *The great white rose to the surface,*

where there was a floating and iridescent smatter of chum:
fish oil and sardines ladled into the water specifically to attract sharks.
A severed seal's head floated nearby.

(Tim Cahill, "Here Sharky, Sharky, Sharky," *Outside,* August 1998)

Sometimes I chose sentences based on the way the writer used imagery:

Early morning at Ultima Thule Wilderness Lodge in south-central Alaska.
    Inside the dining room,
the day takes shape in cinematic perfection:
the steam curling from a pyramid of sourdough pancakes,
the golden April sun shafting through the windows,
and visible beyond,
the snowy peaks of Wrangell-St. Elias National Park glinting in the cold air.

(Daniel Coyle, "The First Law of Gravity," *Outside,* August 1998)

And sometimes I would choose a sentence because of the way it demonstrated skillful use of a particular grammatical structure, as this one does with the prepositional phrase:

Across Rodgers Street
and around the back of the Crow's Nest,
through the door and up the cement stairs,
down the carpeted hallway and into one of the doors on the left,
stretched out on a double-bed in room number twenty-seven
with a sheet pulled over him,
Bobby Shatford lies asleep.

(Sebastian Junger, *The Perfect Storm,* 2009)

Another such example combines a noun-phrase appositive with an adjective clause and a prepositional phrase:

There's only one paved road into Crested Butte Colorado—
Route 135,
a meandering two-laner
that winds up from Gunnison
through wildflower meadows and jittery stands of aspen—
and the locals have always liked it that way.

(Hampton Sides, "Last Seen Heading West on a Vintage Hardtail," *Outside,* September 1998)

By looking at sentences like these with a connoisseur's eye, it began to emerge that the real problem with my students' writing was not the fact that it was "wrong," or strewn with errors—an infraction that had landed them in "remedial" English in the first place. No, you could take most of their sentences and apply all of the necessary punctuation, capitalization, syntax, and spelling, and still have something that's not very good. And this was the case with my at-grade-level and honors students, too. The real problem was not that their sentences were incorrect, but that they were sparse, austere, and bare—even when they *were* correct. By using the previously noted sentence models, I was asking my students to consider some of the possibilities of writing, rather than its limits.

As much as I would like to report that the students' writing ability exploded into view, that I'd tapped into a dormant facility for writing and beheld an awesome eruption of writing talent, this was not the case. A few well-written sentences fed my hunger, like a jungle insect in the hands of a TV survivalist; but many students had real difficulty distinguishing the grammatical differences between the chunks I had provided, often conflating them in such a way that drove the sentences off the road into a grammatical ditch. Many of them could not resist their tendency to move too fast, getting to the verb long before it was called for and compensating by adding all kinds of nonsense in the remaining portions. Sometimes, the point of imitating the kind of phrasing was completely lost on a student, who would simply put in any old combination of words. When this happened, I was at a loss for what to do, since we didn't share a language that would allow us to discuss these essentially grammatical problems. Traditional grammatical terms like "verbal phrase" meant little to me and my students. I could not simply say, "You need a prepositional phrase there," especially when I barely understood such terms; I didn't know what a phrase like *the steam curling from a pyramid of sourdough pancakes* was called.

I was happy with the effort—getting the students to think about their sentences, and some of them were indeed creating wonderful examples—which provided tantalizing promises of what could come with better, more informed instruction.

Todd Rafalovich

Martin Brandt

This "better, more informed instruction" began when I first participated in the San Jose Area Writing Project's 2003 Summer Institute. I saw I was not alone in the struggle to teach writing effectively and to find meaningful, stimulating instruction. That summer, I was surrounded by colleagues from all levels of education, all willing to share their discoveries as teachers of writing. Andrea Katz, a brilliant elementary school teacher, shared how she adapted the work of Dr. William Spivey to fit her instructional needs. Andrea led a demonstration in which she did not just *chunk* the sentences, as I had been doing with my students, but actually *charted* them, using lines and boxes to separate the grammatical elements, providing a workable scaffold for her students to use. Across the top line of this scaffold, she had written the names of each chunk: *subject, verb, preposition,* and *object,* below which appeared a sample. Students were to complete the chart, following the model established in the sample. The chart looked something like this:

Subject	Verb	Preposition	Object
My mother	took me	to	the dentist.
The dentist	looked	at	my teeth.

I had the second great part of my sentence-level instruction: scaffolding. Andrea's scaffold was actually a preliminary assignment, used to create sentence parts that would be written on strips of paper and then stapled into a small booklet, the strips of which, when peeled back, would reveal the interchangeability of the grammatical chunks. "My mother took me to the dentist" could become "The dentist took me to my teeth," a sentence that's nonsense semantically, but sound grammatically.

This demonstration was fun; I wanted to integrate such a chart into my sentence modeling exercises, which were lacking any comprehensive point or sense of direction. The scaffolding element would accommodate larger phrases or clauses that appeared in my *Outside* magazine examples. The problem was my knowledge of grammar was not sufficient; I didn't know what the chunks were actually called.

Since I didn't really know the names, I'd just have to come up with new ones. For the basic grammatical building blocks, I went back to Andrea's references to Spivey. Any slot that required a noun (subject, direct or indirect object) could be substituted with "who/what"—a direct object is as much a "who/what" as a subject is. Time or place reference nouns would get a "when/where"; "predicate" or "verb" = "action," and adjectives = "description." For the verbal phrase, I'd use a question that the students would have to answer with an "-ing" verbal phrase, like "Doing What?" Here's an example of how I'd scaffold a sentence:

A powerful storm hit the Bay Area Friday, knocking down power lines,
flooding city streets, and creating gridlock on the highways.

Nerd Libs: The Triple Decker

Who/What	Action	Who/What	When/Where	Doing What?	Doing What?	Doing What?
A powerful storm	hit	the Bay Area	Friday,	knocking down power lines,	flooding city streets,	and creating gridlock on the highways.

I called this creation a "Nerd Lib," since students do it like they might do Mad Libs—that delightful road-trip game using parts of speech to create absurd and humorous sentences. I put the chart on an overhead transparency, leaving the projector off while, Mad Lib style, I solicited the students' ideas. We came up with sentences like this:

My friends and I went to McDonald's after school, acting stupid, talking shit to one another, and getting high.

The content is questionable, but more importantly, notice how I've divided the chunks into very small, manageable parts. Here was the solution to my grammatical terms problem: no need to engage in lessons on verbal phrases—the sort of mistaken pedagogy so ably dismissed by Braddock, Lloyd-Jones, and Schoer (1963). Just answer the "Doing What?" question, and start your answer with an "-ing" verb of your own.

The initial results were encouraging enough that I used the Nerd Lib chart for all my classes. I also used the Nerd Lib to address particular moves in academic writing that my students found problematic. For instance, my students could not write with enough authority to produce a truly impressive thesis. "A good thesis should make a strong argument," I'd tell them. Or "A good thesis should sound authoritative." I didn't understand that what I was asking requires specific academic writing—a particularly formal variety of English some call "academic English," others call "analytical writing," but which I call "Nerd." "Nerd" is characterized by the frequent need to establish subtle distinctions, using qualifying phrases and concessive clauses—part of what the Common Core State Standards mean by "clear and coherent" writing (CCSR Text Types and Purposes: 4)—to identify the important-though-latent features of whatever happens to be under examination. I needed to teach a series of grammatical and rhetorical tricks common to this language style, which writers and scholars use *all the time* in order to add layers of meaning to their declarations, making their opinions sound measured, considered, and authoritative. The Nerd Lib chart would help me do that.

Here is a thesis-style sentence, which relies for its effect on some garden-variety Nerd structures that may seem quite exotic to our students, but which they can master with a little bit of practice:

Who/What/ Title	Shows/ Suggests That	What	Is Not	But Is in Fact	What It Is!	What It Is!
To Kill a Mockingbird	suggests that	true virtue	is not just the ability to get along with everyone	but is in fact	the courage	to stand up for what you believe in.

I call this sentence the "What It Is!" sentence. "What It Is!" is a hip-hop expression that I co-opted, an affirmation of overall well being within the world; I use the name because the sentence does two things. First, it establishes the writer's authority by providing an opportunity within its structure to dispute what the writer sees as a commonly held misconception—in this case, the notion that it is a virtue to simply "get along" with people. Second, the sentence creates a sense of anticipation. It declares what something is *not*, before clarifying *what it is*. The reader is led to pose the question: If virtue is not in fact what I thought it was—the ability to "get along" with people—what is it?

There is a grammatical term for such constructions: they're called "correlative conjunctions." It's a fancy term for those two-part constructions ("not only/but also," "either/or," "neither/nor") that are common even in ordinary informal discourse, but which require careful presentation in formal writing. In order for the construction to work in writing, the two parts being emphasized ("the ability to get along" and "the courage to stand up") should be as near to one another as grammatically possible, and they should be parallel—that is, composed of identical grammatical syntax.

However, I didn't need to know the term "correlative conjunction" to come up with the structure. I just noticed that the "not this but actually that" construction is common in Nerd, and that my students, in their attempts to re-create such structures, often tripped over the rules I just noted. The chart functions as a scaffold for practicing the structure and promoting discussion of the rules. Such discussion, on top of the writing, can help fulfill the requirements of the Common Core State Standards, which for example expect 11th and 12th graders to "Use words, phrases, and clauses as well as varied syntax to link the major sections of the text, create cohesion, and clarify the relationships between claim(s) and reasons, between reasons and evidence, and between claim(s) and counterclaims" (CCSR Text Types and Purposes: 1d).

I borrowed from hip-hop lingo again when creating a chart for making comparisons, "The Biter." In my students' slang, "to bite" is to consciously imitate someone else's choice in clothing, music, or speech style ("Why you bitin' my style?"). Given this definition, the meaning of "The Biter" sentence should become apparent:

Like	Name #1,	Name #2	Too	Action	What	What
Like	Jay Gatsby,	Myrtle Wilson	too	feels	the need	to play rich.

The notion that Myrtle Wilson and Jay Gatsby from *The Great Gatsby* (Fitzgerald, 1995) are engaged in a very similar act (however crudely Myrtle tries to pull it off) is a simple but powerful idea, certainly within the reach of my students' powers of observation, but few of them might use this syntax. They would save the "like" comparison for the end of the sentence, probably because this way preserves the order in which the idea occurs to them. By moving the adjectival phrase "like Jay Gatsby" to the beginning of the sentence, the writer has added a mostly stylistic texture—one that adds an authoritative tone to an acute observation.

It's never a bad thing to show students the flexibility of English phrasing, how the phrase "Like Jay Gatsby" can have the same function grammatically in different places within the sentence. For example, the phrase could also be placed after the name Myrtle Wilson—expressing the same idea, but with different emphasis and effect, in this instance burying the operative point of the sentence.

I have also used the chart format for teaching contrast structures, like the "U-Turn Sentence." The "U-Turn" comes in various configurations, but is so-called because it always begins by proceeding in one direction, yet signaling through a subordinating conjunction the writer's intention to veer 180 degrees opposite by the sentence's conclusion. It's an ordinary complex sentence, but I avoid the term "complex sentence" (which emphasizes structure over function) in favor of emphasis on the grammatical and rhetorical effect. Here are some examples:

Although	Name/What	Action	This Doesn't Necessarily Mean That	Who/What	Action	What/ Description
Although	Mr. Brandt	tells a lot of jokes,	this doesn't necessarily mean that	he	considers	his job a joke.

Just Because	Who/What	Action	Don't Think for a Moment That	Who/What	Action	What/ Description
Just because	Jefferson	owned slaves,	don't think for a moment that	the Declaration of Independence	has	no meaning.

"Night and Day"

In Stark Contrast To	Who/What	Who/What	Action	Description	What/ Description	What
In stark contrast to	Frederick Douglass,	Malcolm X	feels	liberated	by his new-found	literacy.

"The Over-Easy"

While It May Be True That	Who/What	Action	What/ Description	Who/What	Action	What/ Description
While it may be true that	school	can be	boring,	the importance of a good education	cannot be	overestimated.

and "Ebony and Ivory"

Whereas	Who/What	Action	What/Description	Who/What	Action	What/ Description
Whereas	Forty-niner fans	show up	in spiffy mini-vans and SUVs,	Raider fans	arrive	on roaring Harleys.

The names of all these structures simply identify their purpose of establishing contrast.

Perceptive readers will notice that all of my examples so far have been divided into seven grammatical chunks each. This is how I did it over the years—clinging tenaciously to seven chunks because I didn't want to change my chart. The beauty of charting your sentences like this is that anybody can do it, including your students. To borrow an idea from Donald Killgallon's wonderful *Sentence Composing* series, just take a sentence you like and have your students try to divide it into grammatical chunks. You'll be pleasantly surprised at how well they can distinguish the different functions within the sentence. Where they can't, you can engage them in some valuable discussion. Let's consider again Jon Krakauer's opening to the magazine article that would eventually became *Into Thin Air*:

> Straddling the top of the world, one foot in Tibet and one in Nepal, I chipped the ice from my oxygen mask, hunched a shoulder against the wind, and stared absently at the vast sweep of earth below.

Most of my students rightly guess that the commas mark off grammatical chunks. The sentence opens with a verbal phrase, moves on to an absolute phrase (a phrase which introduces a separate subject, but with no verb or with a verbal), then introduces the subject followed by three coordinate verb phrases—a triple-decker! In the end, you can chart this sentence into six chunks:

ingbomb	Wannabe	Who/What	Action	Action	Action
Straddling the top of the world,	one foot in Tibet and one in Nepal,	I	chipped the ice from my oxygen mask,	hunched a shoulder against the wind,	and stared absently at the vast sweep of earth below.

You could chunk this into even smaller parts, but I wouldn't. As the students become more confident with your terminology—especially with regard to different names for phrase and clause structures—and as they begin to develop their phrasing, the chunks should become larger, wider units, to the point where eventually they won't need them at all.

In the previous Nerd Lib, I didn't call the absolute phrase in the second slot by its proper name, calling it a "Wannabe" instead. And a broader contradiction: for a guy who claims not to know the grammatical terms, this Brandt fella seems to have picked them up from somewhere. The two points are related, and I use them to address a final purpose: that of naming things, which I have come to see as one of the most essential acts of both academia and teaching.

After a few years with the Writing Project, I found myself fascinated with the professional problem of teaching writing in general, and sentence-level instruction in particular. It had been 10 years since I had my students model that Jon Krakauer sentence, 10 years of sentence modeling and Nerd Libs. Was I doing the right thing? I didn't know, but I was willing to find out, so I enrolled in a Master's Degree Program in Composition at San Francisco State University, where the dots of pedagogy were finally connected by research and theory—particularly the work of Kellogg Hunt, Francis Christensen, and William Strong.

Hunt's research (1965) found that clause length was a reliable indicator of syntactic maturity: that is, that mature, confident writers write longer sentences. Writing teachers would do well, he argued, to find ways to help students develop the length of their clauses. A few years later, Christensen (1978) proposed a way to do this, pointing out that those longer sentences are filled with what he called "Free Modifiers" (adjective clauses, noun-phrase appositives, verbal phrases, absolute phrases, etc.), common phrase and clause structures that could be attached with commas to the base clause of the sentence. One could teach these structures through a method called Generative Rhetoric, Christensen argued, and this would be one way to develop students' syntactic maturity. William Strong, author of the widely used *Sentence Combining: A Composing Book* (1994, now in its third edition), proposed instead that we use sentence-combining exercises to develop our students' syntactic maturity.

The work of these researchers liberated me; I had not been wrong to focus on sentence-level instruction. There is indeed a substantial body of research suggesting that sentence development is an important key to improving student writing. What was missing from my pedagogy, however, was names for things. The Nerd Libs relied solely on generic terms like "Who/What" or questions like "Doing What?" for creating the models. But what generic term could effectively identify something like that absolute phrase in the second slot of the Krakauer sentence?

Consider the noun-phrase appositive, one of Christensen's "Free Modifiers." It's a fancy grammatical term for something quite common. A noun phrase is considered an "appositive" when it's placed next (apposed) to the noun it's modifying. However valuable knowledge of these terms may be, they mean nothing to my students. This is the great paradox of grammatical terms: our students would benefit greatly from knowledge of Free Modifiers, but the terms used to name them are so abstract as to be almost useless. And there's another layer to this paradox: You don't need to know what these structures are called in order to use them. I was 43 before I learned what an adjective clause is, though I of course had been using them for decades. But if you don't know how to use them, how do you learn? How do you teach those who don't already know them?

The answer was to invent a name for the noun-phrase appositive, something less abstract that addresses its function: "The Smack-Talker." Why "Smack-Talker"? Well, "talking smack" is another bit of hip-hop slang I've co-opted from my students for my "Nerderific" purposes. Along with its more vulgar cousin "talking shit," it means, "saying bad things about somebody." So why "The Smack-Talker" for NPA's? Because the noun-phrase appositive is as appropriate a place to inject *opinion* as it is to inject *fact,* and that opinion can of course be negative as well as positive. All the fun of writing happens between the commas. Here's a basic Smack-Talker sentence:

Name	Who Dat?	Action	What?	What?	When?	Where?
Jon and Kate Gosselin,	the despicable stars of the reality series *Jon and Kate, Plus Eight*	announced	their merciful decision	to file for divorce	yesterday	on their show.

Speaking for myself, it felt good to call these people "despicable." If you are fans of Jon and Kate or supporters of their TV marriage, it probably didn't feel so good to read it. You could use a Smack-Talker to respond with something equally passionate, something like "Marty Brandt, a spiteful self-styled arbiter of other people's relationships, really has no business pronouncing judgment on them." For defenders of Jon and Kate, that sentence would feel good to write, too. The Smack-Talker gives writers the structure to vent a little.

Smack-Talker phrases are quite common in obituaries. In such instances, the Smack-Talker phrase is usually combined with an adjective clause, in order to tell not only *who* has died, but also what life achievements make his or her passing noteworthy. In this manner, journalists can summarize an entire life's achievements between the subject and verb of the base clause "So-and-so died." I call this form "The Smack-Talker Dime-Dropper Combo." In underworld parlance, a Dime-Dropper is one who "drops a dime" and calls the cops on somebody—a snitch. In my class, it's a term for the adjective clause, that tremendously useful tool which modifies a noun by introducing a clause with the relative pronouns *who, whom, whose, that, which, when,* and *where* (the "dimes"). To take the instance of Jon and Kate, who will in a few decades have slipped mercifully into obscurity, it will require such an adjective clause to remind future readers of their obituaries just who they were and why their demise is using up valuable column-inches:

Name	Smack-Talker	Who	Did What?	Why?	Action	How?
Jon and Kate Gosselin,	the long-forgotten "reality TV" stars	who	sold access to their family of eight	in order to make a quick buck,	died	broke and alone.

In the course of a year, my students became very adept at Smack-Talker Dime-Dropper Combos—which were extremely useful tools for summarizing. Application of the Smack-Talker Dime-Dropper Combo can also satisfy multiple items on the Common Core State Standards for Language Arts: Comprehension, Presentation of Knowledge and Ideas, Conventions of Standard English, and Knowledge of Language. Students can show growth in all of these areas with mastery of this simple, yet sophisticated form. Here's a student sample, written by Adrian, a junior:

Who?	Smack-Talker	Dime-Dropper	Action	Who/What
Abigail Williams,	a miserable young woman	who tells a fake story in court,	sets up	Mary Warren.

Adrian is a strong and confident writer, but I don't think that he would have thought to use this structure until it was shown to him.

Here's Clarissa, a junior, executing a Smack-Talker Dime-Dropper with a triple -ingbomb:

Name	Smack-Talker	Dime-Dropper	Action	-ingbomb	-ingbomb	-ingbomb
Abigail Williams,	a lying tramp	who is the reverend's niece,	brought tragedy upon a town,	accusing innocent people of witchcraft,	avoiding punishment,	and causing misery for all.

Of course, you cannot expect all students to write at this level. But even the problematic sentences provide insight as to where or how a student is struggling and valuable perspective on the nature of error. Here's an example that addresses both issues:

Who?	Smack-Talker	Dime-Dropper	Action	-ingbomb
Reverend Samuel Parris,	a middle-aged priest	whose daughter and niece were caught dancing in the woods,	who claims about not being payed a lot.	

I could point out a number of things wrong with this sentence, from its religious inaccuracy—Puritan ministers are generally not called "priests" (except by Hawthorne)—to the faulty subject/verb agreement. The greater problem is that even though the student has written an effective Smack-Talker Dime-Dropper Combo ("a middle-aged priest whose daughter and niece were caught dancing in the woods"), he has not completed the base clause. Does he not understand basic sentence structure? I doubt it. Chances are he does not yet *hear* the incomplete nature of the modifiers he's added: they appear to be substantive—because they are—so he thinks that he's got a complete sentence. He needs to be reminded that free modifiers are *additions* to already-complete sentences.

In other instances in which the student goes far beyond his or her usual sense of sentence limits, other errors, once so grating, now seem quite small. Here's a sentence written by Tuyet, a long-term English learner:

Who?	Smack-Talker	Dime-Dropper	Action	-ingbomb
Proctor,	a farmer in Salem	who having an affair with Abigail,	comes to the court,	defending his wife from being accused in the witch trials.

Anyone who's had any experience teaching English learners will recognize the missing "is" or "was" from the Dime-Dropper. But what is most important to recognize is the fact that Tuyet has successfully executed the "-ingbomb," a grammatical structure that is quite complex.

Nerd Libs are introductory in nature. Heavily scaffolded as they are, they belong at the *beginning* of an instructional sequence. I follow them up with signaled sentence-combining exercises—William Strong's (1976) term for sentence-combining problems with a specific solution in mind, whether it be a noun-phrase appositive, a verbal phrase, an adjective clause, an absolute phrase, or some combination thereof. What I am trying to do here is use signaled sentence combining to introduce these Free Modifiers. An early version of such an exercise on noun-phrase appositives, for example, would ask the students to combine simple pairs of sentences, reducing one to a noun phrase and placing it next to the noun it's about:

1.1 *Mr. Brandt was sick yesterday.*
1.2 *Mr. Brandt is the greatest teacher ever to draw breath.*

I'm joking, of course, and my students know it. Anyway, the solution is, "Mr. Brandt, the greatest teacher ever to draw breath, was sick yesterday." (I like to hear them say it out loud.) With signaled sentence-combining exercises, I'll continue to up the ante, adding new layers of phrasing to get them thinking further on the function and rhetorical possibilities of the Smack-Talker:

1.1 *Mr. Brandt was sick yesterday.*
1.2 *Mr. Brandt is the greatest teacher to ever draw breath.*
1.3 *This was naturally the most important day of the semester.*

The specific solution I'm expecting is, "Mr. Brandt, the greatest teacher to ever draw breath, was sick yesterday, naturally the most important day of the semester." Students' solutions go on the board for discussion.

After the sentence-combining course, I'll introduce various sentence manipulation exercises: scrambles of the sort Donald Killgallon uses and a scramble exercise of my own invention, the idea of which I borrowed from those poetry refrigerator magnets. I've started a pool of such sentences; actually, I started collecting them a long time ago, before I knew the names of their features or what to do with them besides showing them to my students in an impotent attempt to get them to "write like this." Now I have something to do with them: chunk them up, scramble them, and see what the students can do.

My own scramble exercises demand the same ability to identify and manipulate the different sentence elements. Here is a pool for one such exercise, asking students to choose between the subject, verb, noun-phrase appositive (Smack-Talker), and adjective clause (Dime-Dropper) to create a "Smack-Talker Dime-Dropper Combo," the pattern of which is *Subject + Smack-Talker + Dime-Dropper + Verb*:

climbed Mt. Everest	Hermione Granger	carved a pumpkin	who hates carrots
Dizzy Gillespie	who plays trumpet	Tupac Shakur	the teacher
William Butler Yeats	the plumber	Cuauhtemoc Blanco	the king of rock'n'roll
the greatest artist ever	Chief Sitting Bull	the beautiful lady	the poet
Lindsay Lohan	who's a vegetarian	are three hamburgers	the movie star
George W. Bush	who drinks Starbucks	Charlie Brown	scored three goals
who ate too much	earned straight A's	the guitar player	the polo player
won three Oscars	who starred in Fargo	Napoleon I	who drives a Subaru
skis cross-country	the painter	travelled to Vietnam	won the SuperBowl
eats only vegetables	who makes me laugh	who rides a bicycle	who went to the beach

Using the previous pattern and drawing from the previous pool, students can compose any kind of foolishness they like: *Dizzy Gillespie, the painter who drives a Subaru, scored three goals*. Semantically, it's nonsense; grammatically, it's sound. The key is to give them the practice in identifying and manipulating (in this case) NPA's and adjective clauses. I've got similar scramble sheets that include verbal phrases and absolute phrases as well. The best way to create them is to simply write a number of different sentences that use the same grammatical pattern, depending on what free modifier you're trying to teach. Once you have enough of them, chunk them up and scramble them into a chart like the previous one. Once students have composed their sentences, they can build on their knowledge further by creating posters divided into four comic-strip style panels, one panel for each sentence element, written and illustrated within the panel.

Where does it all lead? I'd like to report that my students immediately start decking their base clauses with all of these structures, but at first, one of two things happen instead: most of the students *do not* automatically transfer their knowledge from the sentence manipulation exercises into their actual writing; others over-do it, adding noun-phrase appositives where none are needed, such as when they use them to identify someone whose identity is not at issue: *Martin Luther King, an important person in history, once said. . . .*

Do not despair. Mistakes like this, which are a part of growth, should be anticipated and understood for the sign of development that they are. In the 1970s, Kellogg Hunt did research suggesting that the ability to execute different writing tricks comes with age and practice: that is, it's developmental. Progress will be slow, and mistakes will happen. We should keep doing all we can to help our students transcend whatever sentence limits they exhibit at the moment. Will it transfer into their essays? Eventually, especially if we provide them opportunities *in revision* to go back into their essays and see where they might develop some of their sentences even further, with some of the structures they've practiced. In revision, I've found Free Modifiers helpful for showing my students ways to add layers of phrasing to their sentences, extending their length without lapsing into their preferred method of redundancy or unnecessary filler. I do not go as far as requiring my students to include Smack-Talkers, U-Turns, or What It Is! sentences in their writing—as a student, I always found such requirements burdensome—but the structures give a lively diction for the discussion of grammar and rhetoric, so that I can say upon reading something, "I see what you're trying to do here. Do you think maybe this sentence would work better with a Smack-Talker?"

Skeptics may justly wonder why I would want to adopt this weird slang nomenclature for age-old grammatical units. Why not just call it an adjective clause, Mr. Brandt? My answer is that as tools for teaching, grammatical terms would make a lot more sense if they clearly addressed *function*. A term like "adjective clause" says almost nothing to students about its function. But (ironically, in this age of cell phones) they do know what it means to "drop a dime" on someone. The term "Dime-Dropper" addresses *function* in a way that "adjective clause" does not. When I suggest that a student "Drop a dime on that noun," the student has a good idea what I'm asking for. And the fact that I was 43 before I learned what an adjective clause was never once hurt me as a writer; it did, however, hold me back as a teacher of writing. I needed to know what it was, not so that I could teach my students what it was, but to find ways to help them use it in their writing.

Ah, but what about the tests? Won't the students need to know the traditional terms for taking standardized tests? The answer is no. Even the California High School Exit

Exam (CAHSEE), which seems designed almost exclusively around the concept of rooting out error and testing knowledge of orthography, does not ask the students to go as far as *identifying* things like adjective clauses or distinguishing them from other forms. It mostly tests the students on recondite punctuation questions that a good number of adults couldn't answer correctly. (And with all of the Free Modifiers, the punctuation is easy: the humble comma.) And isn't it preferable that students approach the essay parts of exams as confident writers who are able to use these tools to express their ideas clearly? *That* may be the true difference between a pass and a fail. In the end, we are not really in the business of teaching our students grammatical terms; we are teaching them how to write, using whatever tricks we need to help them see the possibilities hidden within their sentences. If we've done this well, we will reap a reward far greater than improved test scores. We will know our students better for the delightful, clever, and engaging young people they are.

If in your professional judgment you prefer traditional grammatical terms, by all means use them. If you can think of better terms that speak to function more clearly to your students, do not hesitate to do so. The real issue is not one of terminology so much as finding ways to stretch the boundaries of your students' sentence writing abilities.

Part III: Using Nonfiction to Empower Students to Move Through and Beyond Formula Writing
by Brook Wallace

Introduction

Formula is dry, dull, and constraining, or so think many of our students, especially the reluctant and personal writers Maria Clinton profiled earlier in this chapter. So how do we convince them to not only learn and utilize a formula for writing, but also see its advantages? It often starts with the content. Invite students to join a textual conversation about a compelling issue and they will be more motivated to employ the formulas most valued by the participants in the conversation. They will be more motivated to try to speak "Nerd," as Marty Brandt puts it.

Although some students are motivated to write by their interest in responding to literature, I have found that more of my students, especially reluctant writers, are hooked by nonfiction. I have seen previously apathetic students make great strides in their essay writing when drawn in by compelling works of nonfiction. These students put in more effort, that is, when given the chance to join a conversation about a real world issue.

In creating units and writing exercises centered on real world issues, I have practiced the same skill of synthesis that I teach my students. Nothing I do is completely novel—any good teacher, if she or he is being completely honest, will admit that her or his most successful practices are a combination of techniques gleaned from student teaching, observing colleagues, professional development, and a myriad of other sources. Even those ideas a teacher feels are completely original are probably just combinations of these influences. In this chapter, I acknowledge my sources, as I teach my students to do, to the extent that I am conscious of them. For those readers who would like to explore some of the excellent resources I have counted among my influences, I mention them throughout the text and list them in the References and Resources section at the end of this chapter. However, I begin by acknowledging my main inspiration, the program that started me on my journey toward teaching nonfiction: the Expository Reading and Writing Course (ERWC) of the California State University system, a program that is itself modeled on the processes and ideas shared in Bean, Chappell, and Gillam's *Reading Rhetorically* (2010). As a participant in some of the original workshops of this program, I was so inspired that I eventually became a trainer and unit writer. That opportunity, combined with my reading of a variety of other sources, has led me on a journey toward becoming a more effective writing instructor. In what follows, I share what I have learned about the best ways to inspire passion and improvement in high school writers.

Rationale for Nonfiction

I have experienced great success by focusing on exciting and stimulating content. From my freshmen reading and analyzing articles on teenage behavior and school policies, to my sophomores weighing in on the debate in Germany over the treatment of Turkish Muslim immigrants, my students' writing blossoms when they are asked to share their opinions on serious real world issues.

I realize my own experience will not prod many English teachers into incorporating more nonfiction into their courses. For those who need additional convincing, therefore, I present the following objective facts. First, by many national measures, high school students are not presently being prepared to meet grade-level writing or reading demands. The scale of this problem is nicely outlined in two recent publications from the Alliance for Excellent Education, *Writing Next* (Graham and Perin, 2007) and *Writing to Read*: *Evidence for How Writing Can Improve Reading* (Graham and Hebert, 2010).

In addition, beyond such grade-appropriate expectations, one of the goals of a high school education is to prepare students to succeed in college and in their careers. College students are expected to read complicated nonfiction texts; analyze, evaluate, and synthesize those texts; and then turn that work into coherent, persuasive writing. Increasingly, workplaces of all sorts are requiring similar skills. The remediation data for the California State University system support a consistent finding that 45% of the students entering this largest of all systems of higher education need remediation in English. Similarly, the National Center for Education Statistics reports that 20% of incoming college freshmen in four-year institutions are not sufficiently prepared, and must take remedial courses. The percentage of those needing remediation is even higher for students entering community colleges.

This lack of skills affects those high school students who are planning to attend college as well as those destined for the workplace. Over a decade ago, Hall and Birkerts (1997) confirmed the ubiquity of expository writing, pointing out that exposition is the most common form of writing produced by professionals as well as college students. The focus on expository or explanatory writing has only expanded since then. Even before they reach the workplace, students will find that most of the standardized test questions they encounter will be based on nonfiction informational passages. In fact, many of the tests currently being created to assess the new Common Core State Standards use nonfiction reading selections and persuasive and research-based writing prompts. Such a focus on nonfiction is part of the current assessment plans set forth by the two groups awarded Race to the Top funding: the Partnership for Assessment of Readiness for College and Careers (PARCC) and the Smarter Balanced Assessment Consortium. (The PARCC and Smarter Balanced websites, listed in the References and Resources section, have more information about the groups' planned assessments.) In addition, increasingly, these current and future test questions determine not just a school's ranking but also a student's ability to earn a high school diploma or to take college-level classes. So even if increased student motivation could not be cited as a reason to focus more on writing about nonfiction, the demands our students will face in the future could be.

Text Selection

So, where to begin? The first step is selecting appropriate and engaging articles that lend themselves to analysis. Obviously, it is best to consider the reading level of one's students when choosing texts, and having selections of varying reading levels on a common topic is even more helpful. I keep topic folders in which I save electronic copies of related articles. Often there will be a flurry of articles on a "topic du jour," and I can find multiple articles from multiple sources that express similar ideas addressed to audiences of varying reading levels and backgrounds. Then, when I come to a unit centered on that topic, I have a collection of articles, usually of varying levels of difficulty, from which to draw. In a unit centered around the question "Does the media portray adolescents accurately and fairly?" I had saved so many articles commenting on adolescent behavior that I was able to assign my students different articles matching their reading levels and appealing to their current interests. Students then became the class "experts" on their articles, giving some struggling readers more credibility and confidence than they had previously experienced in English classes focusing exclusively on works of literature.

Using media-based texts as part of a nonfiction curriculum is especially useful, since today's secondary level students do most of their everyday reading and writing online, yet often lack the ability to critically evaluate the products seeking to influence them. Advertisements, cartoons, movies, current songs, and public blogs offer rich opportunities for analysis, evaluation, and written response. I particularly like working with blogs (many major newspapers, such as the *New York Times,* now have online-only content and regular blogs or online columns that solicit reader feedback), or with the comments left in response to these blogs, as they demonstrate to students that even the supposedly "lawless" internet has rules of discourse, and poorly written blog posts tend to be ignored. In addition to their real world credibility, these online sources are usually available free of charge—another plus in these times of tight budgets. However, along with the availability and currency of such online content comes a limited shelf life. For example, I recently capitalized on the ubiquity and popularity of Eminem and Rihanna's song, "Love the Way You Lie," by centering an entire unit on an analysis of it, its accompanying music video, and the reaction of bloggers and the entertainment media to both the song and video. This unit produced some of my on-level sophomores' best analysis, debate, and writing. Sadly, I estimate this unit will only have a two- or at most three-year shelf life before the song and music video become so dated that they no longer hold students' interest.

However, there are still many articles and media messages that address issues likely to engage my students for years to come. For instance:

- the media's portrayal of adolescents
- government and school policies about adolescents
- parenting trends and behaviors
- cyberbullying and how it should be handled
- the criminal justice system's treatment of adolescents
- abortion
- the treatment of animals
- universal human rights vs. respecting others' cultural practices
- racism and sexism
- grading policies
- discrimination based on appearance

Writing About Texts—Writing as Process vs. Product

There are several initial stages of writing, or "pre-writing," that students should utilize—all the less formal, short pieces of writing we do when analyzing or evaluating a text, winnowing our ideas, or exploring our own thoughts. The ultimate goal, however, is the formal essay or report that is generally the end result of "writing as a process." I contend that while moving beyond formulaic writing is important for final products such as reports and essays, sticking with a consistent formula for the process itself is not just acceptable but desirable. In fact, not enough time is spent on teaching these earlier stages of the writing process, and as a result many students' end products lack insight and inspiration.

So, ironically, teaching a more formulaic process and structure for one type of writing can lead to more creative and inventive writing as the end result. In other words, analyzing multiple texts and recording one's analysis in predictable ways can provide the basis for more creative essays and reports based upon those texts. Indeed, *Writing to Read* (2010), cited earlier, confirms that smaller writing tasks such as quick-writes, journal entries, and the answers to analytical questions not only help improve students' writing but also their reading comprehension.

Employing Formulas for "Writing as Process"

A major stumbling block many students encounter when attempting to write with passion is a lack of things to say about a text. Although the choice of text often plays a critical role in this struggle to find an authentic writing voice, an inability to analyze a text can serve as an equal hindrance. No matter how interesting the text, students who cannot move beyond simple agreement and disagreement will quickly run out of things to say about it. One benefit of using formulaic writing structures when analyzing a text is that they can help students focus on the many aspects of a text they can pick apart and consider when crafting an essay or the content of a report. The following sections will describe writing templates that students can use to make sense of their initial encounters with texts, and will also show how those structures can lead to less formulaic writing as an end-product.

Annotation

The first and simplest level of writing is annotation, which I define for my students as "first underlining or highlighting sections of a text, then writing analysis of and responses to those highlighted sections in the margins." Although annotation is not usually considered a formula, I believe that teaching students to employ a formula when annotating helps them pay attention. This idea is nothing new—it has been discussed extensively in excellent publications such as *Reading Rhetorically* and is now presented in a myriad of online forums (see References and Resources). However, it is usually considered as a part of the reading process rather than as a key part of the writing process. In fact, it is inextricably linked to both, for annotation often provides the first germ of ideas and analyses that will become integral to the full-flowering plant that is the exceptional essay. When teaching annotation, agreement and disagreement and questions are good places to start with reluctant readers.

Next, students can note the presence of main ideas and the types of evidence used to support those ideas. Then students can add comments on the appropriateness, reliability, and logic of that evidence. In this sort of sequence, students' annotation becomes increasingly more complex and focused on the details of a text, details (such as evidence reliability) that will later help them to support their initial agreement or disagreement with textual critique. Other textual aspects students should be taught to notice in their marginal annotations include evidence of the author's bias, "loaded language," and rhetorical appeals. Once all these layers are reinforced by checks of students' understanding, students begin noticing these features of the text independently, leading in turn to more precise and effective writing about those texts.

Although my students are often initially reluctant to write while reading, preferring to only underline or highlight a text, many eventually embrace it in some form or another once they experience the power of being able to successfully critique a published author. After such focused annotation, I even found two of my usually tepid freshmen, Chantal and Devin, having an enthusiastic discussion of the flaws in the author's organizational structure, complete with textual examples and detailed analysis. Chantal pointed out, "You see, here, she doesn't transition between this section and the text. She just picks up with a new metaphor." Then Devin added, "Yeah. She's confusing. She does that later on too. Her conclusion seems completely detached from the rest of her essay. It undermines her argument. I get her overall point but she doesn't connect the dots very well." As Chantal and Devin illustrate, students love criticizing adults, and published authors are no exception. Annotation can give students the ammunition to back up their criticism, both verbally and in writing.

Todd Rafalovich

Brook Wallace

Analysis of the Organization of a Text

Another element that can be added to annotation or developed into its own writing exercise is organizational analysis. Bean, Chappell, and Gillam call such organizational analysis "descriptive outlining." In this practice, students map out how an author structures his or her text and evaluate the effectiveness of this organizational structure. The organizational unit students examine can be as small as a sentence or as long as a chunk of sequential paragraphs. Regardless of whether they are looking at sentences or sections, students should always look at two elements: the sentence/section's content (what it "says") and the sentence/section's purpose (what it "does"). At first, students often have difficulty distinguishing between content and purpose (they usually lament, "but its purpose is to say [content]"). Therefore, before they can work independently, most students need a list of common purposes for sentences or sections and some modeling of how to identify a sentence or section's purpose. With some prodding, students can even come up with their own lists of what a section of a text might "do." A sample list of purposes created by my on-level freshmen includes such items as:

- stating the author's thesis or main point
- providing background information
- providing evidence to support a main point
- acknowledging the other side's viewpoint (a counterargument)
- responding to prove the other side is incorrect
- introducing a problem
- providing a narrative example of a problem
- introducing a solution
- listing the possible causes of a problem
- transitioning from one idea to the next

This list of purposes can be expanded depending upon the sophistication of the students. But most students can generate a list that includes the basic elements they have been taught to include in their own writing: main points and evidence.

Depending upon the length of the text and the students' needs, organizational analysis (often called "descriptive outlining") can be done on three levels:

1. **Sentences within paragraphs:** Students who struggle with writing coherent, clear paragraphs themselves or who are working on the skill of close-reading analysis can benefit from analyzing how others structure their paragraphs. At this level, students paraphrase the content of each sentence (what the sentence "says") and then determine each sentence's purpose (what the sentence "does"). Such a micro-level analysis helps students see what types of sentences tend to be grouped together in a paragraph and how sentences are ordered within a paragraph.

2. **Paragraphs in a section of a text:** Most students benefit from analyzing a text's organization at the paragraph level. Bean, Chappell, and Gillam have written about how to do organizational analysis at this level. Instead of focusing on sentences, students summarize the content of each paragraph (what it "says") in a discrete section of a longer text. Then, they determine the purpose of each paragraph (what it "does"). Once they have a list or a chart with each paragraph's content and purpose, students should look for overall patterns in the author's organizational structure, asking questions such as:

    a. What ideas does the author tend to clump together? Why?
    b. Does the flow of ideas make sense to you? Why or why not?
    c. How does the author move from one idea to the next?
    d. Do you notice any patterns in the author's organizational structure (for example, does the author always give a narrative example of a problem, state the problem, and then end with evidence demonstrating the extent of the problem)?
    e. How effective is the author's organizational structure? Can you follow his or her ideas? Would you have put the paragraphs in this order? Why or why not? Do you think another order or sequence would have been more effective? Why?

3. **Several paragraph chunks in long text:** For extremely long texts, the teacher or students can chunk paragraphs into sections by purpose. A teacher may choose to chunk paragraphs into sections ahead of time, asking students to identify the content and purpose of these predetermined sets of paragraphs. Otherwise, the teacher can instruct his or her students to chunk paragraphs into sections by identifying paragraphs' purposes first, grouping adjacent paragraphs that have the same purpose, and then summarizing the content of those grouped paragraphs. After the students have listed or charted the content and purpose of these chunks, they should look for patterns, answering the questions in the previous list.

While analyzing another text's organization can help students become aware of the diverse structures authors use, and those structures' relative effectiveness, organization charting can also be a powerful revision tool when applied to students' own writing. As a peer revision exercise, students can chart the content and purpose of each of the paragraphs in a peer's essay. More self-aware students who will notice what their paragraph is actually doing (not what they wanted the paragraph to do) can also evaluate their own drafts using this method. When students who have practiced organizational analysis with published texts become confused about the purpose of a peer's paragraph, that confusion often stems from flaws in the student author's organizational structure. Therefore, revision exercises that include some form of organizational analysis can provide important feedback to student writers who are struggling to move beyond rote essay structures and into more flexible, yet clear and effective organization.

Evidence Charting

Another aspect of the writing process that can be used for analyzing both others' and one's own writing is evidence charting. Once they have identified the type of evidence the author is using, the students rate the evidence's reliability on a scale of 1 to 10 with 1 being completely unreliable and 10 being completely trustworthy. Students can use the following questions to help them make their decision:

- Is this true for all people and all situations? If not, how common is this experience/viewpoint/situation?
- What viewpoint(s) are missing?
- What information is missing?
- How reliable is the source of this evidence or information? Is the source credible?
- Does this comparison or analogy make sense?
- How many people were subjects in this study? Is the number of people large enough for the researcher to be able to draw a general conclusion?
- Where did this statistic come from? How many people were interviewed or situations looked at to come up with this number?
- Could someone else easily verify this evidence?

Taking into account the type of evidence and their answers to the questions in the previous list, the students then must justify their reliability rating. More sophisticated students can also add an additional layer of complexity by evaluating the evidence's effectiveness. While many students conclude that less reliable evidence is less effective, more astute students often point out that less reliable evidence, such as hypotheticals, can be very effective due to their appeal to the audience's emotions.

By asking students to consider an author's use of evidence, "evidence charting" makes students more aware of their own ability to prove their points and can therefore help them improve their own writing. In fact, just like organization analysis, evidence charting can be employed as a revision tool to help students evaluate their peers' and their own use of support. In addition, focusing on common types of support can open up a conversation about the evidence valued by different audiences in different genres, enabling students to more consciously choose the proof they will rely on when engaged in different writing assignments. Those more sophisticated students mentioned above can even choose to eschew traditionally reliable forms of support in favor of perhaps more rhetorically effective personal anecdotes or other appeals to emotion. As long as the choice is conscious and motivated by sound reasons, the writing it engenders will most likely be passionate and convincing.

Textual Ideology

Although detailed analysis of an author's organization and evidence can help students "write to learn," a more holistic approach to textual analysis can also help students understand the larger context of the text they are reading and of the conversation they are joining through writing. Examining textual ideology—the ideas and beliefs valued by the author and implicit in the text—can be a stepping-stone to deeper understanding of the text's content.

Students often need some explicit modeling and examples, however, before they fully grasp the idea of textual ideology. I usually start by selecting several quotations or passages and asking students to infer from those passages what the author thinks about a particular topic or group. For example, when asked to infer what author Clark-Flory (2010) thinks about teenage girls, based on the following paragraph, students can conclude that the author believes teenage girls are attracted to and titillated by dangerous boys and are unable to clearly see the dangers they may face as a result.

> *Part of me cringes thinking of all the teenagers who will watch this [the music video "Love the Way You Lie"] and, if they're anything like I was at their age, find it incredibly sexy— sexy being anything that is extreme, frightening and hard to comprehend. It makes me think of "Fear," that mid-'90s flick starring Mark Wahlberg as an older guy who is romantically obsessed with a high school virgin played by Reese Witherspoon. I was titillated by his predatory, caveman persona and, woo boy, the Marky Mark abs didn't hurt, either. But when I recently watched the movie again for the first time in over a decade, I was horrified. Horrified! The dude is an abusive psychopath, as the end of the movie makes painfully clear—but I didn't care, I just filtered out the part where he terrorizes her family and kills her dog.*

(Hormonal teenage girls and their immense capacity to forgive bad boys—Clark-Flory)

These narrowly focused and guided inferences can slowly give way to open-ended questions about a paragraph's or a section's ideology and then an entire article's ideology. Students who still struggle with identifying the author's underlying beliefs often make progress by referring to questions such as the following:

- What does the author describe positively? Negatively?
- What assumptions does the author seem to make about his or her audience? About men? Women? Other groups?
- What information does the author leave out or not mention?
- What group or groups does the author leave out or not mention?
- Does the author mention part of a group or population as if it represents the whole group or population?
- What topics and ideas come to mind when you think about the author's main topic or point? What do you think the author thinks about these related topics or ideas? Why?

Beware, however—bringing to light the underlying ideology of a series of texts can lead students to write meandering essays if one does not teach them how that ideology fits into the overall argument to which the student wishes to add his or her voice. Although students can identify what an author might believe about a topic, they may not always see how that author's belief contributes to a larger debate. Some explicit instruction by the instructor may be in order or, at least, questions such as "why does it matter what the author thinks about x?"

For example, when analyzing bloggers' responses to Eminem's song "Love the Way You Lie," students identified the following aspects of authors' ideologies:

- A belief that portrayals of abusive relationships should be primarily negative and shocking.
- A belief that portrayals of abusive relationships should be as authentic as possible, including both positive and negative aspects.
- A belief that adolescents are not able to critically analyze songs or music videos.
- A belief that adolescents are attracted to dangerous, extreme emotions and situations.

However, when writing drafts of an essay about whether or not the song and its accompanying music video glorify abusive relationships, my students revealed a tendency to incorporate these authors' views tangentially rather as making them integral parts of their own main arguments. Students struggled with how to articulate the relationship between different bloggers' ideologies and their agreement or disagreement with the bloggers' points. Therefore, a whole class discussion was needed to help students explicitly examine how each author's ideology could be used to critique the author's argument and credibility (if the student disagreed with the blogger) or to affirm the author's argument and credibility (if the students agreed with the blogger). With a little bit of guided questioning, students were able to see that the author's ideology could be used as a sign of the author's bias or as evidence supporting the author's reasonableness. For example, many students pointed out that Clark-Flory undermined her overall argument because her lack of respect for teenagers made her less credible as a commenter on teenagers' possible reactions to the music video. Alternatively, others saw how Clark-Flory's admission that she was once an impressionable teenager (and that her view of current teenagers was shaped by her own experiences) could be used to establish her credibility as an honest, self-reflective adult who is willing to admit that some teenage girls are attracted to "dangerous" men (an attraction that other, current teenagers might share but not admit to). This explicit discussion helped students choose to either jettison their mention of the author's ideology or more clearly incorporate it into their arguments, resulting in more focused and nuanced final essays.

Connecting Persona, Audience, and Purpose

An awareness of audience and some strategies for effectively reaching that audience also lead to more effective student essays. However, many students lack the genre awareness necessary to tailor their writing to a variety of audiences. They may be vaguely aware of differences in writing styles among genres but few have thought about the finer points of genre conventions such as preferences for passive versus active voice, appropriate diction, and common organizational structures. Teaching students to become more aware of other texts' audiences and purposes and other authors' personas and to critique these elements often helps make students aware of more subtle genre conventions and in turn choose to employ such conventions in their own writing.

One way to encourage students to explore the connection between audience, persona, and purpose is to ask students to write about an idea or a text from the point of view of different possible readers and/or to present the text's ideas to different audiences. For example, students can practice writing responses to an article about "beauty bias" by taking on a variety of personas including:

- a beautiful woman who bristles at the idea she was hired partially based on her looks
- an overweight man who experiences discrimination based on his size
- a clothing store employer who wants his sales staff to "positively represent his brand"

Depending on class time, students can even read each other's writing and discuss which responses were the most effective and why. After they have written from the imagined point of view of various persona for varied purposes, students can analyze how they wrote and what information they included in their writing. By self-consciously changing their reasons for writing and the different audiences they might be writing to, students can become more aware of how their writing structure changes as a result. Of course, some students may not change their structural organization very much when writing from these different perspectives for these different purposes. If this happens, a guided discussion of different audiences' needs and expectations and more exposure to different textual genres may be in order. But often, engaging in this exercise helps students recognize the knowledge they do possess and empowers them to choose structures for writing based on their purposes and the effect they hope to create.

Students also benefit from examining how rhetorical appeals (sometimes called persuasive appeals) fall into three broad categories: appeals to logos (logic), pathos (emotion), or ethos (character or credibility). Ethos encompasses the character of the speaker or author, including his or her attempts to present himself or herself as a credible, trustworthy, and ethical source. Therefore, appeals to ethos are an important way authors communicate their personas. There are many excellent and detailed websites and texts focused on identifying and analyzing elements of rhetoric. One of my favorites is Jay Heinrichs' book, *Thank You for Arguing* (2007).

As Heinrichs demonstrates, almost all of the stylistic choices an author makes can be seen as appeals to logos, ethos, or pathos. Different genres' stylistic conventions also tend to privilege certain types of appeals over others. For example, scientific journal articles appeal almost exclusively to logos and ethos while political speeches often rely heavily on appeals to pathos and ethos. Therefore, students who learn to identify the rhetorical appeals being used in a given piece of nonfiction writing raise their awareness of these appeals, and can begin to consciously include the same appeals in their own writing.

Too often, students either write without a sense of their audience's needs (without a clear structure or transitions that will help their audience follow their argument) or in such slavish devotion to supposedly universally effective organizational structures (the five-paragraph essay) that they undermine their own points or bore their reader. Of course, having students first master a given writing formula subtly conditions them to look for the organizational structures most valued in both school and non-school settings. However, the problem with such formulaic structures is that they often do not exist except as school-based writing assignments. By examining real world writers' purposes, audiences, and personas, however, students can guide their decisions about everything from structure to evidence to vocabulary, and can begin to consciously move beyond the formulaic in their own school essays.

Nonfiction Discussion Circles

In addition to focusing on persona, audience, and purpose, students can begin to pull all their analytical writing skills together by engaging in nonfiction circles. Nonfiction circles are my adaptation of literature circles, with a focus on expository analysis. While Harvey Daniels has discussed using literature circles with nonfiction texts, and suggested which types of nonfiction texts will work best with literature circles, he has not changed the original literature circle roles and instructions to suit a wide range of nonfiction texts. Therefore, nonfiction circles are my attempt to synthesize several different writing tasks to scaffold students' analysis of nonfiction texts.

How Do They Work?

Before the Nonfiction Circle

1. The students are assigned or choose a nonfiction circle group of no more than five students.
2. Each student in the group is assigned a different role.
3. The students read and annotate an assigned article.
4. After they have read the article, the students answer the questions associated with their role and type up their responses to these questions.

During the Nonfiction Circle (in-class)

1. The discussion director summarizes the reading.
2. The group members ask any clarifying questions they may have and the group answers those questions.
3. Each group member shares the **key points** of his or her prep work.
4. The group discusses interpretive, analytical, and evaluative questions (this should take the majority of the discussion time).

After the Nonfiction Circle (in-class)

1. Each student writes an individual reflection that includes a summary of the discussion's main points and an evaluation of the quality of the group's discussion.
2. Group members decide on a group question and conclusion to share with the class. The group question is a question the group still has about the text or the author. The conclusion is the best insight or analytical or evaluative conclusion about the text that the group came up with during their discussion.
3. Group members set a group goal for improvement for the next nonfiction circle.

4. A group spokesman shares the group's summary, question, conclusion, and goal with the class.

5. The teacher shares the positives she saw during the nonfiction circle meetings and the areas she thinks need to be improved.

Nonfiction Circle Goals

These goals are written on the board and announced to students. The teacher observes the nonfiction circles looking for these things, provides feedback to the students based upon these goals (see step 5 above), and assigns a participation grade based on her observations:

1. All students participate equally.
2. All students support their ideas with textual evidence.
3. All students discuss ideas in-depth rather than superficially.
4. The majority of the time is spent discussing the answers to analytical, evaluative, and interpretive questions.

Nonfiction Circle Roles

I use seven nonfiction circle roles:

1. Discussion Director
2. Bias Finder
3. Rhetorician
4. Evidence Evaluator
5. Diction Detective
6. Structural Analyst
7. Connector

Students do not use all seven roles during each nonfiction circle. Instead, I choose a sub-set of the roles based on which analytical skills we have covered so far and the text(s) students will be analyzing. I usually assign students roles (at least at first) as certain roles are easier than others. Struggling readers tend to have the most success with the Connector role as it frees them from their fear of not getting the "correct" answer when examining a text. However, with some modeling, I have found that even remedial freshmen can experience success with more difficult roles such as Bias Finder.

Using the Writing Process to Inspire Less Formulaic Writing

By engaging in the previously outlined writing exercises, students not only practice important analytical reading skills, but also practice writing about their analysis and evaluation of complex texts. These smaller, less formal writing tasks in turn give students the ideas and ammunition for more empowered, interesting formal essays. Furthermore, these exercises make students more aware of the varied writing strategies sophisticated writers employ and encourage them to both critique the effectiveness of those strategies and examine the same elements in their own writing that they have scrutinized in others'. Is their/my use of evidence sound and convincing? Does a descriptive outline of their/my essay reveal problems with their/my organizational structure? Does their/my diction make them/me seem overly biased? Are they/am I making conscious choices that help them/me achieve their/my writing purpose with their/my audience? Asking students to answer such questions about their own writing gives them a roadmap as they struggle to move beyond five-paragraph formulaic writing. Using a "formulaic" structure of initial written responses as a roadmap, as well as providing my students with stimulating nonfiction texts, has led many of my students to produce excellent results. I hope your students will find similar success.

References and Resources

Bean, John C., Virginia A. Chappell, and Alice M. Gillam. *Reading Rhetorically*. 3rd edition. New York: Longman, 2010. Print.

Braddock, Richard, Richard Lloyd-Jones, and Lowell Schoer. *Research in Written Composition*. Urbana, IL: National Council of Teachers of English, 1963.

Cahill, Tim. "Here Sharky, Sharky, Skarky." *Outside,* August 1998.

California Common Core Content Standards for English Language Arts and Literacy in History/Social Studies, Science, and Technical Subjects. California Department of Education: Tom Torlakson, Superintendent.

California State University. *Expository Writing and Reading Course (ERWC)*. http://www.calstate.edu/eap/englishcourse/

Christensen, Francis, and Bonniejean Christensen. "A Generative Rhetoric of the Sentence," in *Notes Toward a New Rhetoric: 9 Essays for Teachers,* 2nd edition. New York, HarperCollins, 1978.

Clark-Flory, Tracy. "Megan Fox Sexes Up Domestic Violence in Eminem's Video." *Salon.com.* Salon Media Group, 6 August 2010. Web. 15 September 2010.

Common Core State Standards. http://www.corestandards.org/

Coyle, Daniel. "The First Law of Gravity." *Outside,* August 1998.

Fitzgerald, F. Scott. *The Great Gatsby*. Scribner, 1995.

Graham, Steve, and Dolores Perin. *Writing Next: Effective Strategies to Improve Writing of Adolescents in Middle and High Schools: A Report to Carnegie Corporation of New York*. Washington, DC: Alliance for Excellent Education, 2007. Print.

Graham, Steve, and Michael Hebert. *Writing to Read: Evidence for How Writing Can Improve Reading: A Report from Carnegie Corporation of New York*. Washington, DC: Alliance for Excellent Education, 2010. Print.

Hall, Donald, and Sven Birkerts. *Writing Well,* 9th edition. New York: Longman, 1997. Print.

Heinrichs, Jay. *Thank You for Arguing: What Aristotle, Lincoln, and Homer Simpson Can Teach Us About the Art of Persuasion*. New York: Three Rivers Press, 2007. Print.

Hunt, Kellogg W. "Early Blooming and Late Blooming Syntactic Structures." In Charles Cooper and Lee Odell, eds., *Evaluating Writing* (Urbana, Illinois: National Council of Teachers of English, 1977): 91–104.

Hunt, Kellogg W. "A Synopsis of Clause-to-Length Factors." *The English Journal,* 54.4, (April 1965): 300, 305–309.

Junger, Sebastion. *The Perfect Storm*. W.W. Norton, 2009.

Killgallon, Donald. "Sentence Composing." http://userpages.umbc.edu/~killgall/

Krakauer, Jon. *Into Thin Air*. New York: Anchor Books, 1998.

National Center for Education Statistics. http://nces.ed.gov/

National Governors Association Center for Best Practices, Council of Chief State School Officers. *Common Core State Standards*. National Governors Association Center for Best Practices, Council of Chief State School Officers: Washington, DC, 2010.

Partnership for Assessment of Readiness for College and Careers (PARCC). http://www.achieve.org/PARCC

Rosenthal, Nadine. *Speaking of Reading*. Portsmouth, New Hampshire: Heinemann, 1995.

Shaughenessy, Mina. "Diving In: An Introduction to Basic Writing." *College Composition and Communication*, Vol. 27, No.3 (October, 1976).

Sides, Hampton. "Last Seen Heading West on a Vintage Hardtail." *Outside*, September 1998.

Smarter Balanced Assessment Consortium. http://www.k12.wa.us/smarter

Stillman, Peter R. *Families Writing*. Cincinnati, Ohio: Writer's Digest Books, 1989.

Strong, William. "Sentence Combining: Back to Basics and Beyond." *The English Journal*, 65.2 (February 1976): 56–64.

Strong, William. *Sentence Combining: A Composing Book*. New York: McGraw-Hill, 1994, 3rd edition.

4

Creative Reading in Support of Writing: Developing Meaningful Response to Literature

by Jay Richards, Brenna Dimas, Marie Milner, and Mary Warner

Introduction

Each writer of this chapter reinforces the essential theme that students can and will develop meaningful response to literature when they find books with which they connect. Additionally, the writers emphasize the complementary nature of reading and writing. If we expect students to write better, they need to read more. As Kelly Gallagher (*Readicide,* 2009) and Jeff Wilhelm (*You Gotta BE the Book,* 1997, and *Reading Don't Fix No Chevys,* 2002) assert, students need to experience "book floods" and continually have their "brains stretched" by longer, challenging works.

Jay Richards sets the framework for the chapter in Part I with his discussion of the essential question: How do you teach a book? In Part II, Brenna Dimas describes how she modifies the traditional Literature Circle roles to evoke greater engagement from students. In Part III, Marie Milner describes strategies she uses to promote writing in response to independent reading. In Part IV, Mary Warner explores the power of the "Book Pass" to build a passion for reading.

Part I: Want to Be a Better Writing Teacher? . . . Then Take a Closer Look at How You Teach Reading
by Jay Richards

If you want to be a better *writing* teacher, take a closer look at how you teach *reading*. Do you treat reading and writing as distinct, separate parts of the English curriculum? Do you find that when you teach a book, the main assessment is through multiple-choice or fill-in-the-blank quizzes that check students' comprehension? If you incorporate writing, is it mainly to complete one short-answer essay question at the end of the test? How often do you ask your students to consider, through writing, how the experience of reading the book might change their lives?

For too many middle school students, school becomes a place where interest in both reading and writing decline. English class becomes more about assessing understanding of plot than a place to learn how to have meaningful experiences with books. Books, which were often so meaningful in the elementary classroom, are treated essentially as containers of information. From state tests to programs like Accelerated Reader, students are evaluated by their ability to answer multiple-choice comprehension questions, not by writing substantively about what they have read.

So How Do YOU Teach a Book?

Surprisingly, one of the least frequently asked questions among English teachers is, "How do I teach a book?" Follow 10 different English teachers who teach *Call of the Wild* and you'll see 10 different approaches. Check out middle or high school English course syllabi or attend back-to-school nights, and chances are that while the books "covered" in the course will be listed, any explanation of HOW those books will be taught will not.

"How do I teach a book?" is a question teachers should be able to explain to their students, their students' parents, their fellow English teachers, and themselves. In the absence of a thoughtful teaching philosophy, many teachers end up presenting the same kind of activities to their students as they themselves experienced in school. These activities too often focus on basic comprehension rather than why the events of the story happen or why it matters.

Comprehension, like memorization, should not be the *only* skill we develop in readers. Students need to comprehend, yes, but more importantly they need to learn how they might live differently based on what they've read. Students should understand characters in books like they understand their best friends. They should be able to answer the question, "How has my life been changed because I read this book?"

As Keene and Zimmerman (2007) remind us, "We must have the goal of educating children to become real readers, not simply students who answer test questions correctly but leave school with no interest in picking up a book ever again" (*Mosaic of Thought,* 30).

Beyond Basic Comprehension

A score of "proficient" or "advanced" on a standardized reading test does not necessarily mean a student enjoys reading or is able to think critically about what he or she has read. It's important that students and parents alike know that a standardized test score measures basic comprehension and vocabulary—not inferential critical thinking ability. Over the past 20 years, too many people in and out of schools have come to judge "success" in a reading program primarily by students' scores on standardized tests rather than by meaningful pieces of writing. If reading scores go "up," students, parents, and the community as a whole assume students are developing into more thoughtful, analytical readers.

Some schools focus so much on getting higher scores that students' reading experience in their English classrooms becomes dominated by simulated state reading tests, answering multiple-choice questions about basic comprehension. The problem is that such activities are not in and of themselves rich reading experiences. Students rarely race home from a state reading test and say, "Mom, Dad, let me talk to you about this amazing passage we read in the latest state reading test!" As Kelly Gallagher says in *Readicide,* teachers who rely on such tests "systematically kill the love of reading with inane and mind-numbing practices."

By elevating the place of writing in the reading curriculum, however, teachers can change this test-driven, comprehension-only culture. Teachers can provide meaningful reading experiences that promote reflection and critical thinking by staying true to what reading really should be—an analysis of *why* characters do what they do.

"It's Not About the First Read"

The first time my students and I read a book, we read it straight through primarily to find out what happens to the main character. We're motivated by plot in our first read; our driving focus is discovering how the conflict facing the main character will be resolved. The desire to know how a book ends is a natural one.

For my students and for me, however, it's only *after* we have read the book and know what has happened that truly meaningful reading can begin. When we go back to the story, we can see *why* the author inserted this character or this scene, realize the significance in early portions of the book, and get a deeper understanding of why the characters do what they do.

In most English classes, students read a book once. Teachers approach a book by breaking it down into sections, discussing the plot as it happens, then putting the book back on the shelf. However, when students read a book only once they miss out on all the intentional choices the author makes as the story unfolds.

In my classroom, when students are first presented with a book, I tell them they will have a certain time period (typically one to two weeks) to read the entire book.[1] Middle

---

[1] Most of the books we read in middle school are fewer than 250 pages, so it's not particularly daunting to read it at home. Frankly, reading is one of the more enjoyable assignments students get for homework.

school students so used to the "one chapter at a time" approach to reading a book often look at me quizzically when I tell them that I want them to read the whole book *before* we'll talk about it.

After students have read the book on their own, it's time for my instruction to begin. "It's Not About the First Read" doesn't mean that we reread the entire novel in the same linear fashion that we did during the first read. Lucy Calkins (2000) talks about how reading a book is like taking a long mountain hike. When hikers arrive at the top, they don't usually immediately turn around and go back. They will often look back, reflecting on where they've been. So it is with reading.

On the day when students have completed their first read, we begin discussing what they may have missed. One of the best ways to show the value in going back for a second read is to focus on secondary characters.

Focus on Secondary Characters

Students often don't pay much attention to secondary characters. During their initial reads, they focus on how the conflict facing the main character will be resolved. But secondary characters matter. They mattered to the author, and they should matter to us. A powerful benefit of going back to a book is to understand the significance of those characters, both in their own right and in their relationship to the story as a whole.

Consider "main characters" and "secondary characters" in your classroom. You've got main characters—the vocal, usually confident students who love to participate, whether they've been called on or not. And then there are the secondary characters—students who rarely speak, often because they're more comfortable taking things in rather than hearing

Todd Rafalovich

Jay Richards

the sound of their own voice. If we take the time to get to know these "secondary" students, we find a richness there that we may have overlooked had we only focused on our "main characters."

Example of Secondary Character Richness: Mayella Ewell

I had an epiphany in my 30s about integrating writing into my reading curriculum. I was attending the Invitational Summer Institute of the San Jose Area Writing Project, where Director Jonathan Lovell was conducting a workshop on *To Kill a Mockingbird*, and asked me to focus, along with several other participants, on the character of Mayella Ewell.

I read and listened to passages about Mayella, then "took on" her character while conversing with other characters from the story. When I read *To Kill a Mockingbird* in high school, I didn't pay much attention to Mayella beyond her basic role as the young white woman who frames Tom Robinson.

But in this workshop, I had to go beyond basic comprehension and focus on Mayella as if she were the most important character in the novel. It was about putting myself into her shoes and trying to experience her feelings. As I explored her character, Mayella became real to me, and I felt strong empathy for the lack of love and beauty in her life. After role-playing Mayella in a small group of other participants, I was asked to write about her. The result, reproduced in the following poem, struck me as far more meaningful than rote comprehension:

Mayella
While pain and injustice shadowed Tom and Boo
I know neither one would trade places with you.
Born into neglect, your backyard a dump
Your life severed early, leaving only a stump
Your father, brute drunkard, your mother, long dead
Too alone to bear children, you bore flowers instead
Some see your geraniums as a hope for escape
Those flowers small specks in your barren landscape
So des'prate for love that you dared to kiss Tom
A kiss not returned, now it's shame you live on.
So you lie to all Maycomb, there's pain in your breath
It's so easy to lie when you're scared half to death.

In exploring Mayella's condition and why she makes the choices she does, I came to understand what a meaningful response to literature might look like, and it certainly was not like the quizzes I'd been giving for years. From that point forward, *writing* about the human condition and how we could enlarge our lives through what we read became my primary approach to teaching reading.

Highlighting Every Reference

One approach I've used for secondary characters is to have students highlight every reference to these characters. Since the secondary character is not on every page of the book, the highlighting offers students a way to revisit the book with a focus. Students are scouring pages looking for the name of the character. When they find a reference to the character, they highlight the section. Most of the characters chosen (Mayella Ewell, for example) don't have more than 25 references in the entire book, so this task is not daunting. As students highlight those sections, they generally reread that passage and discover meanings that they originally missed.

The need to highlight provides a reason to go back to the book. Even reluctant readers who may not read the book closely the first time can relate to highlighting. It's like a game. As students highlight passages, they have a focus as they read, and each subsequent passage offers deeper insight into the character.

An obstacle to the highlighting process—which is all too common with the limited funding for education—is having student copies they can highlight. One alternative is to have students work in groups on a single character and have them create a poster or other visual of all the references. Such a visual could be an excellent way for students to discuss and agree on what characteristics or themes are represented through the words, actions, or thoughts on the page. Students also could use the wide range of sticky or Post-it notes to temporarily highlight passages or important details for class discussion or comprehension quizzes.

In important relationships in our lives, we want to learn everything about the people with whom we're in a relationship. Suggest to students that they can apply this same idea to the characters they meet in their reading. This strategy of looking for all references to secondary characters helps hone that skill of paying close attention to everything the character says and does.

Once students have highlighted every reference to the secondary character in the book, it's my turn as teacher to facilitate opportunities to write about them. One activity I do to prepare for secondary character passage discussion is to highlight the passages

Palmer's Father
Reference #5 – page 30

Why wasn't Dad at the earlier party
With the boys?

Why did Palmer feel that the toy soldiers
Were the most valuable things in the house?

What promise does Dad ask of Palmer?
Why does Dad ask that promise?
Why doesn't Palmer keep that promise?

Todd Rafalovich

*Questions Regarding
Palmer's Father*

myself, scan those pages into my computer, and—using PowerPoint or Pages—write in questions to accompany the passages. My role as teacher is to prepare questions to go with each passage (see the example above from Jerry Spinelli's *Wringer*, 1998).

Students can see the highlighted passages on the overhead screen or document camera with teacher-created questions beside them, designed to explore the character. As we look at each reference to the secondary character in the book, we answer such questions as:

- Why does the character do or say what he or she does here?
- What does the main character learn through his or her interaction with the secondary character?
- What do you think the character is thinking right now?
- Does the action or response of this secondary character surprise you?

After discussing every passage dealing with the secondary character, students have a wealth of ideas about the character to answer in writing: they've observed, and they feel like they really know the character. After all, we learn about "real" people by spending time with them, noticing their actions, words, and mannerisms, and asking them questions.

Another benefit to studying secondary characters is that secondary characters always interact with the main character at some point(s) in the book; we not only learn about the secondary character, but also about the main character.

Because writing is the key element in our reading curriculum, we'll usually conclude our study with an essay that analyzes the secondary character. Common questions that drive these written responses include: Who is this character, really? What does the main character learn from this character? Sometimes the secondary character teaches or models behavior that the main character lacks. Other times the secondary character is flawed or tempts the main character in some way. Either way, the main character uses his or her interactions with the secondary character to learn something that we as readers can learn as well.

Essay Assignment: Who Is Henry, Really?

Henry is a fascinating secondary character. Why is he in the book? In this essay, explore what Palmer (and therefore we, the readers) learn from Henry that will help us lead more meaningful lives. Answer Palmer's question from p. 198, "Who are you, really?" There may be two sides to Henry, but who is he, really?

Student Sample Essay—opening paragraphs

Henry is a young boy, but he is so much more than that. He is a complex character, with many personalities and emotions. One side of Henry is the quiet wallflower, which follows Beans and Mutto as if he is their shadow. Another side of Henry is the original good-natured older brother who pulls his sister in a wagon. This is when he is George.

Henry doesn't quit because he doesn't know how to be himself. He has little courage, which makes it hard for him to quit. Also, Henry probably already feels alone, because he is obviously kinder than Beans and Mutto. He does not fit in with his so-called friends. Henry would rather be with people who are not good friends than be by himself.

Palmer had courage, which Henry lacked. Henry and Palmer could have been friends outside of the group, but Henry was too chicken. Courage is not the only thing that helped Palmer quit the group. Henry showed him that if he does not quit soon, he could end up like Henry, "a captive." The group transformed the happy George who played with his sister, into a timid boy when they are around him.

Henry shows us the importance of courage and being true to you. If we all act like Henry, then no one will be ourselves. Everyone would have fake friends and no one would show their true emotions. New ideas would not form, but most importantly, no one would be happy because they were hanging out with people who they do not belong with. Sometimes, we need to be strong and stand up to people even if it is hard sometimes.

—Rachel Reisman

An alternative essay assignment, based on the secondary character essay shown above, uses two passages rather than one. The following assignment is based on *Roll of Thunder Hear My Cry* (1991).

The "Two Passage" Essay Analysis

- You've each been given a booklet of every TJ Avery reference in Mildred Taylor's *Roll of Thunder Hear My Cry*. Now that you've read the book once, mostly to discover what happened to the main character, I'd like you to go back to the booklet and review (look again at) all the TJ references.
- I'd like you to select two passages that you feel best show insights into who TJ really is. At least one of your chosen passages should be a passage that you think most of your classmates will not have chosen. [Note: The purpose here is to encourage students to avoid "climactic scenes" or obvious quotes. Choosing a passage that others may have missed is a challenge to realize that every passage matters and can unlock insights into the character.]
- Be prepared to talk about the passages you chose with the group.
- Why did you select the passage? What significance do you find in the passage? What insights about TJ does it unravel for you? Why does TJ do what he does? What does TJ want more than anything else in the world?

Observe and Infer

Unfortunately, basic comprehension often gets more focus than inferential understanding. Programs such as Accelerated Reader provide multiple-choice comprehension quizzes taken on the computer to demonstrate an "understanding" of the book. While good comprehension is an important goal, the books that generally matter to us as readers don't matter because we've demonstrated that we comprehend them. Reading should be about greater questions that need to be discussed, explored, and written about. In my evolution as a teacher, I've begun to focus on:

- insights over comprehension
- multiple analyses or approaches to the same story instead of a single big question or idea
- "everything matters"—looking beyond the obvious—rather than focusing on a main theme or single key passage

An easy way to incorporate inferential skills is to create a two-column chart. On the left is the observation, the actual passage or literal statement from the text. On the right is the inference, where students write their insights, reflections, and conclusions about the passage. Again, while it's important to know *what* happens, it's more important to learn *why* it happens.

I want students to observe and infer. Some students mention things they see in a book (observations) without explaining what conclusions they draw from what they see. Other students make strong opinions (inferences) without sharing what they see in the story that causes them to come to that conclusion. Encouraging students to do both—observe and infer in tandem—helps them to provide textual support for their inferential thinking. One assignment that helps teach the concept of observing and inferring is observation/inference poems.

Sample Assignment—8/8 Observation/Inference Poem

- Please craft a 16-line poem about your character. Eight of the lines must be observations from the text. These are words you could point to on the page—actual images from the book. The other eight lines are your inferences about the character. These are your conclusions or thoughts about the character that are not directly stated in the book.
- At the end of each line, include the page number of the observation in parentheses. You do not have to include any page numbers for your eight inference lines.
- You can arrange the eight inference lines anywhere you'd like in the poem.
- The challenge here is to see how much insight you can show in the eight lines of inferring.

Answer Characters' Questions

Another strategy for revisiting the book is to have students pay attention to the questions that the characters ask in the book. Just as I have students go back and highlight every reference to a secondary character, I also have students highlight every question posed in the story. Again, students can simply look for question marks—they're not literally rereading the whole text.

Authors want readers to consider the characters in the book and to learn something about them. One way authors do this is by having their characters ask questions. When characters in a book ask questions, the author wants us, the readers, to answer these questions ourselves.

Selected Questions Spoken by Characters in Wringer

- "Why did he do that?" (wring the neck of the pigeon)—Palmer to his mom (40)
- "How am I supposed to act normal in a town that murders pigeons?"—Palmer to himself (93)
- "Why didn't you pick a different place to land?"—Palmer to Nipper (106)
- "Why are you doing this to me?"—Dorothy to Palmer (112, twice) and (115)
- "Do you like my father? Do you think he's nice?"—Palmer to Dorothy (127)
- "I'm going to be ten in seventy-one days, and then I'm going to have to be a wringer too but I don't want to. So what kind of kid am I? Everybody wants to kill pigeons but me. What's wrong with me?"—Palmer to Dorothy (129)
- "Palmer, be honest, did you really spit on the floor?"—Henry to Palmer (143)
- "Why would anyone want to shoot him?" (Nipper)—Palmer to Dorothy (150)
- "Why are you, really?"—Palmer to Henry (198)

Everything Matters

Focusing on secondary characters or answering characters' questions leads to the key concept that everything matters. What *doesn't* matter in a book? If a scene were unnecessary, a good editor would have taken it out. Yet many readers don't read with a close understanding that everything matters.

A way to challenge students to look beyond the obvious is to have them consider passages that other students overlook. When considering evidence about a certain character, there are invariably some important passages that jump out. However, my most thoughtful readers also include passages from anywhere, not just passages in climactic scenes. Analyzing every passage about a secondary character actually demonstrates why every passage is important.

In every book there are small things that seem insignificant at first. However, after analyzing them more closely after the first read, we begin to see their significance. In Jerry Spinelli's *Wringer*, the main character receives a gift of toy soldiers from his father early on in the book. These soldiers are referenced in only four other pages in *Wringer*. The final reference to these soldiers comes just before the climax of the story. In reading the book only once, it is possible to miss the toy soldiers because they are not critically tied in to what happens to the main character at story's end. However, when we reread the book and focus in on these toy soldiers, it becomes clear that they matter. Obviously, the author wants us to consider the soldiers and what they mean, since they are referenced and re-referenced at crucial points in the narrative.

How Can I Change My Life Because I Read This Book?

State reading assessments don't promote particularly thoughtful readers, those who read to gain wisdom, to learn about what matters in life. As a father, I'm always looking at the parent characters in the books I read to see how they handle both their marriage and

Todd Rafalovich

Toy Soldiers

their relationship with their children. I can learn things by considering the actions of these fictional characters. As we learn more about the human condition, we can learn how to improve our own relationships. "To infer as we read is to go beyond the literal interpretation and to open a world of meaning deeply connected to our lives" (Keene & Zimmerman, 2007, 149). Reading can be a path to wisdom if we are constantly observing what characters are doing and learning from them.

Ellin Keene and Susan Zimmerman ask, "How often do you give students a chance to discuss, ponder, infer, and write about what they read?" This is an essential question for English teachers. The deeper we get into books, the more students enjoy the experience. They want to read and they want to write about what they read.

When I ask students to go beyond basic comprehension and to write about what really matters to them, they become readers with the skills to perform well in many types of assessments—including standardized tests. More importantly, students leave my class with rich pieces of writing they want to keep, as well as a desire to want to read in and out of class.

Part II: Varying the Literature Circle Roles to Evoke Authentic Response
by Brenna Dimas

I hate grading papers. I've yet to meet an English teacher who loves it. On the days when papers must be collected—because unfortunately they must be—I bemoan my fate, asking myself, "Why, oh why did I decide to become an English teacher? What could have possibly led me to think this was a good idea?" Some days it seems like there are no good answers to those questions.

Other days are different. Those are the days when the writing assignments are strongly tied to the literature and the discussions we've had. On those days I remember exactly why I teach English. I decided to get my credential in English because I wanted to share with students the joy of reading and communicating. I wanted to help them develop as readers of text and life; I wanted to watch them grow into insightful individuals who understood their world a little better because of the texts they encountered in my class, the discussions that led them to new ideas, and the writing that helped them convey these newly acquired understandings.

When I first started teaching, I thought that Literature Circles would be a great way to impart these things I so desperately wanted for my students. But the more I used them in my classroom, the more I became discouraged by the awkward conversations and forced connections that filled the discussion time. I'd heard Literature Circles touted as an engaging format for students to interact with texts, but that was not the reality of my classroom. Instead, student discussions were being strangled by the recommended roles, which take the processes used by good readers and dissect them into discrete parts, making reading and thinking a less dynamic experience. I had almost given up on Literature Circles when a fellow teacher explained the way she used them with her students. Her method removed the stringent rules about the Literature Circle roles while maintaining the heart of this teaching practice. Since then, I have taken her method and developed it further, finding ways to make the experience meaningful for my students.

The Role of Young Adult Literature

Middle school is a time of extreme contradiction for students: They are no longer children, but they are not yet adults. Mixed messages abound as students try to find where they fit into their ever-expanding world and teachers try to strike a balance between maintaining their charges' innocence and opening their eyes to the realities and responsibilities of young adulthood. It's no wonder that middle school students are very wary of adults' understanding of their world. Consider that we expect our students to assume new responsibilities such as managing six classes worth of assignments or understanding how grades are earned, but don't trust them to engage their minds with content in the classroom without a great deal of handholding and coaxing.

Many young people mistrust adults' experiences, adults' priorities, and what they see as adults' literature. In the English classroom, this is problematic. To add even more complexity to the issue, much of the writing students are asked to compose requires a relationship to reading. Thus, their mistrust and misunderstanding of adults in general has the capacity to carry over into the two essential concerns of the English curriculum—reading and writing.

If this is the reality of the middle school language arts classroom, what is a teacher to do? The solution of using Young Adult (YA) literature in class—a frequent answer to this question about engaging students with content—while a start, is insufficient for many reasons. Not all YA literature is created equal. If one of our main goals as middle school teachers is to address standards that will be the foundation for literary analysis of canonical texts in high school classrooms, we have to find texts that offer rich literary experiences that challenge students' analytical skills while meeting them "where they are" when it comes to topic and voice. This requires teachers to be familiar with what's out there—a particularly ambitious goal as it is a constantly evolving genre that, like many things in the teen world, is prone to fads and fashion. Simply assigning YA literature can prove more or less fruitless if the texts are not meaty enough to explore for such components as theme, symbolism, character development, and figurative language. In many instances, books written specifically for preteens and teenagers are simply too superficial for the level of analysis we need our students to be prepared to do. On a positive note, once a teacher finds a powerful text that meets both the student and teacher criteria of a "good" story, it can be used year after year.

In my eighth grade classroom, the curriculum centers heavily around YA literature. I choose books with either sarcastic, wisecracking narrators or emotionally charged events that rely on themes of identity and acceptance. This is my side of the compromise that must happen if I am going to bridge the aforementioned mistrust: I agree that the texts we read should be relevant to my students' lives, not necessarily to my own. Students see that I am willing to let their interests, concerns, and experiences at least partially guide my choice of texts.

Their side of the compromise requires they "stick it out" with me. I make a concentrated effort to bring students literature that, among other things, challenges their view that

Todd Rafalovich

Brenna Dimas

a reader can determine whether a book is good within the first 10 pages. At the beginning of the year, I work with them to break down texts at a deeper level than they would while reading solely for entertainment. I require an understanding of literary devices and their application when analyzing a piece. The truth of the matter, regardless of what students would like to believe, is that middle schoolers need a significant level of structure and guidance when they are first learning how to be thoughtful readers. Eventually, however, I let them prove that they're able to put what I've taught them into practice.

My final piece of the compromise comes toward the end of the school year. My students leave the protection of teacher-expert interpretations of texts and navigate through literature on their own—with no one telling them what to think or focus on. So I put my faith and trust in my students and relinquish my control; I allow students to explore on their own by using a modified version of Literature Circles. To get started, my students are given Book Talks on several novels. They are asked to list their top five choices of Literature Circle books. From these lists I work to set students into groups. I then "teacher tweak" the groups, moving students around until I have workable combinations. While it can be tempting to tweak the groups to be heterogeneous in gender, skill level, and clique, I try to avoid imposing my own feelings about what would be best in order to allow students to make their own decisions. As long as groups are the right size (four to seven readers), the books are not terrible matches in terms of reading level, and the groups have no obviously extremely toxic pairings, I let the groups form organically. Once the Literature Circle groups are formed, the students find out which title they are given and proceed from there. No student is asked to read a book that was not on his or her list.

A Variation on the Literature Circle Roles

With the help of another teacher in my district, I have worked out a method for using Literature Circles without the roles that are generally part of this teaching strategy. While some may consider it unwise to separate the roles from the practice of using Literature Circles in the classroom, I have found that, for me, the roles tend to lend themselves to lazy reading and inadequately developed assignment completion. In a typical Literature Circle, each member of a group is assigned a role and a task in relation to the role. A "passage picker," for example, is in charge of picking three brief passages from the reading for the group to take a closer look at and discuss at their Literature Circle meeting. Generally, the roles are switched so that the next time a different student will be in charge of selecting passages from the text. Theory suggests that these roles represent discrete but complementary skills that good readers perform as they engage with a text.

Looking beyond the theory and considering the premise more closely, this way of responding to and discussing reading is flawed in several ways. For one thing, many students work just to the specifications of an assignment and not beyond. Further, some students search for loopholes in reading assignments that allow them to meet an expectation without really becoming engaged with the material. A student who has been given a "vocabulary enricher" role, for instance, can completely bypass summarizing the segment of the novel being discussed, as an important way to check his or her understanding of what the group has read, and still be meeting the assignment's expectations.

Another flaw in the usage of roles is that it can discourage rather than encourage discussion. If a student is only "in charge" of one discrete part of a discussion, it is very possible that his or her only contribution will be this one discrete part. For instance, if an "illustrator," need only illustrate a scene from the segment of the novel being discussed on a certain day, what is there to keep him or her involved in the discussion about how another member of the group made a personal connection to the story? In a discussion organized around Literature Circle roles a student can contribute minimally before checking out of the conversation entirely. I find these student behaviors both understandable and unacceptable. If I really want students to interact on an independent level with a text, I can't expect them to do so when the opportunities afforded them to do so are extremely limited.

To be fair, the roles offer structure and a level of accountability. This is why I have combined and repackaged them. When my students begin their Literature Circle unit they are given a menu of Literature Circle discussion prompts upon which they can find questions that utilize many of the skills the roles highlight (e.g., *Prompt 10 Describe the main character. Consider what s/he looks like, what s/he likes to do*—Illustrator; *Prompt 3 Is there any character in the story that is like you?*—Connector). Before they begin the week's reading, each Literature Circle is required to select three questions from the questions menu. They scan through the questions talking about which ones sound interesting and would elicit the best conversations. All members of the group answer these three questions before their end-of-the-week meeting, so students seriously consider their choices before coming to a final decision. This collaboration eliminates the need for a full-fledged discussion director, as each member weighs in and helps decide the group's focus for the week's reading. Further, this empowers the students and creates buy-in for many, as they were part of the process that determined the purpose in their lesson for the week.

I set two limitations on my students' choice of Literature Circle questions: Early in the reading, students cannot select questions that cannot be adequately answered until the book is finished (e.g., *Prompt 14 Does the title fit the story?*); and students cannot repeat the same questions week after week. After the Literature Circle group has selected its three questions, they decide how much of the reading they will accomplish during the week.

Students are presented a deadline by which the book must be finished, so they make their page selections with this date in mind.

A Weekly 3-2-1

Apart from the questions menu, the students answer a weekly "3-2-1." Because I am working with a limited number of texts and cannot send books home, students do all their reading in class; for teachers working with students who can take their books home, I would suggest having students fill out the "3-2-1" more frequently. For each week, my students must provide, based on what they encountered in the text: three (3) words they didn't know; two (2) connections they made to the text; and one (1) question they have as a result of their reading.

The three words are listed out along with the page numbers upon which they appeared and a definition the student found. This portion of the assignment takes the place of the vocabulary enricher role, though it is accomplished in a nearly identical fashion as that role. The benefit to approaching the role in this manner stems from the fact that each student is looking for unknown words. Thus, they are filling in gaps in their personal vocabularies. Further, when multiple students are highlighting vocabulary, the scope that the group covers varies more in size, vocabulary type, and level than it does when only one student is charged with finding previously unknown words.

For the connections portion of the 3-2-1, the students are each fulfilling the connector role. As with the vocabulary, the varied scope covered by the group rather than a single individual allows for fuller understanding of the text. Group members hear from each other how their experiences have aided in comprehending the material on various levels. This allows students who have not had the same experiences to begin to see the Literature Circle novel in new and interesting ways without forcing a particular viewpoint on them.

The "1 question" students must ask in order to complete their "3-2-1s" gives them the right to determine what they find confusing or intriguing about the text. A student may ask why the narrator describes herself in a consistently negative tone or what happens on page 117 because she doesn't understand who is fighting whom. Many times I have seen students become absorbed in a lengthy conversation about another group member's question; I watch as they honor each other's curiosities and concerns.

A Chance to Discuss

When the Literature Circle group meets together, their three questions taken from the discussion prompt menu and their 3-2-1s should be completed. In order for the questions to be "done," students must write at least a paragraph in response to each one. These paragraphs, they are instructed, must meet certain writing requirements besides length. First, the students must answer in a way that leaves the paragraph understandable. In other words, students must start their paragraphs with complete sentences that identify what question is being asked or restates the question in the answer, instead of simply starting with terms like "Yes" or "Because."

Another requirement of this mini, weekly writing assignment is that they call upon examples from the text to support their answers. While students often struggle with this skill when writing essays, the questions menu format makes it more manageable for them to do so in part because their writing, being short, is more focused. The level of engagement students have with the book also aids them in being able to use textual examples. They are often enthusiastic about the book to the point that their attention is more focused as they read and their memory is consequently sharper.

The group begins their Literature Circle discussion by hearing each other's answers to the three questions. Because they all answered the questions, they immediately have a structure for discussion. With this format, one student will start reading her answer; upon hearing it, another student will find a connection to what he wrote down, which compels him to start sharing his ideas with a statement such as "I didn't think that at all because. . . ." In other words, the students actually have a discussion about literature rather than faking one.

When the discussion of the three questions begins to die down, students can move to the 3-2-1s. Even sharing from these worksheets tends to have a fluid dynamic with students readily interjecting their thoughts in relation to what others have stated. When reading off the "3 Words I didn't know," students who were unsuccessful in finding definitions will often get help from others who had chosen the same word or have a sense of the word's meaning. With the connections, students hear a lot of "me too" agreements. When they read the "1 Question I have," students will use it as a springboard for more discussion.

I've varied the final unit assignment from year to year. Sometimes it is an art assignment such as redesigning the book cover to reflect understanding of the novel's characters and themes. Other times the assignment is a presentation of the character's life-line. Still other times, it is the writing of a skit that highlights a pivotal scene in the text. To this unit assignment, however, I always add an essay test based on five quotes from the novel they read for their Literature Circle. They select two of the five quotes and write a short essay about each of their selections.

Because they have spent so much time during their discussions interacting with the text, very rarely do they fall into the trap of summarizing the story instead of analyzing it. Every year, these essays are the most insightful and analytical pieces my students write. Having engaged so thoroughly with the text and their own ideas, the learners in my classroom offer up a wealth of insights and analyses that show their skills as readers, thinkers, and written communicators.

The YA literature book selections give the students the material with which to work. The discussion questions and 3-2-1s help them focus their reading, utilizing the skills that make someone a good reader. The process as a whole develops them as writers by helping them see the connections between deep thinking and communicating ideas to others. But the autonomy—the break from "teacher says; I do"—allows them to engage. Running Literature Circles in this manner allows the students to embrace fully the compromise of trust. Whether they realize it or not, they agree to use the skills I give them to talk about a world which I, as part of the compromise, have to admit I cannot completely comprehend. We tell students that reading allows them to explore life, but so often we set them on a pre-selected path. What is wonderful to see is that if students are simply given a little structure and some necessary tools with which to explore independently, they will find their own way to the teacher's end goal, with no designated path needed.

Part III: Independent Reading: To Read or Not to Read—No Longer a Dilemma
by Marie Milner

Everyone, even the non-educator, has heard a story about how someone "got away" with not doing his or her book report in school. I've even heard adults admit that they turned in the same book report repeatedly in their junior and senior high school days. Well-known YA author Chris Crutcher (2002) claims he "recycled" his older brother's book reports throughout his high school years, but that this "crime" went undetected. Although these stories are always entertaining, we English teachers don't assign independent reading just to torture students or to hone their skills in stealth or creative plagiarism. What, then, do we hope to accomplish when we ask our students to read independently and write about what they have read?

Brenna Dimas, in her discussion of Literature Circles, alludes to the contradictions faced by middle school students. These contradictions continue as adolescents move through secondary school; at the same time, however, these older students are beginning to make more coherent sense of their world and are looking for models and guidance. We want them to be exposed to a far greater pool of quality literature in a given 10-month academic school year than we can reasonably address in that time. We also hope, while examining the human condition through literature, they will recognize even more thematic connections than we can reasonably discuss in the classroom.

When students write in their end-of-year reflections that they didn't know they liked to read until they took my class and completed the "book reports" I describe below, I know that I've struck a form of pedagogic gold.

In *Pathways to the Common Core: Accelerating Achievement*, Lucy Calkins, Mary Ehrenworth, and Christopher Lehman (2012) point out one particular strength of the new Common Core State Standards with regard to reading: "The CCSS call for proficiency, complexity, and independence. It is important to note that the emphasis in the Common Core is on students learning to read and write complex texts *independently* at high levels of proficiency and at a rapid enough rate to be effective" (12). In the past, the practices in many schools have worked against this expectation. In *Readicide: How Schools Are Killing Reading and What You Can Do About It,* Kelly Gallagher (2009) defines "readicide" as "the systematic killing of the love of reading, often exacerbated by the inane, mind-numbing practices found in schools" (2). Gallagher later states that, "A curriculum steeped in multiple-choice test preparation drives shallow teaching and learning" (8). Gallagher's book validates much of what I've always embraced as empowering pedagogy with regard to independent reading. Not only do I allow students a choice in what to read independently, but by giving them various writing approaches for their responses I also strive to deepen their enjoyment and grasp of what they have read. As a result, my students write with more voice and passion when engaged in the types of literary responses I suggest to them, and because I conduct personal interviews about each student's independent reading, he or she has the opportunity for an oral response as well.

It is highly unlikely that a conventional book report summary would have elicited the kind of voice-filled response that the following excerpt of a letter written, and mailed, to author Dave Eggers provides:

Dear Mr. Eggers,

I love your book. It's hilarious and insane, and maybe hilarious because it's insane. You said the silliest things so seriously, shamelessly, and never—I'd never read anything like that.

So to be honest I've never written anyone with a big, or even big (ish) name before, but there was something about you and how you sounded that was more accessible. You sounded like me, like all of us. Do you ever wonder how you got to writing like that? I feel like it should be the natural thing, for people to let loose and just write, in a manic frenzy and it would end up sounding sort of like yours. But no. What do you think influenced you to write like this? I'm kind of thinking of being a writer myself, but there's a lot I want to read, and if you have any influences, I think I'd enjoy checking those out.

Chuc manh khoe, ban!

Andy Nguyen—15-year-old learning out of your book (11th grade)

Andy makes my point. When students have some choice of what to read and in how to respond to that reading, they take ownership of the assignment. When they are offered unconventional approaches to literary response, they are able to write with far more passion.

In-Class Book Report

Over 20 years ago, a mentor teacher of mine shared several of her book report strategies. I've valued them ever since, adapting them to the language development levels of my students, most of whom are either English language learners (ELLs) or students who are currently referred to as RTI (Response to Intervention) students. What follows is a brief outline of the strategies I use to encourage students to read and engage with their independently read books. Several excerpts of student work demonstrate how my approach allows them to both write and speak with passion and voice.

These assignments also allow students to demonstrate their comprehension of characterization; plot elements such as conflict, climax and resolution, setting, and theme; and literary devices such as foreshadowing, suspense, figurative language, symbolism, and irony.

Letters of Recommendation and Condemnation for Characters

In this activity, the student writes two letters, each approximately two pages long. One is a letter of recommendation for the protagonist. This letter can be written by another character in the book or by the student as himself or herself. The student can create the circumstances under which letters might be written. The second letter is a letter of condemnation for the antagonist of the book. Sometimes a character in a book is both the protagonist and antagonist, so this gives the student the unique challenge of writing both a letter of recommendation and one of condemnation for the same character, allowing an examination of the character's complexity. This topic allows students to access characterization and thematic elements.

Because many of these literary responses are read aloud to the rest of the class on another date, the students are able not only to use more voice in the more informal genre of letter writing, but also to write for an authentic audience of their peers.

For example, in a letter of recommendation for Liesel Meminger, the protagonist of *The Book Thief* (Zusak, 2005), Emily demonstrates a deep grasp of the protagonist's character as she recommends Liesel for university acceptance.

> When Liesel was almost ten years old, she lost her only family. Liesel was lucky in a sense because she gained a new family, an occurrence that rarely happens. The Hubermanns treated Liesel as their own child. [. . .] Though losing one's family is very hard, the experience gave Liesel the courage to fight for justice.
>
> Liesel is far more than just an unfortunate soul. She was able to gain knowledge and a strong education during a time when doing so took a great amount of patience and perseverance. [. . .] As a youngster, Liesel had no hope of an education, so she could not read or write. When she arrived on Himmel Street in Molching, she was finally given the opportunity to be educated. [. . .] I'm sure if she sets her mind to it, Liesel can become the writer of the age. I hope you will consider everything I have said and give Liesel a place at your university because with a strong education, Liesel Meminger could change the world.
>
> *—Emily Rakhmilevich, 11th grade*

By writing in the more accessible letter of recommendation format, students like Thao, who wrote the following letter, are able to easily grasp and state theme as a more natural result of a defined goal—in this case, to recommend a character from Amy Tan's *The Bonesetter's Daughter* (2001) for university acceptance.

> I still remember Luling's bravery, and I'm still astonished by it. At that time, women were seen as very vulnerable and not capable of many things, but no, not Luling. When the camp was burned to ashes, she disguised herself, the [youngsters,] and elders to be able to pass the strict and cruel examinations of the enemies. Luling knew that young girls were in danger of getting taken away, abused and raped, so she dressed them up in dirty clothes and had them disguised as sick and capable of spreading [deadly] diseases. Luling's brilliant idea led them to safe ground at last. To many, Luling Young is a hero.
>
> *—Thao Ho, 11th grade*

Likewise, with her college recommendation letter for a Mexican-American immigrant, Vanessa uses the letter of recommendation format to capture the characterization and themes of T. C. Boyle's novel, *The Tortilla Curtain* (1996).

> America Ricon is a young woman who is looking for a bright future. Believe me when I say that she truly would make an amazing student in a college like this. [. . .] We grew older together and spent a long period of time trying to make a living in a ravine in Los Angeles. We crossed to America looking for a better life and trying to find work, and many times it felt that we would never afford anything more than a few groceries per week. America is only seeking an opportunity to receive an education and make a career out of it.
>
> *—Vanessa Salas, 11th grade*

Often when students assume the "voice" of a character in fiction in order to write a letter of recommendation or condemnation, their own voices and self-reflection shine through. James, a highly responsible, diligent young man, takes pride in his maturity and with the challenges he has chosen to face in Advanced Placement courses. He seems to recognize himself with his letter about the protagonist of Robert Louis Stevenson's *Treasure Island* (2010), Jim Hawkins:

> When we reached Treasure Island, I have to admit that Jim made some mistakes. [. . .] However, Jim was the first one to recognize the danger of his actions, and he accepted responsibility for them when he kept his word of honor to Silver that he would not try and escape his captivity during the brief time he was in the custody of the pirates. [. . .] He was determined to make good on his mistakes. Thus, I am convinced that Jim's experience on Treasure Island transformed him from a reckless boy into a decisive young man of character.
>
> —*James Leet, 11th grade*

The letter format is particularly effective in encouraging student voice in writing. The reading and writing connection becomes stronger when students can project themselves into the thematic content of a work of literature by conceiving of an appropriate letter of recommendation or condemnation for a character.

"Where I'm From" poem (George Ella Lyon) for novel characters

Inspired by the lovely George Ella Lyon poem "Where I'm From," the student creates a poem about one of the characters in the book, focusing on characterization rather than plot.

Because students will have already written their own "Where I'm From" poems as part of a class assignment, they readily make the leap from writing their personal poems to writing ones based on characters in the texts they are reading. Several excerpts from student poems follow. They reflect the connection between their earlier personal poems and the ones they wrote based on the literature they read independently.

An 11th grader, Celeste, focuses on the happy memories of her childhood. The experience of accessing these memories and crafting them in heightened language, however, helped her access the themes in Tim O'Brien's Vietnam War novel *The Things They Carried* (1998) and further develop her own growing poetic and passionate voice. From her personal childlike poetic lines of "I'm from sunny days at the beach, /from barbequed burgers and cold soda. /I'm from trips to Happy Hollow, /from ladybug rides and koi ponds," Celeste, in one week's time, moves to a profound grasp of O'Brien's themes:

> *"I'm from a belief that true war stories/are never about war, /From a passion that pushes me to write, /I'm from the story that Mitchell told me/with the moral that nobody listens. /I'm from a hope that you will listen to my stories, /to reflect upon the memories I have, /so that, together, we can resolve the pain of my past."*
>
> —*Celeste Rodriguez, 11th grade*

In her personal "Where I'm From" poem, Yesenia remembers the sweet cultural memories of her Mexican-American family: "I'm from the bedtime traditions/and the love our family shares. /From 'Que suenes con los angelitos, /In an accented / Spanish, /From 'Hasta mañana." This writing project helped facilitate her move into powerful writing about literature, in her "Where I'm From" book report about *The Things They Carried:*

> *"I am from the mud/From the field of feces that was our bed. / I'm from the longing for home/(every spare moment/spent thinking of home.)/ I am from the trees/hiding us from our enemies/and the sun whose rays could be tortuous. / [,,,] I'm from killing a man/because of a truth I made up."*
>
> *—Yesenia Jimenez, 11th grade*

Movie Time

Most students love movies, and this assignment taps into that excitement. Each student writes a paper in which he or she not only casts the book based on living actors, but also describes the filming of either the book's climax or a particularly poignant scene. The student needs to justify the casting choices for the book's characters and the cinematic choices for the imaginary "filmed" scenes. Many contemporary students are avid movie fans whose point of reference about storytelling comes from their repeated viewing of films and their general interest in popular cinema. While teachers often complain that students no longer have the capability to visualize what they are reading, if students are asked to "film" a scene from a book, this facility is addressed. Showing the students a filmed version of a novel the class has enjoyed together also goes a long way toward demonstrating the power of "visual" literacy before this particular book report activity is assigned.

Book Recommendation Letter to Another Student

In this popular and entertaining activity, the student writes a letter to another student in the class recommending the book he or she read independently. Sometimes I ask the students to make an allusion to another work of literature by comparing the book's protagonist to a character from a core work read in class. Today's students are especially adept at writing to peers in the sense that they love to email or "text" each other and use social media sites such as Facebook. Thus, the letter to another student generates rich voice because students

Todd Rafalovich

Marie Milner

see another opportunity to have their voices recognized by their peers. Here are the first two paragraphs of a letter originally hand-written during class time from one freshman girl to her peer in another of my freshman classes:

> Dear Nhi Chu,
>
> I have recently read The Alchemist by Paul Coelho. As many of my fellow classmates have suggested, it is quite the inspirational novel: throughout the book, Coelho shows his readers that no goal is impossible and that even the smallest sliver of hope can bring wondrous results. If you are one who wishes to further understand your own mind and reflect on one's self, I highly recommend reading Coelho's masterpiece.
>
> In his book, he speaks much of the meaning of life, as well as one's sole purpose in life: to realize one's Personal Legend. According to Coelho, "there is one great truth on this planet: whoever you are, or whatever it is that you do, when you really want something, it's because that desire originated in the soul of the universe. It's your mission on Earth." Such ideals are conveyed through the voice of a wise old king as he describes Personal Legends. The young shepherd boy, to whom these words of the wise are spoken, becomes greatly influenced and feels empowered to follow through with his goal: to discover the treasure of the pyramids that haunted his dreams the past few nights.
>
> —*Jennie Dinh, ninth grade*

Letter to the Author

The student writes a letter to the author of the book, in which he or she states and supports an opinion about the book's quality and themes. Mailing these letters to living authors often results in personal responses from the authors. Since so many authors have personal websites, the possibilities for emailing a letter are endless. Even if actually sending the letter to the author is impossible, this activity provides students with another opportunity to imagine an authentic audience other than the teacher. What follows is another excerpt from a letter to Dave Eggers. In her letter, not only does Annie's voice shine, but she also makes connections to other works she has read previously from her private library:

> Dear Mr. Eggers,
>
> How did you live like that? After reading your book, A Heartbreaking Work of Staggering Genius, I couldn't fathom how life went on like that for you. Well, I guess I could in a way, since I was reading your biography and all.
>
> . . . However, as I further read into the book, it finally hit me: "This is a real story about a man who just lost his parents in 5 weeks. Oh my god." In the beginning, I knew I was reading your biography, but it never fully processed in my mind that this was your story, that this had actually happened to someone. I thought it was amazing for you to have made such impacting life decisions shortly after what happened. You moved to California, raised your little brother, worked out schedules with your sister to help raise your little brother, and still squeezed in some "down-time" for yourself.
>
> You weren't like Bella Swan from Twilight by Stephenie Meyer who curled up into the fetal position, went numb for months, and then jumped off a cliff when the love of her life left her. You were more like Hermione Granger from the Harry Potter series, who kept searching for the keys to destroy the world's most powerful dark wizard when the love of

her life left her. Well, in this case, you're the male version, and you weren't searching for the keys to destroy the dark wizard. Instead, you were searching for the keys to open the door to continue on with your life.

Mr. Dave Eggers, I applaud you. For overcoming your past and living as a stronger person today, for enduring your hardships, for taking care of your brother, and for giving your mother's ashes a final farewell, thank you. Reading your book was truly inspiring.

—Annie Tran, 11th grade

Talk Show

Television talk shows are popular. Each student writes a script for a television or radio talk show with a character from the book he or she has read. The script not only includes enough plot points to demonstrate that the student has completed the reading, but also allows the student to discuss theme and illustrate characterization. The student might pretend to be an actual talk show host, such as Oprah Winfrey, or may interview the character while assuming the role of a modern adolescent talk-show host.

Similar to the "movie time" writing prompt, there is student buy-in with a talk show format. When they write these pieces, they show how well they have observed the kinds of questions a good host will ask a guest. Because raising probing questions is something a good novelist essentially does with fictional characters, the students are able to more creatively and passionately demonstrate their grasp of their books' themes. In the following example, Austin focused on the themes of George Orwell's *1984*:

> *AN:* Goodbye, Winston!
> *WS:* Wait. Actually, I have something to say.
> *AN:* Yes?
> *WS:* I do not want your country to end up like mine. Keep on voting, keep fighting for equality. Don't let your government oppress you. Stay in school, keep educated! Teach family values, keep teaching how to love, how to fear, how to be happy; keep emotion alive. Keep leading your own lives, doing what makes you happy. You are you, and no one else. That is something that the party has failed to realize. Now I must leave. I don't have much time.
> *AN:* . . . Goodbye, Winston. I hope you evade the Thought Police for as long as possible.
> *WS:* I do too, comrade. I do too.
> *AN:* Well readers, you've seen it right here, clear as day. Oceania is some place we never want to visit, and never want to become. So heed Winston's warning and keep fighting for peace, equality, and above all, your own happiness. Thanks for reading.

—Austin Nguyen, ninth grade

Characters Debate Controversial Issue

For this option, students script a debate between two characters in the book as they discuss a current controversial topic—an alternative debate is one between a major character in the student's book and one from a core novel currently being analyzed in class. Scripting a debate allows students to illustrate characterization, conflict, and theme, as well as express their own concerns about current topics. Students love to argue with each other and assert their identities, so what better format to encourage writing voice and heart than the scripted debate? Their passionate views are crystallized in these debates while they simultaneously access those viewpoints presented in the literature. In terms of the Common Core State Standards, there is an increased expectation that students will engage in writing that emphasizes argumentation. This book report activity addresses those standards that focus on this genre.

Thematic Comparison

For a more conventional approach to the independent reading "report," students can make substantial thematic comparisons between the independent reading book and a core book read in the class. Theme is one of the most challenging concepts to teach students, but with this assignment, students more readily grasp the concept of theme when they begin to recognize how authors employ universal themes. Because the independently read books are ones of the students' choosing, they often write with far more personal investment than they do when providing a response to required reading.

End-of-the-Year Independent Reading Project

As a culminating book report activity, students select five or more of the previous genres and use *each* of them to illustrate their comprehension of a single book's themes and artistry. With these various representations of what they have read, students create a powerful mosaic of understanding, voice, passion, and heart.

Mechanics for Book Selection, Student Interviews, and Written Assignments

Students first select a book from an extensive list of possibilities. My current list has several hundred titles on it, including 30 or so contemporary or recent works. (In her description of the "Book-Pass" activity, presented later in this chapter, Mary Warner highlights ways in which students can be introduced to book possibilities.) My high school students are expected to read at least six books independently over the course of the year and are usually given between four to six weeks to complete their reading. For the first book choice of the year, each student chooses a title and then signs up with me as a commitment to read that book. Inspired by conversations with students, I make recommendations based on their language development levels and interests, while also suggesting that students ask each other for recommendations. It is perfectly acceptable for students to sign up for a book that a friend in the class is going to be reading as well. The nature of my book "reports" is such that they do not permit cheating; consequently, students may choose to discuss the book they are reading with a friend.

Their only commitment to me on book report day is to have read their books and have those titles in their hands. There is no conventional book report assignment that they should have completed at home. The book reports are done in class.

On the day of "book reporting," the students write an in-class "creative" assignment, based on a variety of previously modeled and practiced genres. I recently taught a 100-minute block class, so my students were expected to complete the in-class written book report in that time, minus the three or four minutes I spent interviewing them quietly in a corner about their books. When I teach in traditional classes of 50 to 55 minutes, I collect the written assignments at the end of each period and return those to the students for completion the next time the class meets.

Book Interviews

For the interviews, if two or more students have signed up to read the same book, I summon at least two of them to my location in the room and double the time spent discussing the book with them. This way a more detailed discussion is feasible, and the students have a classmate nearby for emotional support. After the first interview of the year, the students understand that they are not going to encounter any questions they cannot answer if they have read the book. I begin with factual, elementary plot questions to quickly learn whether they have actually read the book and to build their confidence. Then I delve into questions that address characterization, structure, theme, and other literary elements.

When a student is sitting 12 inches from me during an interview, he or she is virtually incapable of pretending to have read the book, and most students learn this the day of the first in-class book report. After that, students either make sure to have read their books or confess to having not done their reading before I call them to my side. I make the book reports equal to a major essay grade in my class, so *not* reading the book does not come up terribly often.

When interviewing the students, I try to honor their integrity and maturity. I may ask them if they have seen the movie version of their book and suggest that they may want to watch it at some time and compare it to the novel. I tell students early in the year that I have questions on each "filmed book" that will quickly determine during an interview if a student has actually read the book rather than just watched the film.

The intimacy of these book interviews and discussions with students is highly gratifying, especially when I am able to interview a few students together and establish a "mini-book club" atmosphere; my students share the same feeling about these teacher-student book conferences. Whatever discussion we hold together during the book report generally informs the students' written assignments no matter what time during the class period I interview them. Thus, the interview serves as a talking pre-write of the kind that often inspires writing.

Modifications for Various Students and Situations

There are a few exceptions to this assignment because I want to encourage, not discourage, student engagement with literature. If a student has almost completed a book of, say, 300 pages, and is a English language learner, I interview him or her on the portion of the book completed, and then schedule another date to interview him or her again once he or she has completed the book. If a student has insisted on reading a fairly lengthy book of 600 pages or more and has only read, perhaps, 300 pages, I generally suggest that he or she complete the next 300 pages for book report number two. This prevents students from being discouraged when reading substantial texts.

If students have been actively writing over the class period and express frustration that they have not been able to complete the written assignment at the end of class (particularly if their interviews came late in the period), I collect the papers and tell them they can come at a later time and complete the written portion. If an English learner and emerging writer has clearly not made much headway during class time, and yet the interview has confirmed that he or she has read the book, I make a confidential agreement with the student that he or she finishes the written portion at home. These students often honor that arrangement with me with a neatly typewritten copy of the book report, even though that is not a requirement of the assignment.

Note: In-class book report interviews are conducted quietly with each of the students while other students continue to write. These book interviews are no more than three minutes each, or perhaps six minutes if two students are being interviewed together about the same book.

Part IV: The Actual Not the Virtual: The Power of the Book Pass to Engage Teen Readers— by Mary Warner

In Chris Crutcher's *Whale Talk*, protagonist The Tao Jones comments on what he's learned from his English teacher about the best way to tell an effective story: "The trick is to dig out the people and events that connect, and connect them." TJ's words express a central premise about the power of a book to illuminate students' lives, to engage students enough that they want to read. Jay Richards and Brenna Dimas, earlier in this chapter, have expressed so well this same principle—creating meaningful response to literature begins with finding ways to help student readers to connect, to come to that wonderful question: How can I change my life because I read this book?

For a number of years as I've taught Literature for Young Adults to college juniors and seniors—many of whom plan to teach high school English—I've routinely done a Book Pass activity early in the semester prior to having each student do a Book Talk. The Book Pass, depending on how many books you have to review and how much time you allow for reviewing a book before it's time to "pass" and get another, allows students to become familiar with about 20 books in a short period of time. My goal in the Literature for Young Adults course is to introduce students, frequently future middle and high school language arts teachers, with as many YA authors, books, and genres as I can. The students always love this activity, ranking it as one of the most helpful parts of the course. They identify books they'd like to read and they get to know, quickly, lots of the best books and writers to "hook" the teens they'll teach. Students consistently comment that they never got to read YA literature in middle or high school, with many reflecting that they may have been better readers if they had had such opportunities.

Going "On the Road"—The Book Pass in Middle and High School

An ALAN (Assembly on Literature of Adolescents of NCTE—National Council of Teachers of English) Research Grant proposal, "Learning From Their Own Stories: Using YA Literature to Build Literacy in English Language Learners," allowed me to test out the

Book Pass in middle and high school settings. I know encouraging adolescents to become readers, especially in a cultural milieu where so many elements compete with reading, is in itself a challenge. English language learners face even more challenges as they meet and try to comprehend texts in English, which is often their third or fourth language. I therefore raised three central questions:

- How might YA literature, which is written in more accessible English, help build language comprehension?
- How might YA literature, with topics that appeal to adolescents, encourage ELLs to do more reading and facilitate their acquisition of English?
- In what ways can YA literature serve as a bridge for ELL into the "canon" of literature in the English courses?

I received the ALAN grant and a sabbatical in the spring of 2009, allowing me to contact middle and high school students to "poll the audience." Building on the principle that "making a connection" is an essential ingredient to get students reading, I created a brief survey:

1. What would help improve your comprehension of English?
2. What topics interest you?
3. What books have you read that you like and would suggest to other English learners?
4. What authors do you know and what books or works by these writers do you enjoy?

A last minute brainstorm before I began my school visits was to do the Book Pass activity. I have a good collection of YA books, but serendipitously, from a wonderful independent book store owner, I got nearly 300 books —advanced reader copies—that I could actually give to the schools I visited after completing my research.

Book Pass Procedure

As in any teaching context, you have to find out what the students know. I'd begin by asking, do you know how to do a Book Pass? And then I'd model the procedure.

- Look at the title. What does it suggest the book will be about?
- Look at the cover or book jacket if the book has one. Do be warned—you can't always judge a book by its cover.
- Look at the back cover. Are there short blurbs or excerpts from the book?
- Read the first pages of the book or skim chapter titles if the book has these.
- Give each book a two-minute review.

For high school classes, I frequently used Han Nolan's *If I Should Die Before I Wake* to model the review process. Starting from the cover's close-up of a swastika in the eye of a young woman and the word "die" in the title, the book grabbed students' attention. With the middle school students, I alternated between Will Hobbs' *Crossing the Wire* (2007) and

John Boyne's *The Boy in the Striped Pajamas*. Though both books evoked students' interest, *Crossing the Wire* was especially resonant with the many Latino/a students.

Before we began the Book Pass, I asked students to go to the flip side of their survey paper and use the space there to write down the titles of any book they saw that they'd like to read. Additionally, since I was collecting the surveys, I suggested they use a separate paper to record the books so that they and their teachers could keep a list. I monitored the procedure for passing the books, kept the time, and watched the students' response to see how quickly the books needed to be passed—though I aimed for a minimum of a minute and a half. In middle school classrooms, the total time for the Book Pass was generally 35 to 40 minutes; in high school classes, students got 45 to 50 minutes to review books.

Students' Response—A Validation of the "Actual"

We always concluded the Book Pass with a quick "round the room" survey, asking everyone to name at least one book he or she would like to read. As students shared titles, I affirmed their choices, frequently giving other titles by the same author or giving more details about the books. If time allowed, I asked students what they liked about the Book Pass. Repeatedly students said, "We got to see these books." They explained, "These books come recommended. You brought the books to us." The response from a middle school student at J. W. Fair Middle School is indicative of student responses to the Book Pass:

> In all my years of going to school I have never had an experience like this. It was honestly a great pleasure to be a part of, if I do say so myself, one of the best ways to get young readers interested in books. . . .
>
> The "book pass" we did was honestly a great way to meet new authors and titles that I've never even heard of!! Starting with *Three Cups of Tea*, *Among the Positives*, and even *The Lion Hunter* . . . I really enjoyed examining books and different kinds of cases of them. I like the way you talked to us about reading and books.

Even though I have yet to completely process the data from the survey of the 1,700 students I engaged in this Book Pass activity, I have tabulated for each school the lists of the books their students found interesting and would want to read. The dominant image that emerges from watching the students participate in the Book Pass is the power of the actual, rather than the virtual. Hearing the students, as they came into the classroom and saw the books they'd soon be reviewing, say, "Can we have these books?" and watching them skim the books confirmed the studies that talk about teens responding to a single caring adult. Yes, most teens are tech-savvy and great navigators of the Internet and they might be able to find the author websites for many of these books. I would argue that they liked the books they saw and "felt" because a person came to their classrooms, brought the books to them, and validated their responses.

Occasionally as I moved among the classes at a single school or when I went to a new school, I'd discover a book was missing—Laurie Halse Anderson's *Speak* (2001) or Royce Buckingham's *Demonkeeper* (2008). Though I'd regret not having the book for the next school's Book Pass, I'd also think that if students saw a book they wanted to read and took it, that wasn't such a bad thing. Often during the actual Book Pass, a student would be so "into" a book, she or he would not want to be "interrupted" by the next book that was passed. Sometimes as the class period ran down, I'd have to wrench a book away from a student.

The atmosphere the Book Pass creates is what Kelly Gallagher in *Readicide* describes as a "book flood." Gallagher confirmed what I'd discovered in my research: students need to have ready access to a wide range of reading materials if they are ever going to develop the reading habit. And it's up to the teacher to provide the book flood and to read enticing excerpts or share just enough of the plot to elicit students' interest. Combining brief Book Talks with the Book Pass make it even more effective.

Eventually you can lead your students to http://teenreads.com or http://authors4teens .com, or to the ALAN website: http://www.alan-ya.org/. Initially, building a passion for reading begins with teachers who know their students and know what books to give them. This starts the connections that will keep students reading for the rest of their lives.

References and Resources

ALAN: Assembly on Literature for Adolescents of NCTE (National Council of Teachers of English) website: http://www.alan-ya.org/

ALAN Picks—reviews of the most recent YA books.

Anderson, Laurie Halse. *Speak*. New York: Penguin, 2001. http://Authors4teens.com

Boyle, T. C. *The Tortilla Curtain*. New York: Penguin Books, 1996.

Boyne, John. *The Boy in the Striped Pajamas*. New York: Ember, Reprint Edition, 2007.

Buckingham, Royce. *Demonkeeper*. New York: Puffin, 2008.

Calkins, Lucy. *The Art of Teaching Reading*. Boston: Allyn & Bacon, 2000.

Calkins, Lucy, Mary Ehrenworth, and Christopher Lehman. *Pathways to the Common Core: Accelerating Achievement*. Portsmouth, NH: Heinemann, 2012.

Crutcher, Chris. *Whale Talk*. New York: Laurel Leaf, 2002.

Eggers, Dave. *A Heartbreaking Work of Staggering Genius*. New York: Vintage, Reprint edition, 2001.

Gallagher, Kelly. *Readicide: How Schools Are Killing Reading and What You Can Do About It*. Portland, ME: Stenhouse Publishers, 2009.

Hobbs, Will. *Crossing the Wire*. New York: HarperCollins, 2007.

Keene, Ellin, and Susan Zimmerman. *Mosaic of Thought: Teaching Comprehension in a Reader's Workshop*, 2nd edition. Portsmouth, NH: Heinemann, 2007.

Lyon, George Ella. "Where I'm From." http://www.georgeellalyon.com/where.html

Nolan, Han. *If I Should Die Before I Wake*. Graphia, Reissue Edition, 2003.

O'Brien, Tim. *The Things They Carried*. New York: Broadway, 1998.

Orwell, George. *1984*. New York: Signet Classic, 1950.

Smith, Michael W., and Jeffrey D. Wilhelm. *Reading Don't Fix No Chevys: Literacy in the Lives of Young Men*. Portsmouth, NH: Heinemann, 2002.

Spinelli, Jerry. *Wringer*. New York: HarperCollins, 1998.

Stevenson, Robert Louis. *Treasure Island*. Calgary, Alberta, Canada: Qualitas Classics, 2010.

Tan, Amy. *The Bonesetter's Daughter*, 2nd edition. New York: Putnam, 2001.

Taylor, Mildred. *Roll of Thunder, Hear My Cry*. New York: Puffin, 1991. http://teenreads.com

Wilhelm, Jeffrey D. *"You Gotta BE the Book."* New York: Teachers College Press, 1997.

Zusak, Markus. *The Book Thief*. New York: Alfred A. Knopf, 2005.

5

Finding Your Writing Voice

by Mary Warner, Kathleen Cohen, and Marie Milner

Introduction

The elusive quality of voice really need not be that elusive—particularly in the technological world so commonplace for our students. Consider the many ways they "voice themselves": their Facebook, Twitter, LinkedIn, or any other social networks. Adapting the slogan for Capital One, we can ask them, "What's on your iPod?" Your students are no doubt well aware of the ring tones they select; however, for a mini-lesson on voice, have your students describe the kind of person who would select a particular ring tone and explain the "voice" that comes through in their own choice. These digital writing contexts are rich in student voice, even though students often see no connection between the personality they present online and the personality they might present in their academic writing.

Additionally, we might think of how often we and our students express the desire to be heard. "Did you hear me?" "Will you listen to me?" "Do you understand what I'm saying?"—these kinds of questions substantiate the importance of developing the writing voices of our students.

Katie Wood Ray, a writer and researcher in the teaching of writing, advocates for "reading like a writer." In her presentations, she demonstrates the importance of giving our students models of the kind of writing we'd like them to do. Katie, a fan of columnist Leonard Pitts, provides numerous examples of Pitts' columns in a writing workshop she conducts for fifth graders. In this workshop, she guides students through an examination of Pitts' rhetorical techniques and the style of Op Ed articles. Once these students "read like writers," they create their own strong writings. However, a significant reason for the strong writing they create is the good models they have seen; through hearing Pitts' voice, they have a sense of how they can make their voices heard as well.

Katie also provides the example of her good friend who is a talented seamstress. When Katie and her friend go shopping, her friend loves to examine dresses, skirts, or blouses, but she never buys anything, much to Katie's frustration. Her friend, though, is reviewing the models, knowing she can always better her craft by examining how other garments are made. She views others' clothing construction to improve her own, just as we want our students to "read like writers" to improve their creations.

Young Adult (YA) author Sue Ellen Bridgers offers another perspective on voice. When I was writing *Adolescents in the Search for Meaning: Tapping the Powerful Resource of Story*, I asked her if she would do the Foreword for the book. Sue Ellen, who has written six YA novels, short stories, and poetry, surprised me by saying, "I have to read Forewords to know how to do this; I've never written a Foreword before."

Katie and Sue Ellen teach what should be obvious—we can't write what we don't know. We as teachers of writing need to help our students hear the voices in the text and then hopefully connect to these voices. The next step involves moving from accessing voice in what students read to helping them develop their own.

In Part I of this chapter, I demonstrate how the use of readers' theatre, specifically Karen Hesse's *Witness* (2001), can help students first "hear the voices in texts" in order to connect and respond to literature with their own voices. In Part II, Kathleen Cohen explores the "snapshot, talk shot, and thought shot" process as a means of empowering the voices of middle school writers. In Part III, Marie Milner describes the value of using mentor texts as models for generating voice in the writing of high school students.

Part I: Using Readers' Theatre to Hear the Voices in the Text
by Mary Warner

In my university Literature for Young Adults course, I've found a powerful way to address the concept of voice through readers' theatre with Karen Hesse's *Witness* (2001). *Witness* is a poetic play in five acts, telling the story of the Ku Klux Klan's attempt to recruit members in a small town in Vermont in 1924, with the events conveyed through the voices of 11 townspeople. Among the key voices in the text are

- Leanora Sutter, a 12-year-old black girl who has recently experienced the death of her mother
- Esther Hirsh, a younger Jewish girl, who is, like Leanora, a target of the Klan's bigotry
- Merlin VanTornhout, a teenager, and Johnny Reeves, a minister, who voice the Klan's hate-filled message of white supremacy
- Reynard Alexander, a newspaper editor who is trying to walk a careful line of neutrality until he has to take a stand

As the characters speak directly to the reader and relate the juxtaposition of acts of hate and love, violence and peace, terror and kindness, they illuminate the full range of human weaknesses and strengths.

Almost any literary selection with multiple characters and sufficient dialogue can be adapted to readers' theatre. Essentially what the teacher needs to do is highlight the dialogue in the text and distribute the parts to students. Depending on the number of characters in the text selected, creating a readers' theatre version allows for greater student participation. I vary the way I assign characters. As we read *Witness*, I give the students a list of the characters about three weeks before we do the readers' theatre and have them sign up for specific characters. I also have three or more readers for each character, depending on how often the character speaks in the five acts of *Witness*. Each subsequent semester it's evident how much the students engage with Hesse's text, how much they "hear the voices" of the Vermonters, and how well they speak these characters' voices. It could be the readers' theatre, it could be that reading and immediately responding act by act helps the students "stay with" the text, or it could be that they don't have to read the text "alone." The "voice" the student readers give to the characters demonstrates how well they understand the text; they grasp the key aspect of *Witness*—it conveys a single experience told from multiple perspectives.

Writing Activities to Identify Voice

During the in-class reading, students respond to the following questions after each act:

1. With which character do you relate or empathize the most? Why?
2. What voice is most powerful? Why? Or what are the "power lines" that capture your response?
3. What lines or words help you to hear and know the voice?
4. For your own character, what lines in the text give your character the voice you are using? Explain.

The first few times I taught *Witness*, I used the typical assignment in most college literature courses—a literary analysis paper. Often the result was writing that barely got beyond summary and lacked the passion the students demonstrated in voicing the characters as they read. In the Writing Project Summer Institute of 2006, as I worked to prepare my workshop for my K–college peers, I revised my approach to find a way to tap my students' voices. I recalled Katie Wood Ray's mantra, "read like a writer." When my students caught the power of Karen Hesse's vignettes, they could replicate her powerful model in their writing.

In the fall of 2006, I experimented with the following approach and have been doing this successful voice activity ever since. After the class reading of *Witness*, I remind my students that what Hesse has done is tell a single story or recount a single event from multiple perspectives. The key is the event has been shared or experienced by many people. Then I suggest that all of us have had shared experiences and direct them to the following prompt. Once we've written (I also write and read my vignette, making sure I'm modeling what I ask of my students and making my voice a part of the class readers' theatre), all of us read our vignette aloud—in any order—depending on who is "moved" to read. By the end, everyone has read—thus creating our own readers' theatre. The following is an example of the prompt I use for the shared event:

Writing Prompt for 9/11—our shared event

In your own voice or in the voice of someone you'd like to represent (for example, a passenger on one of the hijacked planes, a NY fireman or emergency worker, etc.), describe your experience of September 11, 2001. Develop your response in the free verse poetry style of Karen Hesse or in a short prose vignette. Be prepared to read your vignette aloud.

What emerges in the 9/11 Readers' Theatre is a range of voices—real voices of students who remember that day in 2001—and a sense of how students heard the voices in Hesse's text and caught her vignette style while expressing their experiences of the events. These vignettes come from about 20 minutes of writing; the power of the writing attests to the connection with the voices they've heard and to the impact of one of the most horrific experiences Americans have faced. The following two samples of these student voices show their results. The complete 9/11 Readers Theatres are available at http://www.sjsu.edu/faculty/mary.warner/Warnerstudentlinks.htm.

In the first sample, Ahmed Al-Sheikh, a Middle Eastern student, expresses his anxiety and anger, anticipating the inevitable backlash to come. Both student samples, though, convey powerful voice and demonstrate how strongly they connected to Hesse's text. In the second example, Scott Ferris chose to "voice" former president George W. Bush.

> *I saw the future as I saw the towers fall*
> *saw it before because*
> *of Oklahoma.*
> *Americans hate Arabs more than*
> *Russians*
> *Asians*
> *Germans*
> *or any they hated before.*
> *They butcher us in their films*
> *Disregard our culture as backward and oppressive*
> *When the bomb went off in*
> *Oklahoma,*
> *they blamed us all.*
> *Women covering their heads in modesty*
> *Children saying hamdilulah instead of bless you*
> *when they sneeze,*
> *Men with earth tone skin and thick dark hair*
> *They punished us all before it was revealed*
> *to be two*
> *white*
> *Christian*
> *men*
> *I knew it would happen again when I saw*
> *the towers fall*
> *And when one evil man who happened to share*

my faith and birthplace admitted responsibility
it became worse.
They'll kill us all.

—Ahmed Al-Sheikh

I had arrived at the elementary school,
my sole task being to read a book.
A children's book for children about
something they could understand,
something they could cope with.

The children were so excited to see me
and I was excited too.
I began to read
and they began to listen,
nothing more important on our minds
than that story.

Not long after I had started reading
one of my men walked calmly over to me
and whispered something in my ear.
A great tragedy had occurred,
something the children
would not
could not
understand.

I remained calm and
continued reading,
struggling to prevent any change
in my voice or on my face.
They were so young and little
and they didn't need to know what had happened.
Not right now.

A short while later,
the same man came over to me,
whispering once more.
Tragedy had struck once more.
I continued reading.

Perhaps I should have stopped,
perhaps I should have gotten up and left.
But what could I have done?
The damage had been done.
I had been powerless to stop it.

But I was not completely powerless.
Rather than scare the children,

I sat
and I read.
I did what I thought was
the one thing I could do at that moment.
I tried to protect them for just a while longer.
I had failed to protect my country,
but I would not fail to protect them.

—Scott Ferris

Their writing speaks for itself; the students are able to "make themselves heard." The challenge is to keep them using their newfound voices in whatever writing tasks they meet.

Part II: Tapping the Voice of Middle School Students by Kathleen Cohen

I couldn't believe my math homework grade—50%—What would my parents say when they heard the news? They would be hot lava demons and throw me in the fiery pit.

I was in awe. Shi, my English language learner, a writer of "the firstly, secondly, and in conclusion" school, had VOICE.

Voice is a trait shared by almost all middle school students: loud, quiet, accented, and changing. Middle school kids scream and squeal. Their conversations are natural, unguarded, and quite delightful. However, middle school writers begin their journey to adolescence by guarding their thoughts and feelings and carefully protecting themselves from revealing the innate power of their natural writing voices. Amy Tan (2003), long after she finished middle school, wrote, "The hard work of writing is emotional, feeling insecure, feeling stupid. There's a fear that if things don't come out right, it will be a wasted effort."

Imagine those 13-year-olds who feel that their every word, every piece of clothing, every action, is being scrutinized by their peers. No wonder they're afraid to write freely. The only thing they do freely is talk. Middle schoolers filter their written expressions for "correctness," both among their peers and when submitting writing assignments. When given a writing prompt, fifth graders will grab their pencils and fill a page in five minutes. Seventh graders, by contrast, tentatively select their "Alphagel Chrome" mechanical pencils, hover over the page, hesitantly putting pencil to paper to perhaps write their names, their faces screwed up with horror at the task ahead, silently questioning, "What shall I write?"

After being assigned a personal narrative about an incident that took place in school, John drove me crazy when he whined, "I don't have anything to write about." It became his mantra. At least once a day, he would complain, "I still don't have anything to write about." He wouldn't write, so I finally said, "**Tell** me your story. **Tell** me something that happened to you at school." And he did. His story was personal and powerful. Once he had told me his story, I could say to him, "OK, now go write it just like you told it to me." Telling the story liberated him to write it. Since children of this age are consciously self-aware and developmentally diverse, the middle school teacher's challenge is to tap their unique personalities and free their writing voices. Based on Barry Lane's (1992) "snapshot, talk shot, and thoughtshot," here are the steps I take from the first day of school to help my students experience their writing as not only a safe, but a joyful activity.

Creating a Safe Community

At the beginning of the year, we read as a class "All Summer in a Day" by Ray Bradbury (1954). The story, set n an imagined future in which humans inhabit Venus, describes a young girl, Margot, who is isolated and different from her classmates. As is so common in middle school, she is bullied. Margot has had some experience with Earth while her peers have lived all their lives on Venus. She breaks the cardinal rule of middle school: "Thou shalt not be different." The Bradbury story serves dual purposes. "All Summer in a Day" provides a springboard for discussing how to create a safe classroom atmosphere by encouraging students to formulate their own expectations for appropriate behavior. Furthermore, it is an engaging story, modeling great voice, that promotes discussion and is the basis for a personal narrative.

The Journal Writes

Moving students from hearing Margot's voice in "All Summer in a Day" to the reality of their own lives involves a series of scaffolded journal writes, culminating in a personal narrative. These journal writes (JWs) are brief and focused on topics related to the classroom environment.

- JW 1—Describe Margot's classroom
- JW 2—Evaluate Margot's classroom
- JW 3—Imagine your ideal classroom

JW 3, imagining their ideal classroom, allows the student writers to explore a topic on which they are experts and have something to say, thereby assuring voice in their writing. In small groups, they develop a description of the atmosphere and the physical space in their room, creating a communal vision of their ideal classroom. The ideas are posted on a Google survey, and the students can vote for their favorites. In sharing their ideas, these middle schoolers who often keep their writing close to their chests don't realize that they have just shared writing in a meaningful, non-threatening environment.

Moving Toward a Personal Narrative

The next two journal writes ask the students to list memorable school experiences they have had and choose three to develop into a short narrative. Why school experiences? They are common to all. Students have had good, bad, and weird experiences, so no two will be alike. For example, Moumita wrote a story about a sweater her mom knit for her.

Just before recess, I noticed the loose thread. It called to me to be pulled. The bell rang, and
we tore out to recess. I sat on the very top of the jungle gym and pulled out some more red

yarn. By lunch, I was completely mesmerized. The more I pulled, the larger the hole grew. I could see my white tee shirt through it. I consulted with my friend, Megan, "What should I do with the yarn?" "Take off the sweater and put it in your lunch box, so you don't lose the string," she suggested. That seemed logical. We took turns pulling the yarn away from the sweater, watching the pile of red grow.

When Moumita's mom picked her up that afternoon, she was gifted with a lunch pail full of red yarn. While you may end up reading two or three stories out of a hundred about winning or losing a relay race or being late for class, you're not likely to get more than one in a lifetime about a first grader meticulously destroying the sweater her mom knit for her.

The detail that Moumita added in her story emerged from an oral retelling of her simple journal write, "My mom knit me a sweater and I destroyed it." Likewise, the voice that Shi has in the opening anecdote of this chapter, describing his parents as "hot lava demons," developed from the simple sentence: "My mom and dad were very mad at me for getting a bad math grade." The key is that in a verbal pair-share of the short writings about memorable school experiences, the writers are encouraged to become storytellers and to add details, as their listeners want to know more about each experience. The sharing is oral and aural because each pair has a teller and a listener.

Verbal Pair-Share

Teachers should determine the pairs. The best pairs combine students with differing abilities; determining the pairs beforehand assures no one is left out. As students tell their stories to their partners, they typically add more and more detail. This oral/aural process is crucial to developing the emerging writers' voices because it is an honest interaction. The listener knows the person behind the words, and the writer knows the listener. John told his story about how he stuck with the track team even though the coach had confused and humiliated him. After his listener responded to John's story asking for more detail and raising questions to clarify the story, John could then powerfully and clearly write about his hatred of this coach, which ultimately turned into grudging admiration. Shi, my "firstly, secondly writer" who would never think to write about his parents as "hot lava demons," had no trouble verbally describing his parents with this wonderful metaphor after getting feedback from his pair-share partners.

Providing the students with a specific discussion format aids them in staying on task and introduces an academic tone that can liberate students from the shy to the boisterous. According to Kate Kinsella, a professor at San Francisco State University who specializes in developing academic language skills with English language learners, "'Academic talk' is a verbal sentence with appropriate vocabulary, syntax, and grammar" (Kate Kinsella, "Dual Language Workshop" PowerPoint). Verbal pair-shares offer a structure to encourage the academic discourse that English language learners, as well as their native English-speaking peers, need to practice.

These pair-shares are structured learning conversations that encourage the focused response the author needs and help the student listeners move beyond the vague responses like "Cool, Dude" or "It sucks" to specific examples provided in complete sentences. Both the storyteller and the listener have to be engaged in this process for it to be successful, so I model the structured dialogue by writing on the board and acting out each part: "I have three school stories to share. Please listen to each one and help me choose the story that will best develop into a personal narrative." Then, the listener says: "Your idea, _____, can develop into a successful story for these reasons: _____, and _____. Before the pair-shares, we have a practice round. Almost everyone thinks the practice is dumb, but practice helps ease the fear of the actual story sharing. If everyone has to share, and there is no opting out, the teacher can engage all of the students from the start of the year in the process of sharing writing.

Each student gets to share at least two stories. The ultimate goal is to identify the story that will work best for the student's personal narrative. Some stories are too complicated, some are too vague, but among those three stories, more than likely, there is one that the partner will encourage the writer to develop. To assure that the listeners are accountable, they should provide the tellers with written responses.

Once again, structuring the encounter, I ask the students to share with a new partner. This facilitates two learning experiences. The storyteller is more comfortable with her story and will tell it with increasing confidence; meanwhile, the listener gets to sharpen his critical skills, adding his suggestions to those the author has already received. The room is divided into storytellers and listeners. The storytellers go to an available listener and ask, "May I share my story ideas with you?" The listener responds, "Yes, I would enjoy hearing your story." After the author tells the stories, the listener looks at the original comments. He can agree, "I agree with Jason, your first story is more exciting AND_____." This gives the teller additional encouragement and specific feedback. Or a second listener, Henry, wrote: "While I understand that Jason likes your first idea about going to science camp, your second story about your 'first love' made me laugh out loud, and I think you should develop that one." Kevin's story of first love was particularly appealing to his listeners since it sounded exactly like him.

> *In fourth grade, I was a happy little camper. . . . I decided to tell my friends something important. All school year long we had been friends, and we called us, the three musketeers. . . . we were very close, but this was fourth grade, when boys started shaking off the cooties thing and started having crushes. I was going to tell my friends who I happened to like. So there I was, after school, going to tell the other two musketeers the truth. I did it and I was very happy. So I get to school the next day and at least three people come up to ask me, "Do you really like her?" and then I wasn't too happy anymore.*

The very act of *telling* the story develops the writer's voice as well as two other traits of good writing: ideas and organization. I frequently hear listeners suggest to the storytellers what to cut, where to focus, and how to order the events, so students who struggle with writing organization particularly benefit from oral/aural peer exchanges. This oral/aural exchange also functions as a form of differentiation for English language learners. Most of these students are far more confident social speakers than they are writers. Telling a story successfully really boosts a language learner's confidence. The switch from conversation to academic writing is challenging. With the oral exchange, however, before even picking up a pencil, the authors now can shape and organize their ideas. Before they navigate verb tense, usage, agreement, and all the other important mechanical aspects of writing, the emerging writer has a story.

During this time of sharing and listening, the students learn a lot about one another and develop enough trust to share their personal stories. So we begin the year as a community of storytellers and move quickly to a community of writers.

Todd Rafalovich

Kathleen Cohen

After the group sharing and discussion, I assign the personal narrative, and each story becomes a unique, honest personal history. The story sharing has taken the place of pre-writing and outlining and actually eliminates the need for a specific paper length. During the time they are writing, I read them examples from literature that include an engaging beginning, some dialogue, and a thoughtful conclusion or "so what" moment. This modeling helps my students understand how a structured narrative can help to organize their genuinely captivating stories.

Snapshots, Talk Shots, and Thoughtshots

In his book, *After 'The End': Teaching and Learning Creative Revision,* Barry Lane (1992) discusses three ways to build voice: "the snapshot," " the talk shot," and "the thoughtshot." The snapshot can be a word picture that draws the reader into the story. A lively snapshot gives the story a sense of place and person.

To encourage writing with sensory detail have students become aware of it and search it out in their reading. Katie Wood Ray calls this "reading like a writer." Looking for great sentences encourages students to read great authors. My students keep a list of "golden sentences" in their journals. When they find a beautiful, sensory passage, they write it down and cite the author and story. Periodically, students share the sentences in groups and choose one or two to share with the class. In the very helpful anthology, *Telling True Stories*, Emily Hiestand writes,

> Hearing beautiful language . . . engages the visual, physical, and emotional intelligences . . . because our intelligence is so multifaceted. Writing that honors the senses—presenting sea smoke ghosting over a lake; a cool plum; the whir of a fan—engages not only the logical mind but also our visual, physical, and emotional intelligences. . . . It is also respectful of readers, at the core of the "Show, don't tell" mantra.
> (*Telling True Stories* edited by Mark Kramer and Wendy Call, 2007)

Bradbury's "All Summer in a Day" is bursting with sensory detail that engages the eyes, ears, and heart. In their journals, students emulate the author's style and structure with their own sentences. They write the golden sentence first and then write imitative sentences following the same form. They do this writing exercise at least once a month.

Once they get the idea, they're enthusiastic about the outcome and not the least bit shy about sharing. Students can also build their metacognitive skills by using the Six Traits from Vicki Spandel (2008) to analyze the golden sentences as writers. For example, Bradbury gifts the readers with a beautiful snapshot in "All Summer in a Day":

> *It had been raining for seven years; thousands upon thousands of days compounded, and filled from one end to the other with rain, with the drum and gush of water, with the sweet crystal fall of showers and the concussion of storms so heavy they were tidal waves come over the islands.*

A student instinctively knows this is a great snapshot, a golden sentence. But, through analysis based on the Six Traits, he can actually articulate what makes it great. For example, the organization of Bradbury's sentence is concussive and ponderous. Repeating the word "with" makes each phrase louder and heavier. It gives weight to the rain. Bradbury's word choice, especially the metaphor "tidal waves come over the islands" and the comparison between "gush of water and sweet crystal fall of showers," demonstrate the different kinds of rain. The words also give a "drum beat," feeling like rain on a tin roof. Finally his voice, matter of fact and calm yet unrelenting, *"rain, rain for years, rain for thousands of days, ceaseless rain, gushes of rain, rain showers . . . ,"* makes the reader yearn for a bit of sun.

The dialogue is "the talk shot," and developing authentic dialogue is especially tricky for the young author. Students tend to fixate on the form of the dialogue, the placement of the commas and quotation marks, and not on the conversation itself. Good, clear dialogue is about voice, not about using "I said" and "Mom replied." It's about writing conversation as though you were in one. Read lively, engaging dialogue to your students. Children's literature is particularly valuable for teaching dialogue; good children's literature is accessible to all readers and it's meant to be heard. Middle school children love listening to stories and are nostalgic for the good old days of sitting on the rug and looking at the pictures in a child's book. To demonstrate authentic dialogue, I read Rosemary Wells' (1985) *Hazel's Amazing Mother*, *Star of the Week* by Barney Saltzberg (2010), or *Lunch Bunnies* by Kathryn Lasky (1996) and any book by Russell Hoban or William Steig. In *Brave Irene*, Steig (1986) creates a wonderful conversation between Irene and the wind.

> *"Go home!" the wind squalled. "Irene . . . go hooooooooome. . . ."*
> *"I will do no such thing," she snapped. "No such thing, you wicked wind!"*
> *"Go ho-o-ome," the wind yodleled. "GO HO-HO-WOME," it shrieked, "or else."*

The squalling, yodeling wind not only sounds exactly right, but also feels cold and scary, too. Good children's literature models honest, lively dialogue; it can lead to discussion of word choice and how a particular word appeals to the senses.

The thoughtshot in this assignment is the "so what" moment. The thoughtshot in a personal narrative reveals what the author learned or remembers from this experience. It defines why the reader should care about this writing. Authors want readers to connect with their stories, but most middle school kids don't know how to create such connections. Teachers need to emphasize the power of the moment of truth or the "so what" moment and share inspiring examples in literature. "All Summer in a Day" is a great story to teach the "so what" moment. Most middle school students are mesmerized by *The Outsiders* by S. E. Hinton (1997). It's revelatory to them that gang members who are socially bad can be personally caring and thoughtful—the "so what" moment. Through her character Ponyboy Curtis, Hinton converys the "so what" and "why should I care about these characters" moments. Middle school students are just beginning to develop empathy and to consider the impact of their actions. The thoughtshot, then, becomes a powerful tool to help them write reflectively. In her narrative, Christina wrote an insightful "so what" moment:

> *I guess in elementary school, I knew how far I could push it because I knew all of the rules. I went to the same elementary school all my life, and everybody knew me from the crossing guard to the secretaries. Last year was my first year at a new school. Going to a new school was tough, and I got into a lot of trouble. Now I know the rules a lot better and I know what my teachers expect from me and what I expect from me too. Next year I get to start all over again in high school, but I feel confident that I know myself, and I know how to be me and not worry about it.*

Like Christina, students use the thoughtshot to write about how they were changed by an event and why they remember it so vividly. Additionally, the thoughtshot helps the narrative to conclude, not just end.

Peer Editing

If presented as a sacred trust, peer editing can and will be a successful learning opportunity for both the author and peer editor. Editing has to be taught and scaffolded to work successfully with middle school kids.

Because the purpose of this personal narrative assignment is to foster voice through the snapshot, talk shot, and thoughtshot, peer editing should concentrate here. Students will be more helpful editors if they focus on specific aspects of writing rather than on the writing in general. Spandel's *Creating Writers Through 6-Trait Writing Assessment and Instruction* (2008) is my guide—specifically three of her six traits: organization, voice, and word choice. Before the students read one another's papers, I have them read and practice editing on a paper written by one of my former students. It's important to choose a paper that is pretty strong, so the practice can focus on editing rather than disaster repair. The class reviews the meaning of logical organization, authentic voice, and specific word choice. Each student receives a copy of a single page story with the lines numbered and a peer edit form that the students will eventually use to edit one another's work. (See Table 5.1.) The first part of the edit sheet asks the author to explain where he needs feedback. The second part of the form asks readers to ask questions of the author's writing choices. Using questions instead of statements is much less threatening to the author. Some questions that come up are: Can you use a better word than "run" in line 28? Could you add a talk shot in line 22? Can you end the story differently? It just sort of stops. The author might ask: Does my dialogue sound "real"? Does my story make sense? Do I have enough description?

TABLE 5.1   *Peer Review Sheet*

Author _____   Reader _____

Give Me Feedback on...	Peer Commendations	Peer Questions	Author's Next Steps

Revision

Understanding revision is a key step. Middle school students perceive revision as starting over and can get discouraged after working so hard and long on their narratives. If a student has a list of five or six changes, the task is doable. For example, Kuba originally wrote, ". . . entering the room I was greeted by the jumpy and anxious smiles of my classmates. . . ."

His peer editor questioned, "Could you use more action verbs?"

Kuba revised:

> *I slipped into the classroom. It was hot and charged with tension. Everyone sat smiling with closed lips clutching white knuckled to large poster boards. The basket with the numbers perched on the teacher's desk. It might as well have been full of arsenic pieces. No one wanted to present first.*

The End Result

With the personal narrative, almost every student has a successful writing experience early in the year. Students gain confidence in their writing skills. The writing has personality and voice. They have chosen the subject and have had control of its development. They have learned the names of their classmates and shared some school history with them. By the fourth week of school, they have written to six targeted prompts and have about three pages of writing in addition to their narratives. They are willing to attempt other genres. They can see writing as a process filled with struggles, but with ultimate rewards. They have achieved something both collectively and individually. To celebrate the finished narratives, there is "publishing day." I read parts and sometimes all of some narratives aloud, of course with the permission of the authors. I did not honestly understand the power of this assignment and the power of publishing until a father sent me his son's essay written in high school. The subject was pride in developing an important skill. Cameron wrote about having his story published in my class, and he gets the last word here because he sees himself as an author—every writing teacher should be so lucky:

> *The essay I wrote was so good my teacher read it out loud in class. Even then she pointed out many areas of improvement, but I had never had my work read out loud before. It was a great experience for me even though my writing had a lot of holes. Don't be confused, though it was still good writing, like all writing there was room for improvement. That day,*

I learned what my writing could be. It opened up a realm of possibilities for me and showed me that I was good at something. In a sense, it is where I get most of my confidence from. No matter what other people say, writing may be my most important skill.

Part III: "Make Music That Wasn't There Before": Modeling Voice with Mentor Texts
by Marie Milner

"Endure—and make music that wasn't there before." President Barack Obama in his memoir *Dreams From My Father* (2004) makes powerful use of Billie Holiday's music as a metaphor for artistry in the face of oppression. As I read his last line of a chapter on racial identity, I was struck by its applicability to the passion to write. I reflected on the purpose of this book, to encourage writing passion, and thought, "That's it! That's what we want our students to get!" We don't want them to cultivate the craft and artistry of writing only to pass a standardized test. We don't want them to develop strong, passionate writing voices simply to fulfill a teacher's expectations of "college level" writing or to fulfill academic "standards." We don't want them to view writing as a form of academic torture that they will shed like dead snakeskin once they complete their formal educations. Rather, we want them to see that through a strong passion for writing, they will "make music" with words that didn't exist until they conceived of them.

Obama's words moved me to entertain a high school English teacher's fantasy: What if I could not only help students recognize the music in the voices of the authors we most admire, but also inspire them to add their own voices to that literary pantheon? After all, William Shakespeare was an English schoolboy before he ever conceived of Lear. Toni Morrison, who dazzles with her novel *Beloved* (1987), was once a freshman struggling to write. Maxine Hong-Kingston, whose memoir *Woman Warrior* is the quintessential reflection on cultural identity, was once a schoolgirl playing on the concrete playground, and Gary Soto and Francisco Jimenez, who helped define the Mexican-American childhood experience, once played baseball in the streets with young friends. Yet somewhere along the way, these authors were all inspired to add their unique voices to the enduring music of the written word. There is no reason our students cannot do the same.

Four Elements for Generating Voice

When I recall the times when my students have written passionately and with the most "voice," I reflect on those writing assignments that generated this kind of engagement. Four elements emerge:

- The students had been provided with strongly written models to inspire them.
- They had been given an opportunity to write for an authentic audience.
- I had shared my own written work and writing process with them in order to begin to demystify these elements.
- The class had become engaged with professionally written work which specifically invited students to recognize themselves and their own lives.

Model or Mentor Texts

With regard to the first element, I'm the "modeling queen." I adamantly defend and recommend the use of strong models in the writing classroom. After all, my mother was a profound role model in my own life, yet I have not become my mother. I have emerged as my own person with my own voice, although greatly inspired and shaped by the life choices she modeled for me. For the same reason, I object to colleagues who argue that writing models or mentor texts are prescriptive or proscriptive. Actually they are neither. In my 20 years of teaching high school English, I've watched students discover their own voices after finding inspiration from published authors and seen students rapidly acquire craft and display artistry, once a professionally written excerpt has been demystified for them. I've celebrated the voices of once taciturn students as soon as a mentor text has given them the proverbial "something to hang their hats on." The "but, where do I begin?" goes away.

When my students experience such strong, personal poetry models as Linda Hogan's "Heritage" or George Ella Lyon's "Where I'm From," they don't initially write traditional analytical essays. Instead, my students write their own family heritage and identity poems, knowing they will be shared aloud with other students in class. Before they write their own poems, I share my poems and my writing process. I ask them to point out where the professional models provided me with a sound structure through which to express my own ideas, and to explain how my own voice transcends that structure. Then I challenge them to fill their own poems with passion and voice.

When the students read their poems aloud in class, their peers commend their craft, using the academic language they have acquired through examining the professional models. I add my own praise, reinforcing those elements of craft the students have embraced. Even in the poetry of my lower-skilled students, there are gems to be mined and peer models to inspire their classmates.

In my racially and culturally diverse school district the student poems present unique cultural perspectives as well as individual student's voices. Single words, phrases, or entire lines of the poem written in their home languages are often incorporated into the English poems, thus displaying confidence in their own aeristic voices and embracing a multilingual appreciation of the power of language:

> *Where I'm From*
>
> *I am from up on our hangout tree*
> *From white scarves and navy blue uniforms*
> *I am from Granada in Santa Clara*
> *(Nine glorious years, it felt like my second home)*
>
> *I am from white washed rocks and brown Honda*
> *And a game of green light, red light, yellow light*
> *Right over from my brown house*
> *With the palm trees out front*
>
> *I'm from dark and curly haired*
> *From desert people and camel riders*

And Mama and Baba
From Injera and hot sauce

I'm from crazy and loud
On the streets of my friends
From shy and reserved
Insightful or friendly
On classroom desks

I'm from modest and clean
And five prayers a day
I'm from Friday nights
At the MCA

I'm from Dad's peaches in the summer
And tangerines in the winter
From the sound of Mom "la hawla wa la kuwta illah billah"
In every kissing scene

I'm from Taylor Swift's songs
On my bedroom floor
I'm from long summer nights
With my sister
Watching new movies, storytelling, reading,
Or just trying to keep cool in our tangled sweaty sheets

I'm from barbecued chicken
On my Daddies grill
And tea on the lawn
Or meals on the table
With Dr. Joe

I'm from Ramadan nights
With my former classmates
Spent in Crescent Cuisine
And long prostrates

I'm from chapters and chapters of a book you never read
Captured in too many moments
And all it too be said

—Yusra Dawood, ninth grade

Other assignments that inspire student voice are various extensions of these personal poems inspired by the mentor poets. For example, when reading Toni Morrison's *Beloved* (1987), or Andrew X. Pham's *Catfish and Mandala* (1999), students create poems based on the books' characters. From *Beloved*, students might use the "Where I'm From" poem to explore Denver's characterization, and from Pham's memoir about his Vietnamese and American dual identity, students might use Hogan's "Heritage" poem to reinforce Pham's themes. The following expresses some themes and characterization from Gary Blackwood's novel *Shakespeare's Scribe* (2002).

Where I'm From

I am from the orphanage,
From the discards and the forbidden.
I am from a past of secrets.
(Concealed, Dark
A silent ghost lingering.)
I am from the world of horses,
York
The world of "Nays" and "Ayes,"
Whose flavor my tongue wraps around.

I'm from friends of hunger and longing, coughs, thieves, and applause,
From Mistress MacGregor, Dr. Bright, Simon bass, and Lord Charberlain's men.
I'm from a pile of unwanted toys being bartered.
From a hand of theft,
Thieve of words,
Valued only for my knowledge of charactery.
From an unknown identity I carry,
A false ID of Widge.
From a ghost named Sarah,
And a mystery of a crucifix
lingering.

I'm from the land of lies.
From imagination and pretend,
From the world of Hamlet and Ophelia.
Masks and stage,
Myself half boy half girl.
I'm from the orphanage,
From the discards and forbidden.
I am from a past of secrets,
From the unknown mysteries of having a family.

But I'm also from a land of change,
A bright future.
From a leaf
Turned.
A future where the word family is in my vocabulary.

—Allison Chau, ninth grade

Ray Bradbury's "The Long Rain" as Mentor Text

An excerpt from Ray Bradbury's short story, "The Long Rain" (1950), has inspired stunning writing from students. Bradbury's description of the endless rain on Venus is a testament to his brilliance, and students are at first awed by his talent. Although intimidated by the notion of using his piece as a model, students may nonetheless be capable of inspired writing as well.

As we analyze the craft in "The Long Rain," students begin the demystification process. Yes, Bradbury's work is sheer genius, but he employs specific literary devices such as parallelism and repetition in the service of his artistry, and students begin to recognize these elements and take ownership of their application. I frequently write with or share my own writing with my students. Thus, after brainstroming with students about their understanding of the national horror that was Hurricane Katrina, I read my version of Bradbury's text based on the hurricane and the emotional and physical destruction wrought by the storm. I then ask my students to create their own passage, also using the Bradbury excerpt as a model. In the student samples that follow, what is most striking is the infinite variety of student response—herein lies the lyricism in students' voices as they "make music that wasn't there before."

The heart kept beating. It was a jolting heart, a ruthless heart, a kindly and considerate heart; it was a light, a gateway, a break in the sky, a tease to the dead; it was a heart to shine on all the souls and all the beings. It came by the sound and by the feeling, it surged life all throughout the world and brought hope to those who had seen only darkness and put smiles on the faceless and took away sorrow and misery.

—Miguel Vasquez, 11th grade

And the song continued. It was a piercing melody, a mournful melody, a mocking and bitter melody; it was a sorrow, a misery, a deceitful of the truths and a hypocrite of the morals. It was a song bearing pains from racism; a song drowned and filled with suffering, agony, and protest. It was a song to silence all songs, in the memory of songs.

—Thao Ho, 11th grade

When these selections are read in class, they are a revelation. The students' peers compliment their artistry, employing their ever-growing academic language. They point out another student's use of polysyndeton—repeating conjunctions in close succession for rhetorical emphasis—to slow rhythm and create emphasis. They appreciate and acknowledge the use of parallelism by a fellow student modeling Bradbury's use of it in "The Long Rain." That students can learn to make powerful use of metaphor, simile, onomatopoeia, synecdoche, repetition, alliteration, assonance, juxtaposition, diction, and syntax is rapidly reinforced through the sharing of their writing. Because the students know as they write that their work will be read aloud rather than merely "graded" by the teacher, they are inspired to impress their peers. The students begin to acknowledge the voices emerging from their classmates; however, despite the powerful Bradbury model, none of these voices are Bradbury's, as is evident in the previous student excerpts.

Seasonal Model

When the holiday season arrives, I use " 'Twas the Night Before Christmas" as a model for student writing and also as an introduction to poetry scansion. There have been countless parodies written of this traditional and beloved poem; I share many as additional models. We spend a class period exploring the craft and artistry of this charming poem, examining not only the formal elements of rhyme scheme and anapestic tetrameter, but also how Clement Moore developed the poem's whimsical tone.

My students then write a shorter version of the poem, perhaps 20 lines long, employing its formal aspects while personalizing its theme. The students do not write about Christmas because I want them to select other topics and move toward a broader appreciation of the interplay of poetic language. They take up the challenge of writing humorous pieces related to current events, our own school culture, or literature we are currently reading.

During the Y2K hysteria surrounding the turn from the 20th to the 21st century, the students wrote humorous poems based on that experience, " 'Twas the Night Before Y2K." Again, because of the cultural diversity of my school district, each year I see cultures passionately represented in poems such as " 'Twas the Night Before Tet" (Vietnamese New Year). The following is a brief thematic poem based on *The Great Gatsby*, written by two students during a class period of about 90 minutes:

Gatsby Abridged

'Twas the night of his party, when all through the house
The lights were on blazing, and the bright moon was out
Servants were spreading with jazz through the air
As Gatsby stood watching all those who were there.

Well, I was invited unlike all the rest
Who came when they wanted and partied their best
And Miss Baker was looking quite pretty that night
Also Gatsby's great library sure was sight.

But all of these parties he watched from above
They never did help him to earn Daisy's love
And Gatsby's now dead, his parties not to last
As we are all borne ceaselessly into the past

—Alex Ly and Monica Nguyen, 11th grade

Read-Alouds/Publication/Letter Writing/Authentic Audiences

The student poets gain a wider audience for their work because they illustrate their parodies; when I post them in my classroom, other classes and visiting teachers are then drawn to read and appreciate their written work.

The time investment required to have student work "published" through read-alouds is well worth the effort. Even when time becomes an issue, I still find ways to give students authentic audiences for their writing. Sometimes, in groups of three or four, students share their writing aloud. Then each group chooses one selection to share aloud with the class. This way, all the student work is acknowledged, and particular students have their writing highlighted and commended.

When my 11th grade Honors Literature students read Henrik Ibsen's *A Doll's House*, they write a letter of recommendation for one character and one of condemnation for another. When students are writing these letters, they display a very mature grasp of characterization without having to write a formal essay on "characterization in *A Doll's House*."

Here is a creative excerpt from Mary, a quiet student whose writing demonstates the power of her "voice."

Dear Casting Director:

> *I would like to recommend Nora Helmer for the [lead] role for your new movie production. [. . .] Nora is a young woman [who] has been through a rocky marriage. She had to leave her husband and even her children. She was in love and faithful to a man whom she thought she loved, but was wrong. She felt like a bird that was stuck inside a cage when she was with him, but now she is free. The marriage has affected her emotionally, but I know that the best actors and actresses can be those who suffered through much misery in life. [. . .] Her ability to change characters rapidly will be a great asset to a role that requires it.*
>
> —Mary Quan, 11th grade

Using a document camera allows for sharing these entertaining and instructive sample letters with the entire class. These more "informal" assignments can serve as "prewriting" for more formal essays, the more formal essays are ultimately filled with more voice because of the creative process involved in writing the letters.

External Authentic Audiences

As valuable as the classroom peer audience is in promoting student voice and passionate writing, there is no substitute for other external authentic audiences. Any opportunities to assign student writing when those selections will be entered in writing contests are invaluable. My students have won multiple awards in our district-wide Martin Luther King, Jr. Essay and Poetry Contest and Cesar Chavez Writing Contest. I attribute these awards to accomplished students who have been exposed to extensive professional models and have had authentic audiences for their classroom writing.

Freshman Sandy Ngo won a district-wide first place award with her poem about her own neighborhood, entitled "Down this Very Street." Here is an excerpt from her poem:

> *I remember like it was yesterday*
> *Down this very avenue*
> *Virginia Avenue . . . was our world*
> *I could hear from thin lips to thick lips*
> *All sorts of languages*
> *Chinese, Cambodian, Spanish, and English*
> *We taught each other Chinese Jump rope and Double Dutch*
> *We smiled, laughed, and even cried in the same languages*
> *Those were the days when everyone understood each other*
>
> *I remember like it was yesterday*
> *Down these very doors*
> *Apartment number 1, 2, 3, and 4 . . . was our home*
> *I saw black, brown, white, and yellow*
> *My brothers and sisters*
> *Jamal, Mario, Elizabeth and Mei*
> *We went in and out of everyone's house like it was our own*
> *We ate and drank at the same table . . . we were the same*
> *Those were the days when everybody was family*
>
> —Sandy Ngo, 9th grade

Likewise, one year I was teaching 11th graders in their first year of the rigorous International Baccalaureate (IB) program. As their English teacher, I frequently heard in their writing their frustrations with the program. I'm only half joking when I say that if I had asked them to write a humorous piece about popcorn, they would have found a way to use it to complain about their work load in IB. Many of the students felt that the program expectations had not been truthfully represented prior to their enrollment. My revelation: The students would write a letter to our school's IB coordinator, as well as the IB teachers at the school, including me. The students knew these letters would be delivered to the parties addressed; as a result, their writing voices soared. They were explicit, passionate, detailed, and authentic. They were *thrilled* to have an artistic manner in which to give voice to their frustrations. Those of us already supporting the fine IB program also learned a great deal from our students through these letters about the ways we could better support them. Most teachers can find similar authentic audiences to which students can write, such as school or commercial newspapers, magazines, or online sites.

More moving still are the insightful comments I receive from students at the end of the school year. After discussing the concept of metacognition, I have students reflect on their learning experience during the year. What follows is a personal favorite, an excerpt from a reflective essay written by a student who was born in Kenya.

> *Reading* Beloved *was the most emotional part of IB [honors] English. I am the only black person in the IB program, which has always decreased my confidence. I have always wished that more African-American students would be motivated enough to join IB. [. . .] I would have liked to be in a class where someone would understand the struggles and relate to it like I did or at least help me get through it. I was not ready for* Beloved *and when we read the book in class, I had to take deep breaths because I didn't know my ancestors went through that pain. [. . .] I am glad that I read the book because it made me stronger and less ignorant of my past. If black students were to read it, I'm sure that their view would change as it did for me. I'm saddened by what could be but is not.*
>
> —Maryanne Karuga, 11th grade

Granted, not every piece of prose students encounter in their academic or professional careers will "speak to them" personally. Not every opinion stated in an editorial will spark an explosive response from them. Not every essayist's personal journey will resonate with the student reader. What will always be true, however, is that encouraging student voice and passion must begin with an educator's acknowledgment that students want to engage with writing that doesn't seem transmitted to them telepathically from Mars. Many of our reluctant readers appear to experience much of what we read in just such a way.

Students are not going to light up at every piece of nonfiction placed before them, but especially for the reluctant reader or writer, "relatable" content goes a long way toward developing voice. We all know how strong our own voices are *when we really have something to say!* Our students, and especially our reluctant readers and writers, are no different from ourselves in this regard. They respond strongly when provided with a compelling text and something important to say.

In an honors class, students read and write about a recent Harvard study conducted on the negative effects of praise. Interestingly, the study concluded that students who were praised more for their effort and persistence in accomplishing a task fared better than those who were commended for their intelligence. I suspected this essay would spark an interest

Todd Rafalovich

Marie Milner

in my students, but I was unprepared for the passion of their written responses. The majority of students had personal stories that supported the conclusions of the study. As I read, I imagined these students might have partially been inspired to write so convincingly by their considerable relief at knowing their experiences were not unique.

Because of the cultural and ethnic diversity of my students, I read with them a *Newsweek* "My Turn" column entitled, "The Good Daughter." The personal essay describes a young Korean-American woman's reaction upon discovering that she had been mispronouncing her own surname her entire life. From this initial anecdote, the writer extrapolates eloquently about the nature of the "hyphenated American"—the Mexican-American, the Vietnamese-American, the Japanese-American. When the students respond to this piece, they are so emotionally truthful that I will read a set of 35 papers in one sitting because I am so moved by their passion. These candid and well-written responses allow me to engage in a written dialogue with each of these students. Here is an excerpt from an 11th grade student:

I know who I am—I am American, yet I am also Vietnamese. Evidence of Vietnamese culture abounds everywhere in the neighborhood, and it is a strange juxtaposition to go to an American school and immerse in American culture, yet go somewhere or do something that reaffirms the duality of my identity—eat in a Vietnamese restaurant and understand the menu, go to a Vietnamese New Year's festival and gamble my savings away with grizzled men (but then to get it back later—no one wants to take money from a kid), or even something like a family get-together, where deep aluminum trays are stuffed with Vietnamese party food and (though I was often with my English-speaking cousins, playing video games) the aunts and uncles clamored to hear me play piano, hear me sing in their native tongue.

—Andy Nguyen, 11th grade

As evidenced here, my students respond very strongly to this essay, which at only a page long is highly accessible. Additionally, Robin Scarcella, noted ELL scholar, specifically emphasizes the need to reach ELL students through written material that will engage them because they can readily identify with the experiences described therein. The following response comes from a mainstreamed ELL 11th grader:

Having my parents be in control of my life, I was repeatedly warned to have any type of relationship with only an Asian and marriage with a Vietnamese who is equally religious as my family. To have the privilege of being with whomever I please was eventually taken away had struck me hard, as I felt caged like a bird. Their expectations seemed ridiculous but as of learning the truth from my relatives that it was our family tradition that started before my great-grandfather has taught me to be more open-minded.

One important aspect being the first generation American is the understanding of the older generations. Most parents concern lies on the environment of their children's upbringing as well as leading a successful future. Vietnamese or Korean immigrants will go through all means to aid their children to excel in academics. Majority of them wish for the younger generation to take up a field within medicine, law, or business for its long history of top-notch materialistic achievement. In Hwang's situation her parents wished for her to go to law school but instead she received a Ph.D. in English literature, as if I were in her shoes at the very moment my parents urged me to start my career in medicine whereas my desire leaned towards interior designing. Knowing that my life is indebted to my parents' sacrifice, I couldn't find the confidence to defy them nor bring myself to disappoint them any further.

—Monica Nguyen, 11th grade

The students are animated as they discuss this *Newsweek* essay and share their common experiences with this subject. They practice oral academic language and, because they are enthusiastic about the topic, they more readily participate because they are highly motivated to do so.

If a whole group discussion is not practical for any given reason, the students may discuss *Newsweek's* "The Good Daughter" essay with a partner before responding in writing. This pre-writing conversation between students allows them not only to begin formulating and shaping their own ideas for their response, but also to recognize still other commonalities with their classroom peers, most of whom share the *Newsweek* author's frustrations. The students' engagement with the essay is apparent as they bond with other students in discussion of these common experiences.

Likewise, because students fret understandably about paying for college I use a controversial personal essay, also from *Newsweek's* "My Turn" column, entitled "Pay Your Own Way—and Then Thank Mom." The students are generally indignant, and this impassioned writing has engendered some equally astonishing classroom discussion with many students commenting about how radically their initial views of this topic change over the course of this writing and discussion.

Two other "My Turn" essays—"Sleepless Nights" and "Stop Stressing Me!"—elicit a great deal of emphatic response. Exploring the stress that accompanies today's secondary students, especially as they try to distinguish themselves for college acceptance, these two pieces never fail to strike a personal chord with students. The essays argue against students taking on too many honors classes or extracurricular activities, suggesting instead that they try to strike a healthier balance. James's response to these essays could not be more emphatic:

Here is my position: parents should stay out of it! Granted, there are some things, such as chores or how to act in public, that parents should teach and force their kids to do. Nevertheless, parents who force their kids to take on harder classes or to practice piano for hours are doing direct harm to their [children] when they could be accomplishing great good. . . . I do not remember a single homework assignment or extracurricular activity that my mother forced me to do. I am not motivated by fear or a ruler over my knuckles; I want to do these things because when I look up to those I respect and admire, I see the power of knowledge and the value of hard work.

—James Leet, 11th grade

Billie Holiday may have "sung the blues," but no one will ever forget her. She had "voice in her voice," so to speak, as does any great singing artist. When Barack Obama writes about Billie Holiday, there is "voice" in his description of her. What a happy, happy writing teacher I am when I realize my students are accessing their own writing voices and the music therein.

References and Resources

Blackwood, Gary. *Shakespeare's Scribe*. New York: Puffin, 2002.

Bradbury, Ray. "All Summer in a Day." *The Magazine of Fantasy and Science Fiction*, March, 1954.

_____. "The Long Rain." *Planet Stories,* 1950.

Bridgers, Sue Ellen. http://www.sueellenbridgers.com/

Fitzgerald, F. Scott. *The Great Gatsby*. New York: Charles Scribner's Sons, 1925.

Hesse, Karen. *Witness*. New York: Scholastic Press, 2001.

Hiestand, Emily. http://www.ehiestand.com/

Hinton, S. E. *The Outsiders*. New York: Speak, 1997.

Hoban, Russell. http://www.bookfinder.com/author/russell-hoban/

Hogan, Linda. "Heritage." in *Calling Myself Home*. Greenfield Center, NY: Greenfield Review Press, 1978.

Hong Kingston, Maxine. *Woman Warrior*. New York: Vintage, 1989.

Ibsen, Henrik. *A Doll's House*. New York: Dover Publications,1992.

Kinsella, Kate. http://www.sccoe.k12.ca.us/depts/ell/kinsella.asp

Kramer, Mark, and Wendy Call, eds. *Telling True Stories*. New York: Plume, a Penguin Group, 2007.

Lane, Barry. *After 'The End': Teaching and Learning Creative Revision*. Portsmouth, NH: Heinemann, 1992.

Lasky, Kathryn. *Lunch Bunnies*. Boston: Little, Brown and Company, 1996.

Lyon, George Ella. "Where I'm From." in *Where I'm From, Where Poems Come From*. Spring, TX: Absey and Co., 1999.

Morrison, Toni. *Beloved*. New York: Plume, by the Penguin Group, 1987.

Newsweek. My Turn Columns: "The Good Daughter." September 21, 1998.

"Pay Your Own Way—and Then Thank Mom." September 10, 2000.

"Sleepless Nights." September 19, 1999.

"Stop Stressing Me!" January 28, 2001.

Obama, Barack. *Dreams From My Father: A Story of Race and Inheritance*. New York: Three Rivers Press, 2004.

Pham, Andrew X. *Catfish and Mandala: A Two-Wheeled Voyage Through the Landscape and Memory of Vietnam*. New York: Farrar, Straus, and Giroux, 1999.

Ray, Katie Wood. http://www.sdworkshops.org/presenters/katiewoodray.shtml

Saltzberg, Barney. *Star of the Week*. Cambridge, MA: Candlewick, 2010.

Soto, Gary. "Seventh Grade." in *Baseball in April and Other Stories*. San Anselmo, CA: Sandpiper Press, 2000.

Spandel, Vicki. *Creating Writers Through 6-Trait Writing Assessment and Instruction*. Boston: Allyn & Bacon, 2008.

Steig, William. *Brave Irene*. New York: A Sunburst Book of Farrar, Straus and Giroux, 1986.

Tan, Amy. *The Opposite of Fate: A Book of Musings*. New York: G. P. Putnam's Sons, 2003.

Warner, Mary. http://www.sjsu.edu/faculty/mary.warner/Warnerstudentlinks.htm

Wells, Rosemary. *Hazel's Amazing Mother*. New York: Dial Books for Young Readers, 1985.

6

Bringing Passion to the Research Process: The I-Search Paper

by Brandy Appling-Jenson, Carolyn Anzia, and Kathleen González

Introduction

Ken Macrorie's seminal work, *The I-Search Paper* (1988), guided many in English Education programs in the late 1980s and early 1990s to the value of using the I-Search paper for teaching students the research process and the value of being curious. In the era of assessment when many teachers find themselves driven to focus solely on raising student test scores, the value of more comprehensive writing such as the I-Search paper entails has gotten lost.

Standards, and the assessment thereof, are not going away. That doesn't mean, however, that the teaching of the assessed skills has to mimic the bubble-filling tedium that often rules teachers' lives. The beauty of the I-Search paper is that it fulfills the Common Core Standards while engaging students where they live. Guided practice in writing each component of the I-Search paper incorporates the practice of skills such as proper Internet research that will serve students throughout their lives. The structure provided by the I-Search assignment leads students from "I don't care" to "I want to learn." Built on the premise that the "searcher" *needs* to know the information he or she is researching, the I-Search paper by its very nature emphasizes student choice and the authenticity of research. Additionally, many of the topics that middle and high school writers search—finding the right college, the world of video-gaming, saving the planet, or health issues—allow them to explore and use multiple sources. The I-Search encourages them to explore their interests within a set structure, preparing them for a lifetime of engaging with information.

The three writers of this chapter—Brandy Appling-Jenson and Carolyn Anzia, middle school teachers, in Part I, and Kathleen González, a high school teacher, in Part II—do not claim they are doing something new; they have, however, for many years successfully used the I-Search paper with middle and high school writers and share their experience as a guide for teachers leading their students through this compelling alternative to the traditional research paper.

Part I: The Crittenden Middle School I-Search: Introducing Passion Into Research and Long-Term Project Planning
by Brandy Appling-Jenson and Carolyn Anzia

"Ms. Jenson! Ms. Jenson!"

The urgency in her voice makes me spin around, ready to leap into heroic action. I search for something wrong, peering behind her for apocalyptic mayhem or at the very least a skinned knee.

"Ms. Jenson, did you grade my project yet?"

I struggle to avoid a look of exasperation—it's Open House, and there might be parents just behind that student. However, I am actually shocked that anyone would have the audacity to ask. I collected I-Search papers just eight hours ago, but by the end of the evening I have had at least 10 parents asking what grade their child got on the "very cool" project that was turned in today, countless children begging to know their grade, and three emails demanding project grades "as soon as possible, Ms. Jenson." The I-Search generates an engagement with writing for both students and parents, and defines our seventh graders' experience.

The I-Search project has been an institution at Crittenden. In this project, students research one of their parents when he or she was age 12 or 13 and complete a research paper on that year. The I-Search takes two months; however, while the project is the primary focus during these two months, we simultaneously continue working on vocabulary lessons, Literature Circles, grammar and usage and other components of the language arts program.

Why Do the I-Search in Middle School?

There are many compelling reasons to do the I-Search. First, it addresses a number of essential language arts standards and skills. Over the course of the project, students learn how to write a formal research paper, including how to take good notes and document sources; exercise listening and speaking skills in conducting an interview; and engage in extensive personal/reflective writing about themselves and about their experiences with each step of the I-Search. Moreover, they learn how to organize and complete a long-term project. In recent years, in the rush to teach all of the necessary standards, many teachers have given up on such projects as science fairs and social studies symposia due to time constraints. As a result, the I-Search is often the only true long-term project students will complete before high school.

During the course of the I-Search, students complete several components addressing different aspects of the standards. They

- interview their parents (listening and speaking skills)
- locate information in an almanac (critical thinking)
- take notes from Internet and print sources (reading and processing information)
- write Biographical Poems (writing skills)
- write a Sensory Poem (writing and comparing eras)
- complete one research paper (writing, critical thinking, and reading skills)
- assemble an edited and professional final draft

Throughout the process, students reflect on their successes and challenges with the various parts of the project. All these tasks involve basic literacy skills and can be adapted to serve all skill levels. Even struggling writers turn out solid pieces that highlight the writing and critical thinking skills we work on all year.

However, the I-Search has an impact that goes far beyond meeting the Common Core Standards. As every middle school teacher knows, even seventh graders who abhor writing will gladly write about themselves and their own interests. Developmentally, this is perfect for them: the reflective writing in the I-Search helps them define their own growing sense of identity. The project also fosters one-on-one communication between students and their parents at a time in teenagers' lives when meaningful conversations with parents are virtually non-existent. Students often report that the project brings them closer to their parents. Occasionally a student will return from conducting his or her parent interview and say, "That's the most I've ever talked to my dad," or "I've never talked to my mom about her childhood before." Talking to their parents helps them to understand that Mom and Dad were once teenagers themselves and faced many of the same problems that they do.

Upon completing the I-Search, students are amazed at how much they have written. Years later, this will be the one thing that they remember doing in middle school; indeed, many former students (now in high school and college) admit to still having their final projects.

The Process

Now, actually getting to a place where every student is successful with this large project requires significant scaffolding and encouragement. The first step involves sending a letter home to parents with a timeline of due dates and deadlines for the various stages of the I-Search project. Getting the parents on board is vital to the students' success.

Throughout the next two months, students are periodically asked to reflect on the process. We begin this with the Introduction and a paragraph about what the I-Search is and why we are doing it, taking ideas from the parent letter and from the discussion about what the rest of the project will encompass. With emerging writers it is especially important that we write this first paragraph together on the document camera over the course of one period.

By beginning with a success, all students feel more confident in their ability to finish this project; after all, the beginning is easy enough. The second paragraph of the Introduction is essentially a KWL (K = What I <u>Know</u>, W = What I <u>Want</u> to Know, L = What I <u>Learned</u>) in paragraph form. The students write about which parent they chose, why they chose that parent, what they already know about him or her at 12 or 13 years of age, and what they want to find out. This sets the stage for the interview and research portions of the project.

The Parent Interview

The parent interview is vital for a successful I-Search. Almost every other piece of the project draws on information gathered during the interview. To ensure student success, I provide instructions and a list of sample questions that they can ask their parents about their lives when they were 12 or 13. Then I play the role of the brusque parent, forcing them to draw information out of me:

Student:	"Did you ever get in trouble?"
Teacher:	"Yes."
Student:	"Did you get grounded?"
Teacher:	"Yes."
Student:	"What did you do?"
Teacher:	"Lied to my mom."
Student:	"About what?"
Teacher:	"A boy."
Student:	"What was his name?"
Teacher:	"I don't remember."
Student:	"Did you *kiss* him?"

It takes all of my self-control to stifle the giggles I feel as I model the role of the uncooperative parent. After all, part of learning to do interviews well is learning to ask follow-up questions, but it's sooo difficult to control myself and not just spill the juicy details of

Todd Rafalovich

Brandy Appling-Jenson

the 12-year-old me. The process of asking meaningful questions and then asking follow-up questions encourages a level of thinking that students don't often use in conversation. They also enjoy the interview.

When they return to class with the completed parent interview, they conduct a self-interview and answer the same questions that they asked their parents. Eventually, both interviews are typed up and presented as a final draft. It's fascinating to see students' similarity to and difference from their parents at this age. These interviews are followed by the writing of Bio Poems in which students synthesize information from their interviews and present it through a new genre.

Every year, there are poignant stories about the actual interview, and these reinforce that the project is valuable in ways not measurable by any assessment. This interaction, this conversation, is the reason that our I-Search is so successful.

The Search Process

Continuing with the reflection component of the project, "The Search Process" is a three- to four-paragraph ongoing document that explains the hows/whens/wheres of the I-Search. There is a brief introduction to the main parts of the I-Search, followed by a paragraph each about the interview, research, and choice assignments. The interview paragraph details the setting of the interview, how they felt during it, how their parent(s) reacted to it, and one or two things that they learned from it. For emerging writers, it is helpful to provide scaffolding in the form of a paragraph frame, while proficient and advanced writers can be given a list of "must-haves" and then sent to write. I encourage students to include the necessary information, but also to practice using their own voice. Immediately after the research and choice assignments are completed, students write similar reflective paragraphs.

Research!

For this portion of the I-Search, students research what was going on in the world the year their parent was 12 or 13. Of the two months of the project, this is where teachers will work the hardest. Frustrated students will most likely offer opinions like "This encyclopedia thing is stupid! Why can't i just use Wikipedia and be done?" Our students can text prolifically, find and download the most obscure YouTube videos through the school firewall, and, between classes, update a FaceBook status to warn of a tough test, but ask them to find factual information online or through traditional research sourrces and they are completely lost. The idea that Google is not omniscient and that the very first hit may not answer their question boggles their minds. This portion of the I-Search requires very structured scaffolding for all students because the goal is for them to complete the project with research skills that meet the standards and will allow them to succeed in high school. These include finding, paraphrasing, and synthesizing information, as well as documenting sources.

We begin the research by passing out packets with all the directions, a list of re-sources, and a note-taking guide. Reading through the first page of the packet takes about 15 minutes because we answer questions and explain each item in detail. The magic number for research is three: at least three different resources, including books. Three topics must be covered in the research paper, and each topic needs to have at least three subtopics. Each of those subtopics needs at least three pieces of specific, detailed information. For example, a research paper on the year 1963 might include the topics "News," "Music," and "Sports." A completed note-sheet for the topic of music might look like this:

Topic: Music of 1963
1. Beatles
   - Beatlemania in England
   - two hits: "I Want to Hold Your Hand," "She Loves You"
   - John, Paul, George, Ringo
   - followed by screaming teenage girls
2. Billboard Top 10 hits
   - "Surfin' USA"—The Beach Boys
   - "My Boyfriend's Back"—The Angels
   - "Louie, Louie"—The Kingsmen
   - "If You Wanna Be Happy"—Jimmy Soul
   - "He's So Fine"—The Chiffons
3. Other musical artists tried new types of music
   - Folk: Peter, Paul and Mary: "If I Had a Hammer," "Times . . ."
   - Motown: Martha and the Vandellas
   - "Blue-Eyed" Soul: The Righteous Brothers

To get students to this point, together we select a topic and demonstrate how to find the information using the resources listed in the research packet, projecting websites and placing books under the document camera. Students enjoy this activity because they have a sincere interest in what was going on in the world before they were born. They are especially excited by the hairstyles of the various decades; a picture of the "beehive" elicits raucous laughter and the girls always ooh and aah over a picture of Mick Jagger.

We complete one full topic together (they are not allowed to use my sample if the years happen to coincide) before they are allowed to choose their own topics. We spend about one 45-minute class period practicing how to choose information and how to write it in our own words. This lesson provides an excellent opportunity to introduce the concept of plagiarism. We emphasize the importance of citing one's sources and using quotations when necessary, reminding students that when they encounter text that they do not understand, they should ask for help rather than resort to copying the author's words.

Students all begin their research with the topic of "News" because part of the I-Search goal is to teach them about recent history. Using the book *America's Century* (Daniel, 2000) as a starting point and branching out to other texts collected from the school library, the students complete a note-sheet (as above) for the year that their parent was 12 or 13. Research on the news takes place in class so that we can monitor the students' progress. Students get their "News" topic checked before they choose two additional topics, ensuring that they have all grasped the concept and have mastered the note-taking skill before being let loose online. Finally, we head to the computer lab for two or three days to finish the two choice topics. It's surprising how little they really know about the last 30 years of history.

Many students are excited to tell me about the *Challenger* explosion, or to ask me, "OMG, did you know that 'Thriller' by Michael Jackson was written over 30 years ago?" I love that the research engages them and allows for student-led learning to take place. Altogether, the introduction to research, the practice, and the note-taking itself take about one week in class. Anything that the students do not finish during this time is finished at home.

For the most part, we encourage students to stick to U.S. history and popular culture, despite the fact that many of their parents grew up in different countries. One reason is that the school library and online sources contain an abundance of age-appropriate information about the American past; information about musical groups, TV shows, and movies from other countries is much more difficult to locate. Additionally, in researching U.S. history, students learn about important events and trends that are frequently referenced in day-to-day conversations. Their "News" research inevitably leads to brief class discussions about the Watergate scandal, the Vietnam War, the assassination of JFK, and the moon landing. When they research "Music," they are surprised to learn how many songs from the 1970s and 1980s are still popular. Occasionally, a student will be able to find information about a non-American musical group, TV show, or athlete mentioned by their parents during the interview; however, because the information is not always available, it's not required.

Writing the Research Paper

At this point, students are determined to successfully turn in a full research paper and are generally eager to get started. Again, the end goal is that every seventh grader becomes a competent writer, so whole-class instruction is key. Group writing on the overhead projector or document camera allows every student to contribute to a well-written paragraph. I always begin by listing the parts of a paragraph and giving examples of each. Then, using the "Music" notes from our group research, the class writes a sample paragraph. I model the process by thinking aloud about how I am synthesizing and organizing the information. With the emerging writers, I frequently prompt them for each sentence; the more advanced students readily volunteer their own ideas. A sample paragraph follows:

Todd Rafalovich

Carolyn Anzia

The year 1963 was an exciting year for music. To start, it was the year of British "Beatle-mania," when Beatles songs hit the charts in England for the first time. Two of their first hits were "I Want to Hold Your Hand" and "She Loves You." The four young men—John, Paul, George, and Ringo—quickly became so famous that they were being followed everywhere by hordes of screaming teenage girls. Meanwhile, The Beach Boys continued to please their listening audiences with songs like "Surfin' USA," which was a hit single that year. Other musical artists were successful in different genres. A girl group, The Chiffons, had a hit with "He's So Fine." "If I Had a Hammer" and "Times They Are A-Changin'" were two of the first hit songs by folk group Peter, Paul and Mary. Early Motown music groups like Martha and the Vandellas also began to have music aired on the radio. These are just a few of the innovative musicians who were popular in the early 1960s.

Writing a sample body paragraph together helps all students to be successful. We also provide the students with well-written sample paragraphs from previous years, on all of the possible topics (Movies, Sports, News, etc.); they can refer to these models as they work. Finally, we display a list of topic sentences that students can use. It generally takes two or three class days for students to complete all three of their own body paragraphs.

We conclude the research paper portion of the I-Search by teaching how to write the introduction and the conclusion of the research essay. Using the document camera, we give guidelines and examples for both paragraphs; students are expected to complete them during class. Following these guidelines, students are able to produce a complete research paper.

Expanding the Research Process

There's nothing quite as sweet as a room full of preteens singing along to "Build Me Up Buttercup." We rock to a playlist of Billboard hits from the 1960s, 1970s, and 1980s while working on the almanac assignment, in which students hunt through an almanac for facts about their year. We love this assignment because it is the first (and often last) time that our students come into contact with a paper almanac. Students practice the important skills of identifying key words, using an index, and locating information. They also have a lot of fun; at least half of the class time they are given to work on the 12-question worksheet is spent looking randomly through the book, shouting out oddball facts to one another.

The Sensory Poem is yet another easy way to add feeling and voice to this stage of the I-Search process. Students use the five senses in comparing and contrasting the current year and their researched year. They conclude the poem by offering their thoughts about the differences between "then" and "now." One of my favorite final lines is: "And I think to myself that Steve Jobs is a genius and I thank him for the iPod, so that I do not have to deal with records like my Mom!"

For the "Choice Assignment," students are given the option of four ways to express and share what they have learned during this project. For the first option, they may choose to contact a relative or family friend and ask questions (at least five) about what her parent was like at 12 or 13, hopefully eliciting new information and offering additional insight into the parent's childhood. The second option encourages students to compose two paragraphs that compare themselves with their parents. The third option encourages students to collect pictures from the year that was researched and create a labeled collage. For the last option, in the spirit of

Back to the Future, students are encouraged to write a story where they travel back in time and meet their parents at 12 or 13. We also allow students to come up with their own creative projects (getting approval, of course) to showcase some of the things that they have learned.

Wrapping It All Up

Finally, we get to the directions students use for revising their I-Search into a polished final draft. By this point, most students are eager to showcase their work. We go over the grading rubric and directions for the final draft, providing examples of the title page and table of contents. Students are expected to stay within the norms for writing in terms of font and spacing, again preparing them for the formatting expectations in high school and college.

When the students walk in with their completed projects, they positively glow. They are so pleased with their final product and can't wait to show it to me, their friends, and any other audience they can corner between their house and our classroom.

Undoubtedly, this is my favorite assignment to assess because I learn so much about the students. During this project, they share a big part of their true identities—that's ultimately what makes it so valuable. Twenty years from now, the I-Search will serve as a snapshot of their 12-year-old selves and how they saw themselves fit into the world. Their parents comment about how much they have enjoyed the process and often thank us for assigning it. Students share the I-Search as part of their senior year capstone project in high school. In addition, parents who went to Crittenden dust off their I-Search papers and share them with their children. It ends up being writing at its best: writing that satisfies Common Core State Standards but also, much more importantly, demonstrates the power of authentic writing about meaningful topics.

Part II: Demystifying the Research Process: The I-Search Paper
by Kathleen González

When was the last time a student thanked you for assigning a research paper? I'll never forget Derek, who was researching dust mites since he had a terrible allergy to them. He had never before completed a research assignment and thought he couldn't do it. He sat with me after school for a couple days where I could talk him through the process and give him immediate feedback on each section. When he finished, he looked at me with a surprised grin and said, "That's all it is? I never thought I could do a research paper, so I never really tried it before. Thanks, Ms. G."

Many people have written about the I-Search paper, particularly Ken Macrorie. I first read and used his book, *The I-Search Paper,* in a university writing course to conduct my own I-Search. Without presuming to have the only formula for the process, I offer the lesson plan I have used with ninth graders of all skill levels; the process can be replicated and adapted for sophomores, juniors, and seniors. A key component of the I-Search paper is the first person perspective that personalizes the writer's search, incorporates authentic voice, and steers the writer away from plagiarizing. Moreover, students choose topics based on their interests, connecting a school assignment to their lives and allowing them to be experts on a topic.

In "Seeing Academic Writing with a New 'I'," Rebecca Feldbusch (2010), a teacher-consultant with the Southcentral Pennsylvania Writing Project, reviews many arguments for using the first person perspective when writing research papers. She tells the story of winning an award for an academic paper on Shakespeare written in first person: "I made a connection to [the audience] as I embraced the 'I' in academic writing."

When students choose a topic that they care about and that they want more information on, it becomes easier for them to write a successful paper. Assigned topics have their place, but it's not always necessary for teachers to mandate them. Table 6.1 shows the complete assignment sheet; Table 6.2 with Parts 1, 2, and 3 offers an inventory of interests. I actually start by having students complete Parts 1, 2, and 3 to capture their interest and enthusiasm, and only after they finish these sections do I give them the actual assignment sheet; this way I avoid the groans that usually accompany the research paper assignment.

The Process

Students complete the Part 1 list in class by responding to every question; it's helpful to do this step at the end of class so students can ponder topic choices overnight. The next day, in Part 2, they pick one topic for further research and write a paragraph telling what they already know about it. For example, Denise hopes to buy a used Honda Accord; she knows she likes the shade of blue Accords come in, they have four doors, they're supposed to be reliable cars, and they cost around $5,000 for an older used one. She wants to know more about them because she will be getting her license in the next year, and her father has agreed to help her pay for a car. When students' purposes are individually delineated and when they list their research questions themselves, they are also less likely to resort to plagiarizing whole essays. Choosing and defining their topics gives them ownership.

Students often know more than they realize about a topic; however, they don't seem to trust their own knowledge since it didn't come from a book or the Internet. In fact, this aspect of the project is an added bonus because students realize that they do know something about a topic—a surprise to some of them. Violet, who wanted to research Hawaii, claimed that she didn't know anything about it. With prompting, she wrote a paragraph explaining that Hawaii was a bunch of islands in the Pacific Ocean, the people did hula dancing and had luaus, and they grew pineapple and macadamia nuts. This paragraph becomes the first one for the paper. Of course, in the revision process, they can revise to make sure the introduction includes an attention grabber and clear thesis, if these elements aren't already there.

The Part 3 paragraph, where students list questions they have about their topic, becomes the next paragraph; students are often pleased to realize they already have a portion of their papers done before they've even started the research. To begin Part 3, students brainstorm questions about the topic. What do they want to find out? This is an important step because students learn how to ask pertinent questions that narrow their topic. Does the . . . student really want to learn about Hawaii's gross national product, information that she'll surely come across in the encyclopedia? Or does she want to find out how to plan a great two-week vacation there? Now I hand out the assignment sheet and introduce the complete list of requirements and due dates.

TABLE 6.1   *I-Search Paper Assignment Sheet*

Directions:

1. Answer the "List of Ten" questions from Part 1.
2. Choose the one topic you are most interested in and write paragraphs for Parts 2 and 3.
3. Then begin your research. Look on the Internet, in magazines, in books, or interview people to gather information. Take notes for each source, and keep track of bibliography information. Keep these notes to turn in with your final project. Notes should be in your own words; if I have doubts, I may ask you to present me with the book or website copies to prove that you didn't plagiarize. Please do include any quotations (with page numbers) that you plan to use in the final paper.
4. Next, write the paper itself, using your notes and quotations. It should include an introduction, body paragraphs that contain all the research you did, and a conclusion paragraph. Use first person point of view; in other words, tell about your search as well as the facts that you found out, with commentary and analysis to show your learning.
5. Meet with a partner to read each other's papers. Use the response sheet to give each other feedback, and be sure to review the feedback you received when you revise.
6. Turn in the final paper with the outline and notes and a Works Cited page. This is an "All-or-Nothing" grade, which means that if you don't complete all required sections, you will have to re-do each part until you meet the standards. It is essential that you have these research skills before you leave this class.

Requirements:

- Parts 1, 2, and 3 (20)
- Notes (in your own writing and words, not just photocopies or downloads) (30)
- Rough draft (20)
- Response sheet completed by partner (10)
- I-Search paper: at least three pages, with at least three quotations from your sources; typed, double-spaced (40)
- Works Cited page in the correct MLA format (on a separate page) (10)
- One visual aid (downloaded image, magazine cutout, photocopy, picture, etc.) (If you download images, be sure to list the source on your Works Cited page.) (10)
- A folder with cover art and a title page.

    i. Include the final draft, visual aid, Works Cited page, rough draft, response sheet, and notes in your folder.

    ii. Title page includes title, your name, teacher name, course title, and date. (10)

Points Possible: 150

Due Dates   Notes: _____

             Rough Draft: _____

             Final Paper: _____

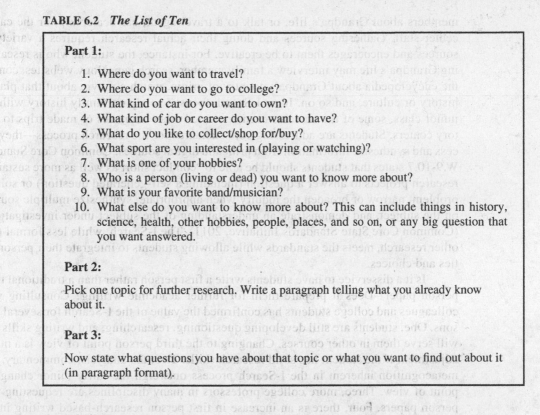

TABLE 6.2   *The List of Ten*

Part 1:

1. Where do you want to travel?
2. Where do you want to go to college?
3. What kind of car do you want to own?
4. What kind of job or career do you want to have?
5. What do you like to collect/shop/for/buy?
6. What sport are you interested in (playing or watching)?
7. What is one of your hobbies?
8. Who is a person (living or dead) you want to know more about?
9. What is your favorite band/musician?
10. What else do you want to know more about? This can include things in history, science, health, other hobbies, people, places, and so on, or any big question that you want answered.

Part 2:

Pick one topic for further research. Write a paragraph telling what you already know about it.

Part 3:

Now state what questions you have about that topic or what you want to find out about it (in paragraph format).

Teamwork: The Write-Around

So far, students have completed each step individually, but the next step takes place in triads. Students take turns telling each other their topics and then brainstorm sources for information. Instead of relying solely on the Internet, as many students are wont to do, this step encourages them to access other sources. Alternatively, students can generate more ideas by doing a "write-around." The process looks like this: All students as well as the teacher sit in a big circle, writing their topics on pieces of paper. Each hands the paper to the right, and the next student adds suggestions or ideas to it, signs it, and sends it on. Having students sign their comments keeps them accountable for writing helpful answers, and then the writer can also find that student later for clarification if necessary. During the write-around, which lasts about 15 to 20 minutes, students may skip topics for which they have no suggestions.

The Search Begins

Generating all these ideas sends students to primary sources, people, brochures—all sorts of places—so that the research process becomes more than just a library or Internet exercise. For example, students may read music magazines, interview family members about Grandpa's life, or talk to a travel agent, car dealership, or the career center staff. Gathering sources and doing their actual research requires a variety of sources and encourages them to be creative. For instance, the student who is researching Grandpa's life may interview a family member, search genealogy websites, consult the encyclopedia about Grandpa's country of origin, watch a movie about that place's history or culture, and so on. In an I-Search focused solely on family history with the junior class, some of the students even contacted other countries or made trips to history centers. Students are addressing core standards for the research process—they access and synthesize information from print and digital sources. Common Core Standard W.9-10.7 states that students should be able to "conduct short as well as more sustained research projects to answer a question (including a self-generated question) or solve a problem, narrow or broaden the inquiry when appropriate, synthesize multiple sources on the subject, and demonstrate an understanding of the subject under investigation." (Common Core State Standards Initiative, 2011). The I-Search, while less formal than other research, meets the standards while allowing students to integrate their personalities and choices.

Is it a disservice to have students write a first person rather than a traditional third person paper? Does it prepare them for further academic writing? Consulting with colleagues and college students has confirmed the value of the I-Search for several reasons. One, students are still developing questioning, researching, and writing skills that will serve them in other courses. Changing to the third person point of view is a minor adjustment if the student has solid research skills. Two, the analysis, commentary, and metacognition inherent in the I-Search process outweigh the fairly minor change in point of view. Three, more college professors in many disciplines are requesting first person papers. Four, there is an increase in first person research-based writing in the mainstream market—from journalism to nonfiction books. Books by Michael Pollan (2007), Marion Nestle (2003), Samantha Power (2008), and Mary Roach (2004), as well as bestsellers such as *The Immortal Life of Henrietta Lacks* by Rebecca Skloot (2010) and *Reviving Ophelia* by Mary Pipher (1995), all show that first person research can be scientific, instructive, informative—and have a personal voice and connection.

Scavenger Hunt: Modeling the First Person Perspective

While students have a week or so to conduct their research and take notes, in class we practice the first person perspective they'll be using in the actual I-Search paper with an in-class scavenger hunt activity. Table 6.3 provides the list of items.

A few rules of the game: Teams consist of three to four students. The group must find all 20 items as quickly as possible. Groups will be disqualified if they steal from another group or damage anything in the room. All items must be found in the room, generally in their backpacks or on their persons; however, if they find a book on a shelf, it has to be returned properly to its place. Each item may count for only one category. Finally, if a group

TABLE 6.3   *Scavenger Hunt Items*

1. autograph of someone wearing blue
2. book by an ethnic author
3. thumbtack
4. #2 pencil
5. grammar book
6. something soft
7. picture of a famous person
8. an "A" paper
9. a word in another language
10. magazine article about another country
11. something red
12. a bottle
13. piece of gum or candy
14. makeup
15. paperclip
16. the word "English"
17. something round
18. an earring
19. a poem
20. tissue

claims to win but does not have all 20 items, it is disqualified. The prize for the winners is small: an eraser, pencil, candy, or extra credit.

The real learning takes place after the room is restored to order and students are back in their seats. Then, each of them must write the "story" of what happened during the hunt: where they found the word "English," who had makeup in her purse, how Emilio tried to steal their tissue, when Nancy had the great idea of looking on the back of *House on Mango Street* for a picture of a famous person (the author), or when Jason removed his new diamond earring and the group promptly misplaced it. The students write these narratives in first person, not realizing at this point that they are practicing the steps of a process that will mirror their I-Search papers: what they needed to find, where they thought to look for it, their successes and failures in the process, and what they gained in the end. Students who have never written a research paper before (or have only written the copy-from-the-encyclopedia variety) experience a process that models their final papers. Though describing this search seems less formal, this is a good opportunity to talk to students about using more formal language rather than informal vocabulary and structures in their final papers.

Todd Rafalovich

Kathleen González

Other Mini-Lessons

I teach a number of other mini-lessons while students are conducting their research outside of class; for example, how to take notes or embed quotations and cite sources, and how to write a Works Cited page, thesis, and introduction paragraph. This is a good time for students to take their first paragraphs, the ones where they chose their topics, and revise them to follow a more standard introduction format with attention grabber and thesis statements. At this point, I distribute copies of the rubric (see Table 6.4) used to score their finished projects so they can integrate this information into their writing, making sure they meet all requirements.

Finally, it is a great time to discuss plagiarism—its temptations and how to avoid them. A helpful resource on this topic is Barry Gilmore's book *Plagiarism: Why It Happens and How to Prevent It* (2008). He discusses the reasons students plagiarize, ranging from laziness to pressure for grades to ignorance (37). One of his most salient points, though, is that the teacher has a responsibility to show students how to paraphrase information and cite sources correctly (28–32). Gilmore offers classroom-ready lessons to teach paraphrasing plus numerous sections listing "Teaching Opportunities" related to ethical research practices. Furthermore, NCTE offers a three-part lesson plan on their Read/Write/Think website (http://www.readwritethink.org), and the Purdue Online Writing Lab (known as the OWL) also offers lessons and practice (http://owl.english.purdue.edu). Following the OWL example, I created a PowerPoint tailored to my students' interests showing the original paragraph, a poorly paraphrased paragraph, and then a properly paraphrased one. I asked my students to select a sentence from the original paragraph, first making sure they understood the idea conveyed by the sentence. I then had them cover up this sentence before writing their paraphrase, so that they were not tempted to use the exact words the author had used. This time spent practicing paraphrasing often prevents instances of plagiarism.

Also, during this time I show students a couple body paragraphs on a topic I am interested in, such as buying a new camera or visiting Venice. Since students may only be

TABLE 6.4 *Rubric: I-Search Paper*

	5 Advanced	4 Proficient	3 Basic	2 Developing	1 Beginning
Report of Information	• Thorough understanding of subject with clear focus • Strong synthesis of ideas; presents interesting & sometimes surprising details • Provides specific textual examples and quotes to support the thesis; uses them effectively and cites them correctly • Four or more sources, which are varied and reliable; works cited correctly • Demonstrates mature use of stylistic devices	• Focused topic that shows understanding of the subject • Shows synthesis of ideas; presents in-teresting details • Provides sufficient textual examples and quotes to support the inter-pretation; uses them satisfactorily and cites them correctly • Two to three sources, which are somewhat varied and reliable; works generally cited correctly • Demonstrates profi-cient use of stylistic devices	• Generally focused topic that shows some understand-ing of the subject • Attempts synthesis of ideas; presents basic facts • Provides some textual examples and details to sup-port the interpreta-tion; uses them adequately; may have some citation errors • One to two sources; may be similar or of questionable reliability; works cited showing some formatting errors • Demonstrates some use of stylistic devices	• Ideas are some-times unclear or off topic • Facts listed with little connection between them • Provides a few textual examples or quotes to support the interpretation; their use does not always enhance the flow of ideas and writing; has citation errors; sometimes plagiarizes • One source, which may be unreliable; works cited inaccu-rately or incorrectly • Demonstrates little use of stylistic devices	• Unclear topic or focus • Few facts listed in random order or unrelated to each other • Does not support arguments with textual evidence or often plagiarizes • One or no sources, unknown sources, or unreliable ones; works not cited or with many errors • No use of stylistic devices

(Continued)

145

TABLE 6.4 *Rubric: I-Search Paper (Continued)*

	5 Advanced	4 Proficient	3 Basic	2 Developing	1 Beginning

Organization	• Thesis idea is clearly understood and unifies the essay
	• Each body paragraph contains a single, focused idea and clearly supports the thesis
	• Sequencing between ideas and paragraphs is logical and cohesive
	• Graceful transition of ideas
		• Thesis clearly stated and guides organization
		• Each paragraph contains a single, focused idea
		• Body paragraphs are appropriately formatted:
		  • Topic sentence
		  • Concluding statement
		  • Embedded quotations
		• Smooth transition of ideas
			• Thesis adequately stated and influences organization
			• Some paragraphs may lack focus or completion
			• Body paragraphs generally contain:
			  • Topic sentence
			  • Concluding statement
			  • Embedded quotations
			• Understandable transitions between ideas
				• Thesis is confusing or incomplete
				• Paragraphs lack focus or completion
				• Body paragraphs generally lacking:
				  • Topic sentence
				  • Concluding statement
				  • Embedded quotations
				• Vague or missing transitions between ideas
					• No thesis or guiding idea
					• Shows a misunderstanding of paragraphs
					• Body paragraphs are missing:
					  • Topic sentence
					  • Concluding statement
					  • Embedded quotations
					• Ideas seem unconnected

Ideas and Analysis	• Main idea demonstrates *in-depth* understanding of the topic • Displays superior critical thinking skills in: insight, analysis, synthesis of ideas, and/or evaluation • Displays clear and thorough development and progression of ideas	• Main idea demonstrates *sufficient* understanding of the topic • Displays competent critical thinking skills in: insight, analysis, synthesis of ideas, and/or evaluation • Displays development and progression of ideas	• Identifiable main idea that suggests some understanding of the topic • Evidence of understanding the topic but lacking advanced critical thinking skills; ideas tend to be formulaic • Displays uneven or inconsistent development and progression of ideas	• Main idea is unclear • Thinking seems repetitive and/or general • Ideas are underdeveloped	• Thoughts in random order with little relation to prompt • Thinking unclear and lacks analysis • Ideas are undeveloped and unrelated to each other

146

	5 Advanced	4 Proficient	3 Basic	2 Developing	1 Beginning
Style	• Purposeful word choice • Precise, clear, imaginative language • Writes with reader in mind • Writing is individual, compelling, and engaging • Purposefully uses a variety of sentence types	• Effective word choice • Generally successful in using precise and rich language • Generally engages the reader	• Acceptable vocabulary • Attempts to use precise language • Writing has discernible purpose but is not compelling	• Ordinary vocabulary • Some incorrect word choice • Author's purpose is unclear	• Simple vocabulary • Inappropriate/incorrect word choice • Language not suitable to purpose

Mechanics/ Conventions	• No spelling errors
	• No fragment/run-on errors
	• Correct use of:
	  • End marks
	  • Commas, colons, and semicolons
	  • Quotation marks
	  • Apostrophes
	• Correct use of:
	  • Verbs
	  • Subject/verb agreement
	  • Pronoun/antecedent agreement
		• Minimal spelling errors (1–2)
		• Fragments/run-on errors do not inhibit understanding
		• Generally correct use of:
		  • End marks
		  • Commas, colons, and semicolons
		  • Quotation marks
		  • Apostrophes
		• Generally correct use of:
		  • Verbs
		  • Subject/verb agreement
		  • Pronoun/antecedent agreement
			• Occasional spelling errors
			• Fragment/run-on errors may distract the reader
			• Some incorrect use of:
			  • End marks
			  • Commas, colons, and semicolons
			  • Quotation marks
			  • Apostrophes
			• Verb errors distract the reader
			• Agreement errors distract the reader
				• Frequent spelling errors
				• Fragment/run-on errors distract the reader
				• Frequent errors in:
				  • End marks
				  • Commas, colons, and semicolons
				  • Quotation marks
				  • Apostrophes
				• Verb errors inhibit understanding
				• Agreement errors inhibit understanding
					• Spelling errors obscure meaning
					• Fragment/run-on errors obscure the meaning
					• No control over:
					  • End marks
					  • Commas, colons, and semicolons
					  • Quotation marks
					  • Apostrophes
					• Verb errors obscure meaning
					• Agreement errors obscure meaning

familiar with the traditional research paper written in third person, using a model is critical. We read through this model together, and I ask them questions to help them see the process I went through, such as brainstorming and narrowing topics, listing what I knew, developing questions, and beginning the research. A sample body paragraph follows:

> *I decided to start my search online since I had time to surf the net. The first interesting site I found was for Digital Photography Review at www.dpreview.com, where it reviews many different cameras. Most of the cameras on their site were larger than what I want, but I am interested in the Olympus PEN Lite and PEN Mini. Casio and Fujifilm also make compact cameras, which was perfect since I wanted a camera that would fit in my pocket. I read through the information for these, but it made me realize that I need to hold the camera in my hands and also talk to an expert about the features, since I don't really know the difference between things like LCD or OLCD or what it means when the camera has "the world's fastest AF" (www.dpreview.com). This site left me with more questions than answers.*

Writing the Initial Drafts

Next, students bring their notes to class and begin to write their rough draft. While they write, I can check their thesis statements, help those who are stuck, review embedded quote formatting, and make sure they tell their search process. At this point, they also incorporate the writing they have already done, which includes the paragraphs on what their topics are and what they already know. They then write up all the paragraphs about their research process and findings. At this point, they may discover that their initial assumptions (from paragraph one) are false, and they can reference this and explain the new information they discovered. Finally, they write a paragraph summarizing what they learned during their I-Search, which becomes the conclusion. These steps are followed by the usual partner response, revision, editing, and final draft steps we would do with any other essay. (Table 6.5 provides the peer response sheet.) Students will turn in a folder, including notes and any brochures, downloads, and so on, as well as all drafts with the final paper, showing their process and proving that they didn't copy from a source.

How the I-Search Prepares Writers for the Formal Research Paper

This assignment, though simpler and less formal than a traditional third person research paper, equips students with all the skills they'll need when they complete a more formal paper. The basic format is the same: introduction with thesis, paragraphs focusing on what they've learned, conclusion, embedded quotations, cited sources, and a bibliography or Works Cited page. Because the I-Search is written in first person, students are much less likely to plagiarize, especially if the teacher takes the time to model and teach paraphrasing and embedded quotations in class. Finally, the I-Search process is often more personalized

TABLE 6.5   *Response Sheet*

Response Sheet—I-Search Paper

Writer:_____   Responder:_____

Writer: What question do you have for your reader? Or what do you want your reader to check for?

Directions: After you have read the paper, check your reactions and write your comments. Remember to make corrections for spelling, punctuation, and grammar.

1. Is there a title? Yes_____ No_____   Does it need improving? Yes_____ No_____

2. What is the thesis statement? Copy it here: (Check that it has preview points!)

3. How many paragraphs are used? _____ How many pages long? _____

    *   Advise the writer if paragraphs are too long or are formatted incorrectly.

    *   Is there an intro? Yes_____ No_____   • Conclusion? Yes___ No___

    *   Is there an attention grabber? Yes_____ No_____

4. Did the author include quotations from the books/resources? Yes_____ No_____

    *   Put an asterisk (*) in the margin where they are. (At least three required.)

    *   Check to see that sources are cited.

    *   Are book/resource titles given and always underlined or in quotation marks? Yes_____ No_____

    *   Are quotations embedded into sentences? Yes_____ No_____

    *   Are page numbers for the quotations given (if available)? Yes_____ No_____

    (Mark these changes on the paper if they aren't done correctly.)

5. Did the writer tell the process of the search? Yes_____ No_____

6. Did the author use transition words? Yes_____ No_____

    (examples: furthermore, then, first, in conclusion)

    *   List four that the author used or suggest where they can be added:

7. Check for "you" and help the author eliminate it!

8. Check the Works Cited page (separate page!) and make any necessary corrections.

    *   How many sources are used?_____ (At least three required.)

    *   Is it alphabetical? Yes_____ No_____

    *   Are all the necessary periods and commas there? Yes_____ No_____

    *   Is all information given, not just a URL? Yes_____ No_____

than traditional research, giving students a gentler introduction to the process and a feeling of success that will propel them into formal research.

These I-Search papers tend to be much more enjoyable for me to read: I also can track students' thought processes, knowing exactly what a student has learned. For example, Caroline wanted to discover how to become a veterinarian. She first visited websites for the American Veterinary Medical Association and Bureau of Labor Statistics to learn about types of veterinary practice and educational requirements. Following this, she wrote, "For the next part of my research, I thought it would be beneficial to interview an actual veterinarian." She learned more about euthanasia and dealing with neglectful owners, stating, "This showed me that being a veterinarian is not just about helping animals but also helping the people that care for them." Finally, she wanted other opinions, so she reviewed a Yahoo! Answers listing where veterinary students posted pros and cons for the profession. Caroline's thought process and learning were more clearly delineated than I would have seen in a standard research paper, and her metacognition will serve her as a student learning to ask questions as well as find answers.

I assess the final papers using two methods: one for points and one for feedback. The I-Search paper is an "All or Nothing" assignment. If students don't meet the standard on each portion, they will receive a zero and have to revise until they meet the standard, which will earn them an A or B. Once they have met the standard for ALL sections, they receive all their points. Table 6.6 shows the grade sheet. I use the rubric as a visual listing of requirements and a quick way to provide feedback to students by highlighting where their work falls on the individual bullet points. The rubric levels of one through five don't necessarily correspond to a particular grade; rather, the grade comes from completing each requirement in the project. Ultimately, students answer these reflection questions: "What research and writing skills did you improve on and how? What will you do differently next time you need to complete research?" Reflection such as this is, again, metacognitive and evaluative so that students may continually grow as writers.

The most gratifying aspect of this assignment is seeing what happens after students have completed it. Often, students are able to use the information they have found to actually reach a goal, such as choosing a college, making a big purchase, helping the family plan a vacation, or finding out more about a person who interests them. Since the requirements can be fulfilled in a variety of ways, this differentiation meets students where they are, whether or not they've done a research paper before and at whatever level they write. Plus, it's highly individualized in terms of topics and research venues, encouraging reflection and metacognition while avoiding plagiarism. Of course, with that kind of freedom, they are able to write with voice, personality, and heart.

TABLE 6.6   *I-Search Paper Grade Sheet*

Student Name _____

Topic _____

	On Time	Late	Points Possible
• Folder/cover & title page			(10)
• Final draft			(40)
• Visual aid			(10)
• Works Cited			(10)
• Rough draft			(20)
• Response sheet			(10)
• Notes			(30)
• Parts 1, 2, & 3			(20)
		Total	(150)

Required Elements:

- Folder/cover with artwork
- Creative title
- Title page
- Typed/MLA format
- Final draft: three pages. You had
- Three embedded quotations. You had
- One visual aid with a caption
- Works Cited page
- Three sources. You had
- Rough draft
- Response sheet
- Notes with bibliography information and quotations

References and Resources

"Avoiding Plagiarism." Purdue Online Writing Lab. 2011. 14 Oct. 2011. http://owl.english.purdue.edu/owl/resource/930/01/

Daniel, Clifton, Ralph Berens, & John W. Kirshon. *America's Century*. East Rutherford, NJ: DK Publishing, 2000.

"English Language Arts Standards, Writing, Grade 9-10." 2011. Common Core State Standards Initiative. 27 Oct. 2011. http://www.corestandards.org/the-standards/english-languagearts-standards/writing-6-12/grade-9-10/

Feldbusch, Rebecca. "Seeing Academic Writing with a New 'I.'" 5 July 2010. http://www.nwp.org/cs/public/print/resource/2371

Gilmore, Barry. *Plagiarism: Why It Happens and How to Prevent It*. Portsmouth, NH: Heinemann, 2008.

Kardick, Maria. "Exploring Plagiarism, Copyright, and Paraphrasing." National Council of Teachers of English. 23 Oct. http://www.readwritethink.org/classroom-resources/lesson-plans/exploring-plagiarism-copyright-paraphrasing-1062.html

Macrorie, Ken. *The I-Search Paper.* Portsmouth, NH: Heinemann, 1988.

National Governors Association Center for Best Practices, Council of Chief State School Officers. *Common Core State Standards*: Washington, DC, 2010.

Nestle, Marion. *Food Politics.* Berkeley, CA: University of California Press, 2003.

Pipher, Mary. *Reviving Ophelia.* New York: Ballantine Books, 1995.

Pollan, Michael. *The Omnivore's Dilemma.* New York: Penguin Books, 2007.

Power, Samantha. *Chasing the Flame.* New York: Penguin Press, 2008.

Roach, Mary. *Stiff: The Curious Lives of Human Cadavers.* New York: Norton, W.W. & Company, Inc., 2004.

Skloot, Rebecca. *The Immortal Life of Henrietta Lacks.* New York: Crown Publishers, 2010.

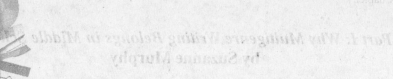

7

Expanding the Boundaries: The Uncharted Territory of Multigenre Writing

by Suzanne Murphy, Maria Clinton, and Marie Milner

Introduction

> "There are very few human beings who receive the truth, complete and staggering, by instant illumination. Most of them acquire it fragment by fragment, on a small scale, by successive developments, cellularly, like a laborious mosaic." *Anaïs Nin (1971)*

Middle and high school students often acquire meaning in fragments; however, they frequently use only one lens when reading and responding to literature. Multigenre writing provides students with options, allowing them to enlarge their scope of thinking "by successive developments, cellularly, like a . . . mosaic." Multigenre products engage students in several levels of response, creating an entire image as they fit together the mosaic pieces.

In Part I of this chapter, middle school teacher Suzanne Murphy presents scaffolding strategies that motivate students to create a highly individual response to texts. In Part II, high school teacher Maria Clinton explores a multigenre capacity to weave together research skills, history, and literature. Marie Milner, in Part III, details how she helps 9th to 12th graders access *Romeo and Juliet* through a variety of writing modes.

Part I: Why Multigenre Writing Belongs in Middle School
by Suzanne Murphy

Middle school students need opportunities to explore questions that puzzle them, build on previous experiences, and begin forging their identity and relationship to the larger world. They need to independently investigate and reflect on what they learn. What better way exists to do this than to encourage writing that communicates their beliefs, questions, and hopes?

While it is important to write with clarity, what if a student's response to literature needs to be communicated differently? Is it possible to find equally credible methods? Highlighting a key concept of the I-Search paper, students need the freedom to communicate authentically and fearlessly, using genres of their choice and integrating technology not only in their process, but also in their products. As Bee Foster states in "Redefining Text," "[E]xpanding what counts as writing compels students to look at everything that contains meaning as text." Foster further explains that the "process that produces the product is the writing." This widens the range of multigenre writing to include music, art, and the spoken word, as well as products created from technology, such as iMovies or digital storyboards.

My writing assignments are structured to encourage students to mirror themselves and view the larger world. While several of the writing assignments seemed successful on the surface, a conversation with one of my students, Chris, surprised me, leading me to discover new and engaging strategies for process and product that students find significant.

Conversation with Chris and Insights About the Traditional Persuasive Essay Assignment

When Chris and I met for a writing conference, he was ready to produce the final copy of a persuasive essay. He had made admirable headway toward his personal writing goal; his paper seemed well crafted and well supported with quotes from the novel. However, something was missing.

My Language Arts class had read Kathryn Lasky's novel, *Beyond the Burning Time* (1994), a historical fiction set in Salem, Massachusetts. The protagonist, young Mary Chase, relates the events of the Salem witch trials as she sees her friends, women neighbors, and her own mother accused and tried as witches. The students were currently studying the colonial period in U.S. history, so the book fit perfectly. During class discussions, students noted the social and environmental forces that produced the hysteria and accusations. At the novel's end, the author lists the historical figures and what happened to them; the students were troubled that the people of Salem Village could let events culminate so tragically.

I asked the students to determine the forces in Salem that created an atmosphere of distrust and fear. Students first worked in small groups brainstorming ideas and contributing at least one to a posted class list; the list included the status of women in society, the role of religion, economic privilege, and superstition.

Todd Rafalovich

Suzanne Murphy

Students then chose three of the forces identified, examined how these impacted the story, and wrote persuasive essays about the forces and social customs leading to the Salem witch trials. They found support from the novel and historical sources from their social studies class.

Back to Chris and his paper—just before he left to return to his desk, I asked a casual question.

> *"Chris, your paper shows you understand what caused the Salem witch trials, so what did you learn from this?*
>
> *"Well, I don't know exactly what you mean, Mrs. Murphy." He started to look a little puzzled.*
>
> *"Could this happen again, in another country, even today?"*
>
> *His brow drew together in concentration, and then he said, "But that's not the point. . . . I was supposed to learn how to write a persuasive essay, so I did." A pause, then, "Just tell me what to write, and I'll do that."*

Chris helped me understand that while he and his classmates could demonstrate their acquisition and mastery of writing skills so that I could assess growth toward a grade level standard, the students and I were ticking off a list of course objectives. They were "consuming" the learning and "digesting" enough to demonstrate academic growth, but it was not "nourishing" their awareness of the larger world. They were not achieving what the National Writing Project defines as literacy—the development of a richness and depth of understanding of one's self and place in the world by reading and writing to learn.

The **English Journal** *Issue on "Multigenre Teaching"*

A few days later, I discovered the November 2002 issue of the *English Journal*, entitled "Multigenre Teaching." Susan Jolley's article about "Integrating Poetry and *To Kill a Mockingbird*" (2002) and "The Ins, Outs, and In-Betweens of Multigenre

Writing" by Nancy Mack (2002) excited me. Although I was familiar with multigenre writing (Avi's novel *Nothing But the Truth*, for example) and I-Search projects, I hadn't used it. Reading the articles, I identified three important aspects of multigenre writing:

- Writing for personal discovery gives control over the media as well as the message.
- When excited by their discoveries, students want to share their findings.
- Having control makes students deliberately conscious of their genre choices and reasons for these selections.

Further, "this type of writing requires much more in the way of academic skills . . . to foster writing as both an art and a skill" (Mack, 2002, 91). In Blending Genre, Alternating Style (2002) Tom Romano describes multi-genre writing as arising "from research, experience, and imagination." He goes on to clarify the nature of this genre by writing:

> It is not an uninterrupted, expository monolog nor a seamless narrative nor a collection of poems. [It is] composed of many genres and subgenres, each self-contained piece making a point of its own, yet connected by theme or topic and sometimes by languages, images, and content. [It] may also contain many voices, not just the author's. The trick is to make [it] hang together.
>
> (x–xi)

Romano's concept of writing pieces, each complete in itself, but working with the others to create a unified experience with literature is applicable for middle schoolers; however, this learning experience requires scaffolding of the following tasks:

1. Defining and identifying multigenre works
2. Practicing various types of writing responses to one literary selection
3. Developing the concept connecting the writing pieces
4. Using an assessment rubric demonstrating student growth

My students needed to experiment with different forms to become comfortable with using several responses to a piece of literature. After gaining skill with a variety of genre "tools," students could craft a concept and shape their writing pieces around that concept into a multilayered body of work.

Define and Identify Multigenre

Before reading *Fever 1793* by Laurie Halse Anderson (2002) as the students began their study of the post-Revolutionary period in social studies, we worked with a short story to develop and practice multigenre writing. Students spent the first day brainstorming every type of writing form to create a class poster of writing possibilities. Table 7.1 shows the class results.

TABLE 7.1 *Ideas for Multigenre Pieces*

Maps	Rules	Poster
Dialogue	Painting	Instructions
History	Interior monologue	Advertisement
Labels	Autobiography	Newspaper
Play script	Will	Symbol
Science fiction	Horror story	Romance
Exposition	Poem	Historical fiction
Mystery	Diary/journal	Warning
Fantasy	Email	Biography
Process manual	Blog	Memoir
Invitation	Folktale	Resume
List	Birthday card	Statistics
Summary	Prayer	Police report
Yield sign	Menu	Song
Psalm	Divorce papers	Comic strip

Begin with a Short Story

The complex construction of a multigenre writing product requires that students begin with smaller, simpler writing. Students first responded to a short story, strengthening their inferential reading skills, so they could "mine" possibilities for writing before handling a longer novel.

From an anthology called *Sudden Fiction* (Shapard, 1986), I selected "Sunday in the Park" by Bel Kaufman (1986). The story involves an encounter between two young boys in a neighborhood park. One boy throws sand at the other child, and the parents get involved in a verbal altercation that threatens to turn physical. Students could read "Sunday in the Park" easily several times within one class period to draw increasingly richer inferences and conclusions from it. They used stem questions—from Jim Burke's *Reading Reminders* (2000)—to start thinking about the story.

> I got confused when . . .
> I was distracted by . . .
> I started to think about . . .
> I got stuck when . . .
> I figured out that . . .
> I first thought . . . then I realized

Their responses included imagining the contrast between the two families, the work the fathers do, and what the two sets of characters do after they leave the park. Finally, students broke into smaller groups, one for each of the five characters, and engaged in the task of drawing a character portrait on large paper as their evaluation.

On the second day, the posted character portraits sparked comments on more general topics and about experiences and ideas that interested them. Several ideas emerged during this discussion including how communities make rules about individual conduct, who decides what is fair, how parental behaviors affect children, the relation of social status to power, and how appearance shapes others' perception. Students created another list of these observations to post.

On the third day, students turned to the "Ideas for Multigenre Pieces" to choose four genres to use and engaged in paired discussions, worked independently on their writing, and researched topics on the Internet. On the fourth and fifth days, students wrote final drafts and used software to design graphics and create a booklet of their four products.

On the last day, every student shared his or her favorite of the four pieces, displaying differing levels of sophistication. The writing levels ranged from emerging to accomplished. As students proudly shared their efforts, they explained their genre choices and how each part represented the "main idea," even though I had not introduced that aspect of multigenre writing. One student informed his peers that because he sometimes had trouble visualizing when he read, he chose to create a scaled map of the setting and "Public Park Rules" signs that he designed after visiting a neighborhood park to see what actual signs look like.

Developing the Concept: Using the Novel Fever 1793

We then began a two-week class study of Laurie Halse Anderson's *Fever 1793* (2002), a book offering rich opportunities for greater complexity and response. Set in Philadelphia, the seat of the new U.S. government, it documents the yellow fever epidemic raging through the city in August 1793. The 12-year-old protagonist, Mattie Cook, relates the horrors of that time; the story details daily life and the precarious state of the new country during the epidemic.

Since several important scenes occur in the newspaper office of one of the novel's characters, I designed the multigenre writing to appear as a "broadside" or newspaper page that reported the news for one day during that gruesome period. Students thus needed to choose from the "Ideas for Multigenre Pieces" those genres appropriate for a newspaper. They conducted research to examine what information contemporary newspapers contained and what they looked like. Technology played an important part in this task, allowing access to actual images of newspapers produced during the period as models for the students' writing. Being able to read actual publications online enriched their understanding of the events. Each student newspaper page would be comprised of five "articles" that derived from a concept the student developed from the novel.

Students developed concepts such as the important presence of the Free African Society in the 18th century, the level and development of medical knowledge and practice, public health awareness, and the connection between social status and power (recurring from the "Sunday in the Park" study).

During the two weeks that students read the novel both inside and outside of the class, they wrote a "List of Things" poem, modeled on Elizabeth Bishop's "The Fish," about one room in the story—the newspaper printing office, the sickroom where Mattie recovers from the yellow fever, the Ogilvie parlor, or the cookhouse kitchen where Mattie helped her mother prepare meals. They also plotted on a city map (taken from Jim Murphy's *An American Plague*, 2003) the path of the epidemic as it moved from the wharves into the wealthy sections of Philadelphia. Again, using extensive Internet searches students located images of building interiors and written accounts of the period.

These two activities encouraged students to think more deeply about what affected them most strongly in their reading of this memorably written novel. For instance, after one student had written about the tea party at which the daughter succumbs to the fever, she explored the ways in which fashion plays a part in social status and privilege. Her articles included a doctor's health warning about burning even precious silks to avoid contagion; a report on the shortages of all kinds of supplies including parasols, Bibles, and iron for smelting; and a eulogy for the fragile young daughter of a wealthy merchant. The author of the following poem focused on rituals and customs of dress for people of the 18th century:

> *Tea Drinking Clothes*
> *First goes on the clean white shift*
> *Freshly laundered*
> *Next she pulls on her best stockings*
> *The ones she wears on Sundays.*
> *Then come the petticoats*
> *She only has a few.*
> *All too soon come the dreaded stays,*
> *Which bite so viciously.*
> *Over those she tugs her loveliest short gown*
> *Ice blue silk with lacy trim.*
> *Her maid brushes her tangled hair*
> *And puts up with a new white ribbon.*
> *New gloves, white as snow*
> *Are shrugged onto her hardworking hands.*
> *She quickly grabs her pale blue fan*
> *The one that's made of silk.*
> *All this work*
> *All this effort*
> *All to go drink tea.*

Lizzie D.

Assessing Multigenre Products

After students shared the finished product with their peers, they submitted their work for assessment. In addition to following the rubric for evaluating a reproduction of a historical document (see Table 7.2), students also reflected on the project in written form (see Table 7.3).

TABLE 7.2 *Newspaper Rubric*

	4	3	2	1
Content	Content of newspaper is compelling.	Content of newspaper is interesting.	Content is readable.	Content is unreadable.
Editing	Writing is free of spelling and grammar errors.	Writing contains one to three spelling errors, but does not distract from fluency.	Writing contains more than three errors that distract from fluency.	Writing contains so many errors the story is not readable.
Historical Accuracy	Historical accuracy is unquestionable.	Some errors in accuracy, but not distracting to story.	Errors in historical accuracy make story unbelievable.	What time period are you writing about?
Graphics	Graphics are appropriate to time period.	One error in graphics.	Missing newspaper masthead or date.	No graphics.
News Style	Style of all five articles is consistent with their genre	Four of five articles have style consistent with the genre.	Three of five articles have style consistent with the genre.	Two of five articles have style consistent with the genre.

http://www.southernct.edu/~ils69313/fever1793/webquest.htm

TABLE 7.3 *Reflective Journal to Accompany Product*

Answer four of the queries to inform me before I assess your product:

1. What did you learn about writing in different genres as a way of communicating what you know?
2. Tell me about your best piece of writing and describe why it is best.
3. Tell me about your weakest piece of writing and describe why it is weakest.
4. What did the multigenre format enable you to learn about your topic?
5. What was hard about writing your multigenre paper?
6. What could have made this writing easier?
7. What did you learn about content and/or form?
8. What surprised you?

Student Response Sample from Chelsey B.

1. I learned that with multigenre writing, I'm just retelling the same story but from different points of view. Multigenre not only expresses different views of the story's characters, but it also shows how the author interpreted the story.

4. The multigenre format enabled me to explore the story deeper but using my own view points. It enabled me to give my own evidence to where I want the story to go. It allowed me to display the topic in different ways.

3. My weakest piece was the sick note. It didn't tell a whole lot of the story. My intent with that piece was to express how the mother was feeling in the story. It did do this, just not very strongly.

8. This multigenre assignment really surprised me all around. At first I thought, "Oh, great, another assignment," but later I really got into it and had a lot of fun doing so. I felt empowered because I could shape the story into what I want.

Using Sudden Fiction *for the Zine Genre*

Then the time came for the students to have more control of the entire multigenre process. Because they had not worked in collaborative groups with multigenre writing, the next unit of study encouraged them to work collaboratively.

"Dinner Time" by Russell Edson, another story from *Sudden Fiction*, contains irony, gore, and shouting, ingredients attractive to adolescent readers. "Dinner Time" portrays an older couple engaging in self-destructive behavior involving kitchen tools. The students read it quickly, laughed at the outcome, and began to read again, looking more deeply into the text.

Students worked in groups of six, brainstorming and discussing ideas they gleaned from initial readings of the story. Each group received a sheet of paper measuring 24″ × 36″, folded to make six spaces, and used whatever tools and resources it had to create a *People* magazine with five pages of text and a cover page; the students would use writing and illustrations to convey the unifying theme of the magazine articles on the cover page. Students used the Internet to find examples of current popular magazines and theme-based publications to help them with the formatting and arrangement of articles, graphics, captioning, and the use of fonts and colors. The group of six functioned as an editorial board to collaborate on the theme; five members each wrote an article, and the sixth member created art and text for the cover.

The next day, the groups had a one-hour period to create their magazine. They spent their time proofreading and making certain that the articles complemented one another. After the students put their magazine together, they posted it either on a classroom wall or on the Language Arts class webpage. Students then engaged in a "gallery walk" to view the work of their peer groups, noting the different ways groups used the same seminal material—the short story—to create widely different results.

To Kill a Mockingbird—*The Centerpiece Assessment*

With the experiences garnered from these three encounters with multigenre writing, students were confident and comfortable enough to respond to Harper Lee's *To Kill a Mockingbird* (*TKAM*) (1960) in ways that were more meaningful than summaries or analyses. I wanted them to examine the rich variety of themes, "walk around in them," and produce a writing product that truly came from their own questions and connected the story with their experiences. This process was aided with a storyboard (see Table 7.4).

Students used sticky notes to identify themes present in the chapters, noticing that the author revisited themes in different ways, especially those of moral courage, ignorance, and marginalization.

I planned three weeks for the *TKAM* study, with a fourth week used for the multigenre writing, clustering the reading into groups that had a "key" chapter: Chapters 1–8, Chapters 9–14, Chapters 15–19, Chapters 20–25, and Chapters 26–31. Students set up their "double entry journal" (a quote from the assigned reading is listed in the left column and a personal response to it on the right side) to keep current with the reading. Students also wrote responses to poetry, including "If We Must Die" (Claude McKay),

TABLE 7.4   *Storyboard (Plot)*

Chapter 1	Chapter 2	Chapter 3	Chapter 4	Chapter 5
Meet Scout, Atticus	Scout goes to school	Meet Ewells	Boo Radley's knothole The gifts	Meet Miss Maudie Boo Radley's history
"there is more than one way to look at something"	"contrast between book and world education"	"blindness"	"superstition"	"acceptance of others"

	Chapter 6	Chapter 7	Chapter 8	Chapter 9
[Sketches are drawn under each chapter as a visual aid to comprehension]	Jem's prank	Nathan Radley seals up knothole	Miss Maudie's house burns The gift of the blanket	Tom Robinson
	"Physical & moral courage"	"Those who look after us"	"Fear"	"Racial prejudice"

"We Wear the Mask" (Paul Laurence Dunbar), and "Strange Fruit" (Abel Meeropol), that correlated with the time and issues. They also conducted web searches using the key terms "Civil Rights," "African American Poets," and "Blues Music" to find music and poetry, which they could present in the class to hear the poets' and musicians' own voices.

The *English Journal* article that encouraged me to use Dunbar and McKay's poetry, "Integrating Poetry and *To Kill a Mockingbird*" (Jolley, 2002), presented the idea of using a poem to express a concept. Remembering the class discussion when I read aloud Lee's description of Maycomb and we talked about how the town itself was actually a character in the novel, I decided to use photographs as writing springboards.

When the students came to class to begin their multigenre projects, I explained they would use the Internet to find a photograph representing Maycomb: a house, small town store, or a government building like a courthouse or post office. They logged onto the American Memory Project site from the Library of Congress, following these instructions:

1. Address: http://memory.loc.gov/ammem/fsowhome.html
2. The site is "America From the Great Depression to World War II"
3. Click on "Black & White Photographs"
4. Click on "Geographic Location Index"
5. Click on any geographic entry of a southern state, especially Georgia and Alabama.
6. Choose any photo of a building that reminds you of Maycomb. Go back to the description in the story to look for further details that can help you make the choice. Choose a photo that does not have farm or rural details or any people or animals.
7. Select and drag your choice to a blank document in Word. Print out a copy for your writing book and save it in your class file on the computer.
8. Write a poem about your photograph, treating Maycomb as a character in the story and using the photo as a visual representation of the concept you are thinking about.

Students were free to use any materials they had already gathered from the *TKAM* study. They would ultimately submit the response sheet (Table 7.3) with their product.

The choices students made were varied, as is indicated by the four different kinds of writing that students composed on the concept of compassion. One student, using the photograph of a home covered with trellis roses and shaded by trees, wrote that the house reminded her of Miss Maudie, a person of compassion and courage. Another piece was a letter from Miss Maudie to Mayella, asking her to be her companion. A third student created Arthur Radley's interior monologue while he stands next to Jem's bed. A fourth student, who chose what looked to be a photograph of a jail, wrote of the importance of the scene outside the courthouse on the eve of the trial, creating a series of poems in the voice of characters that are trapped and find ways to "escape" their prisons:

> **_Dill_**
> *My life is nothing special*
> *But no one really knows it*
> *In a moment I have traveled the world*
> *And discovered something new*
>
> *I've been chained in dungeons*
> *By devil men*
> *Cleaned a camel in the circus*
> *I've seen Dracula too*
>
> *The more stories I weave*
> *The less I can forget*
>
> **_Robert Ewell_**
> *People think I'm low*
> *Dirty and immoral*
> *I'm more, ya know*
> *I'm a father and a workingman*
>
> *So I drink a little*
> *Spend my paycheck a little*
> *That doesn't make me so bad*
> *I got seven kids to raise—gimme a break*
>
> *When I find a way to make some money*
> *Even if it's against the law*
> *I gotta do it*
> *You can't feed seven kids on welfare and farmin'*

Multigenre papers can re-spark the curiosity that students can experience in their reading and writing, a curiosity that on-demand prompts and formulaic programs have all but extinguished. With many types of writing, including a range of digital forms for both process and product, comprising this mosaic, students have the opportunity to work with favorite forms and add new ways of expressing and representing what they know.

While this type of writing is composed of several elements, teachers can focus on one or two components for assessment purposes (for example, the expository writing in the broadside for *Fever 1793*) and can enfold standards-based writing within a larger product that is based on student choice and interest. This eclectic approach offers students a wide range of options for expressing ideas and communicating knowledge. As students explore different avenues for translating what they know into writing, they begin to understand that there is no single "right way" to communicate. Instead, writing demands intelligent, informed choices based on purpose, audience, content, and personal preference.

Part II: The Museum Exhibit
by Maria Clinton

Background for the Project

> *"Fans, for the past two weeks you have been reading about a bad break*
> *I got. Yet today I consider myself the luckiest man on the face of the earth."*

On July 4, 1939, Lou Gehrig, the "Iron Horse" of the New York Yankees, said good-bye to baseball and his fans after a record-breaking career. He addressed a crowd of 62,000 on Lou Gehrig Appreciation Day at Yankee Stadium, saying these immortal, humble words. After his speech, teammate Babe Ruth came out to the field, put his arm around Gehrig's shoulders, and spoke to him for the first time in five years. Gehrig had gotten a "bad break." He had been diagnosed with ALS, now called Lou Gehrig's disease, which cut his career short and would end his life two short years later. This pop culture moment transfixed the audience—not just the audience present at Yankee Stadium, but the radio and reading audiences as well.

While I find Gehrig's attitude in the face of tragedy inspiring, I have never been particularly interested in long-dead baseball greats. I'm much more of a Shakespeare girl. However, the fact is that many of my students *are* interested in Gehrig, Ruth, Peyton Manning, Kobe Bryant, and other huge sports stars. Our students are motivated by sports, music, video games, movies and movie stars, reality TV, gossip, and every other aspect of pop culture. They are so interested in these topics, in fact, that they often read and research as much as they possibly can about their obsessions. When I began teaching in 1990, students would avidly research 'NSYNC and Michael Jordan, and share their information with their classmates and me. Now, in 2012, they gather just as much information about Justin Bieber and Tim Tebow. Truly, many of our students have become "experts in their fields" of inquiry and in accessing a range of digital resources. While some researchers and cultural observers decry students' fascination with pop culture, others point to its potential to aid students in developing both social and critical thinking skills. As Tom Newkirk writes in *Holding On to Good Ideas in a Time of Bad Ones* (2009) of one representative student exhibiting these skills, "Dyson demonstrates the complex way in which children orchestrate the various cultural stories available to them—often performing academic and 'social' work at the same time" (96). Teachers can use this interest to engage students and teach them valuable research and writing skills, while also motivating them to read some great literature.

Earlier in this chapter Suzanne Murphy talked about how multigenre writing gives students ownership and personal interest in their writing. When I consider an activity or project on the high school level, I always ask myself, "How much bang for my buck am I getting?" In other words, how many opportunities for learning and skill practice does the activity provide? Multigenre writing gives an awful lot of bang for my buck.

Why a Museum Exhibit?

As my students begin to read *Of Mice and Men* (Steinbeck, 1993), I have them complete a multigenre "Museum Exhibit" project that capitalizes on their interest in pop culture to help them learn research skills. I use a Museum Exhibit because, while I can read a book on any topic that interests me, going to a museum to learn about a topic is a multisensory experience. When we visit a museum, we find ourselves immersed in a completely different world. For example, if students are able to visit the National Holocaust Museum, they are given a card with the name and age of a Holocaust victim. As they proceed through their visit, they slowly learn about the fate of their European counterparts. They see a boxcar and a giant pile of shoes. They see the hallway of photographs, which is all that is left of one of the Jewish villages that was completely eliminated during the war. Looking into the eyes of the people in those photographs, they can perhaps just begin to fathom the depths of this atrocity. They realize that these were real people, with family and friends who loved them, with hopes and dreams for the future. The victims were not merely numbers or statistics, which is what they are often reduced to in history textbooks. Although students are not likely to forget a visit to the Holocaust Museum, they will often forget the discrete details that they read in a textbook.

A museum is a multigenre experience. It provides the museum goer with many ways of experiencing and processing the information that is presented.

Even though I could just have my students write a research paper, I find that they retain much more information when they create a multigenre project. As they create a Museum Exhibit, they are thinking critically about how they can best convey the information that they want their audience to learn. They evaluate and rank the information they have learned and determine how to present it creatively to their audience. They use and manipulate the information in many more ways in this project than they would in a research paper.

Using the Museum Exhibit to Study Of Mice and Men

Instead of beginning my *Of Mice and Men* lessons with the story of George, Lennie, and their friendship, I begin with a discussion of the Great Depression. While I do give a short lecture on the context of the time period, we move quickly to the pop culture of the era.

Ashley Kidder

Maria Clinton

We listen to jazz and swing, we brainstorm the popular movies of the time, and sometimes we have a Depression-era Thanksgiving party, for which the students bring food prepared from Depression-era recipes which are easily found online. ("Depression Era Cooking and Recipes" at http://www.squidoo.com/depression-era-cooking is one good example, as are online Depression-era cooking shows, such as "Great Depression Cooking with Clara.") These activities help spark the students' interest in the time period in ways that facts about the stock market crash could never accomplish.

The Museum Exhibit requires students to research the life and career of a Depression-era pop culture figure. Once they have gathered information about the person's life, their task is to create at least six artifacts about this person that would be found in a museum. On the back of each artifact, they must glue a paragraph or two identifying the item and explaining its significance to the person's life. Finally, the students need to present their exhibits to the class as though they are museum docents.

This Museum Exhibit assignment not only provides some of the historical and social background that students need for comprehension of the novel, but also allows the students to focus on their research and presentation skills, important language arts standards, without the onus (for both the student and teacher) of a long, complicated report. Actually writing a research paper comes later in the year, after students have honed their

TABLE 7.5　*Possible Research Topics*

Woody Guthrie	Margaret Bourke-White
Walter Winchell	Glenn Miller
Edward Hopper	Al Capone
Jesse Owens	Dorothea Lange
Shirley Temple	Frank Capra
Georgia O'Keefe	Will Rogers
Jimmy Stewart	Marian Anderson
Charles Lindberg	Amelia Earhart

research skills by completing their Museum Exhibit. Table 7.5 provides a list of possible research topics.

The most popular topics are the people who best fit into the pop culture milieu. Students will argue, beg, and bargain over who gets to research Al Capone, while they are not nearly as interested in Marian Anderson, an icon of the Civil Rights struggle. I generally have the students draw their topics from a hat, but sometimes I give particular students a topic that will motivate them. For example, I made sure that Terrence got Al Capone. Terrence was a very intelligent boy in a remedial course for weak readers, but he was too "cool" to apply himself in class; he liked to talk about gangs and try to intimidate his peers. Al Capone was the perfect character to pique his interest.

In the Museum Exhibit, students first do biographical research in the library, allowing me to teach students how to use library resources. Since these topics can be found everywhere on the Internet, as well as in library databases, resource books, and nonfiction books, this project gives us a wonderful opportunity to instruct students on differences among sources, helping students learn to choose the most appropriate source or combination of sources for any given topic.

Terrence did not even give me the chance to take him to the school library; apparently, he went home and researched Capone by himself. He came in the next day with a book and all kinds of information about Capone; he proceeded to quiz his classmates about Capone's rise in the mob culture and his weapons of choice. Since we were headed to our school library, I challenged Terrence to find out what crime finally sent Capone to prison and what eventually killed him.

Six Exhibits to Represent their Depression-era Subjects

Once students have finished gathering information, they evaluate what they have learned, deciding what is most important for others to know. Based on this evaluation, they choose and create six exhibits about their subject that might be found in a museum. These exhibits might include those shown in Table 7.6.

TABLE 7.6 *Potential Exhibits*

Death certificate	School report cards, with teacher comments
Pictures of the person	Pictures created by the person
Diary entries	Wanted posters
Movie posters	Letters written by or to the person
Medical records	Passport, stamped with places the person traveled
Paychecks	Rough drafts of the person's writing
Newspaper obituary	Diplomas or degrees

I encourage students to create a combination of "paper exhibits," such as posters, diary entries, and realia of different kinds. Obviously, students cannot generally obtain actual items that belonged to the character; however, the presentations tend to be more fun and interesting if students have actual items to show us. For example, for Charles Lindbergh, students have brought in model airplanes. For Will Rogers, a student brought a rope and a toy horse. For Shirley Temple, students often show movie clips and bring in tap shoes. Some even bring in Shirley Temple drinks.

Students must write an explanation of each exhibit's significance and attach it to the exhibit before submitting it. The following is Sarah's example:

> This exhibit is a movie. Ginger Rogers was an actress from 1930 to 1965. She appeared in many films, 10 with the partner she got really famous with, Fred Astaire. This exhibit is important because she got famous off of making movies. She started out in dancing competitions and then she moved to Broadway. One of her friends convinced her to become an actress and she listened, but she only had small parts. She was known only as a "bit" actress until 1930. . . .
>
> This exhibit is her quotes. Her quotes were important because it gave an incite [sic] to her mind. Her quotes were mostly about love and life. Some of her close friends even wrote quotes about her. She had nice things to say about her acting and dancing partner Fred Astaire whom she married and later divorced. Her quotes shared what she thought about life and also about love and some people. She also shared a quote about what her mom told her once and that was "you were dancing even before you were born."
>
> Sarah

Finally, students present their Museum Exhibits to the class, practicing the presentation skills that are an important component of educational standards and real-world skills.

I will not pretend that Terrence produced a stellar final product. However, he did actually produce a final product, which was a huge step for him. His exhibits included

- Pictures of weapons from the time
- A picture related to the St. Valentine's Day Massacre
- A picture of Alcatraz, where Capone was imprisoned for a time

He attempted to write his explanatory paragraphs, and he presented to his classmates, taking great pleasure in sharing Al Capone's cause of death: syphilis. Terrence's energy and enthusiasm in this assignment represent a good example of writing that comes from engagement. He did very few other assignments; here, though, he had a topic that intrigued him and a wide variety of choices in the way he presented the material, as well as an authentic, interested audience. He probably didn't realize that he was practicing research, writing, and presenting skills because it didn't really seem like work to him.

The Value of the Museum Exhibit and the Multigenre Approach

When doing research, students too often simply list the facts they have gleaned, without consideration of the significance of those facts. Research generally doesn't matter to our students as much as it matters to us. Much like an I-Search paper, this multigenre assignment requires students to actually think about what they are reading and learning, and apply what they have learned, increasing the chances that they will retain the information. While the evaluation of the information and the selection of appropriate exhibits require the teacher's guidance, this is the kind of critical, analytical thinking that students need to practice.

In addition to developing students' critical thinking skills, multigenre writing allows students to practice their reading and writing skills in a wide variety of genres. For example, a student researching Lou Gehrig might choose to create Gehrig's medical records as an exhibit. The writing skills required for this exhibit involve precise, technical writing. The student may then decide to write Gehrig's journal entries, a task requiring understanding of Gehrig's internal conflicts and an expression of complex emotion through personal writing. Finally, this same student may discover the movie *Pride of the Yankees*, which includes Gehrig's famous farewell speech to baseball. With the teacher's guidance, the student can study that speech for rhetorical effectiveness and clues to Gehrig's personality. The key here is that students choose these exhibits themselves. Because they choose the artifacts and writing styles that interest them, they are more invested in and engaged with the task, while simultaneously improvong their writing.

While writing a research paper is an important skill, I find that the multigenre Museum Exhibit is a less-intimidating, more engaging way of introducing students to high-school research and presentation.

Differentiation

This kind of assignment can be easily differentiated to different grade levels and teaching situations. When I have taught at-risk freshman classes or classes that include several ESL and/or Special Ed students, I allow the students to work with partners on their exhibits. Teachers can require fewer resources of weak readers. For weaker writers, teachers can provide students with sentence stems and paragraph patterns. This is an example of a paragraph pattern.

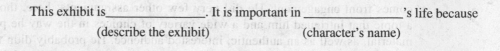

This exhibit is_____. It is important in _____'s life because
(describe the exhibit)   (character's name)

_____.
(give relevant background information about the person's life)

This exhibit shows us/demonstrates _____.
(explain what we can learn about the person from this exhibit)

After students have used the paragraph pattern a few times, they can be guided to expand their paragraphs, adding more information and analysis.

This year, I implemented a new adaptation. I had several students who completed their research, writing, and exhibits, but were terrified to present to the class because they had chosen to work alone. Volunteers from the class stood in front with these timid students. The volunteers held up their exhibits or advanced the PowerPoint. The presence of another student seemed to make all the difference. The assignment can also be adapted to different research topics and/or texts. For example, it could easily be done with Renaissance research to tie in to Shakespeare's *Romeo and Juliet*, or African history to tie in to *Things Fall Apart*. Finally, while I usually have students actually create the exhibit and present it in class to their peers, it could be created as a webpage; that way, the audience could include any web viewer in the world.

In a colleague's class where her freshman students researched the Renaissance era and had to write three multigenre texts, students shared that they got a lot more out of the experience than they had from more traditional research papers. Romi reports, "I felt more of a connection to my topic because I had to create a character, not to mention that the composition of the piece was a lot more fun. . . . It wasn't just a boring set of dates and facts; I had to recreate a very complex person, which makes the writer have to research small details about their character." The texts students produce are more creative as well as more complex and require more synthesis, as Caitlyn points out here: "With a normal research paper, you look up the info and then put it in an essay. With this project, you had to use the info in a variety of ways, so you were constantly re-visiting the information. It really helped me understand the material." Students' writing showed that they often had fun taking on the voices of people or writing in new genres, such as the eulogy, interview, or diary.

Multigenre Writing Across the Curriculum

In addition to the Language Arts classroom, multigenre writing can be adapted to help students demonstrate their knowledge across the curriculum. Last year one of my remedial reading students, Kim, came to me for some help on a project she had been given for her Government class. I discovered that her teacher, J. P. Sampson, had adapted multigenre writing to some concepts he had been teaching. The assignment was to write a fairytale that demonstrated the different systems of government they had been studying (see Table 7.7).

I was very impressed by the creativity of the assignment, as well as the higher level thinking it required; this assignment fit in perfectly with Robert Marzano's research in *Classroom Instruction That Works* (2001), where he speaks about the efficacy of teaching students to create metaphors and analogies. According to his work, having students identify similarities and differences among concepts produces an average effect size of 1.61, translating to an average percentile gain of 45 (Marzano, 2001, 7). Marzano summarizes the research by saying, "Presenting students with explicit guidance in identifying similarities and differences enhances students' understanding of and ability to use knowledge. . . . Creating a metaphor involves identifying abstract similarities and differences between two

---

TABLE 7.7 *Government Systems Fairytale Activity*

For this lesson you will develop a "fairytale" that examines *EACH* of the governmental systems we have studied so far in class. You will work individually on this. The groups are democracy (representative and direct), monarchy, and dictatorship.

What is it that makes a story a fairytale?

There are several elements present in most fairytales. For your assignment, you will need to focus on the following:

Each fairytale has most or all of the elements listed below.

- Special beginning and/or ending words—Once upon a time . . . and they lived happily ever after.
- Good character
- Evil character
- Royalty and/or a castle
- Magic
- Problem and a solution
- Things that often happen in "threes" or "sevens"

Your fairytale needs to address aspects of how EACH of these governmental systems function. Here is an example:

Once upon a time there lived a proud and peaceful tribe of people who valued each other's opinion. Because they were given the right to vote, these citizens had to make tough decisions on which was the best way to run their society. One of them believed a direct democracy. . . .

Your fairytale must:

1. Address each of the governmental systems. (6 pts)
2. Have at least five key different government vocabulary terms included (use the vocabulary organizer you worked on to help you with this). (5 pts)
3. Use a visual. If you want to make it a book, then go ahead. You can also make a poster or pamphlet. It is open ended, so be creative. (2 pts.)
4. Follow the fairytale elements listed above. (2 pts)

elements" (15–16). Creating a fairytale that illustrates governmental systems is an elaborate, extended metaphor that requires very high-level reasoning and creativity.

To help Kim with the assignment, we brainstormed about different fairytale movies she had seen. Because English was not her first language, the source of her confusion about the assignment was the term "fairytale." However, once we started talking about "Cinderella" and "Beauty and the Beast," she understood exactly what she was being asked to do and was much more engaged with the assignment than she would have been if she had simply been asked to write definitions. Clearly, multigenre writing has the potential to be adapted for a wide variety of subject areas, as a way to both engage students and increase the depth of their thinking.

Standards

In addition to engaging students with what they are learning and increasing the depth of their understanding, both the Museum Exhibit assignment and the Fairytale/Government assignment meet several of the Common Core State Standards (2010), as shown in Table 7.8.

TABLE 7.8   *Reading Standards for Informational Text (Grades 9–12)*

7	Analyze various accounts of a subject told in different mediums (e.g., a person's life story in both print and multimedia), determining which details are emphasized in each account.
8	Delineate and evaluate the argument and specific claims in a text, assessing whether the reasoning is valid and the evidence is relevant and sufficient; identify false statements and fallacious reasoning.

Writing Standards (Grades 9–12)

2	Write informative/explanatory texts to examine and convey complex ideas, concepts, and information clearly and accurately through the effective selection, organization, and analysis of content.
3	Write narratives to develop real or imagined experiences or events using effective technique, well-chosen details, and well-structured event sequences.
4	Produce clear and coherent writing in which the development, organization, and style are appropriate to task, purpose, and audience.
7	Conduct short as well as more sustained research projects to answer a question (including a self-generated question) or solve a problem; narrow or broaden the inquiry when appropriate; synthesize multiple sources on the subject, demonstrating understanding of the subject under investigation.
8	Gather relevant information from multiple authoritative print and digital sources, using advanced searches effectively; assess the usefulness of each source in answering the research question; integrate information into the text selectively to maintain the flow of ideas, avoiding plagiarism and following a standard format for citation.

Speaking and Listening (Grades 9–12)

4	Present information, findings, and supporting evidence clearly, concisely, and logically such that listeners can follow the line of reasoning and the organization, development, substance, and style are appropriate to purpose, audience, and task.

(http://www.corestandards.org)

Part III: **Romeo and Juliet** *Brought to Life Through Multi-Modal/Multigenre Strategies* by Marie Milner

Through a *Romeo and Juliet* unit, I've found that expanding the text with a multi-modal/multigenre approach not only facilitates the accessibility of challenging text but also inspires meaningful writing. The language of a Shakespearean play is challenging to all students—native speakers or English language learners. However, the multigenre approach guides them to deeper levels with the play and its universal themes. In what follows, i describe the basic steps that make up the unit, which can run from six to eight weeks depending on my students' developmental levels. This unit, which is adaptable to the teaching of any of Shakespeare's plays, incorporates a variety of genres and modalities including formal and informal letter writing, poetry, children's literature, prose and dramatic fiction, and filmed musical and dramatic film.

Demystifying the Poetry of the Bard with "'Twas the Night Before Christmas"

To introduce the concepts of meter and scansion in a fairly stress-free environment, I use the poem, "A Visit from St. Nick" ("'Twas the Night Before Christmas"). Students first study the poem informally, and then we identify anapestic tetrameter appearing in the poem. For ELL students, Total Physical Response (TPR) is an effective strategy often used in such activities; however, even in mainstream classes I lead the students in physical activities such as tapping their desks or counting on their fingers, to help them develop a sense of poetic rhythm and meter.

Students then create their own parodies of this traditional poem, using what they have learned about meter and scansion to compose their own "Night Before" poems on such topics as "the Prom," "the SATs," "Ms. Milner's Test." Student voice is further strengthened when many of the ELL or first generation students choose to highlight a significant event in their own cultures: 'Twas the Night Before Tet (Vietnamese New Year) or Cinco de Mayo. This entertaining emphasis on anapestic tetrameter allows easier access to the iambic pentameter of *Romeo and Juliet.*

Empowerment Through Schema

On the first day of the actual *Romeo and Juliet* unit, we brainstorm what students already know about William Shakespeare and his times, as well as what they know about *Romeo and Juliet.* Building on their prior knowledge, we talk about the life and times of William Shakespeare. I don't present a formal lecture, but instead hold an informal discussion with student input to foster his or her confidence in oral participation.

Visual aids and realia play a significant role in lowering student anxiety and helping them access language and content through hands-on materials. Using a Globe Theatre poster, I introduce the theatrical conventions of Shakespeare's era, having students role-play with me to grasp such theatrical elements as "asides," the "fourth wall," and the "soliloquy." Although improvising with the teacher can be intimidating, students can participate in nonthreatening ways. (See the Folger Shakespeare Library website: http://www.folger.edu/ for a virtual tour of the restored Globe Theatre in London.)

Incorporating Letter Writing Through the Great Motivator, Will Shakespeare

Using what they have learned in the Globe Theatre lesson, the students adopt the role of "Shakespeare the Younger" of our era and write to "Shakespeare the Elder" of Elizabethan times, sharing with him how different he would find the theatrical conventions of today. This activity gives ELL students a chance to practice their newly acquired academic language in written form. To prepare for writing, I re-post the Globe Theatre poster and students take turns reviewing theatrical conventions with their classmates.

When students write their letters to Shakespeare about his theatre, they not only demonstrate an academic grasp of theatrical conventions of Elizabethan England, but also far more voice than they might in a conventional essay. One student memorably told "Shakespeare" that when he time traveled to Elizabethan England, he chose to attend a comedy (which he identified by the white flag flying above the Globe Theatre) because he was lonely as a time-traveler and needed a comedy to cheer him up.

This assignment explaining a time-traveling experience to Elizabethan England, and then writing a letter to Shakespeare about how his theatre compares to ours, allows students to write humorously and imaginatively.

This assignment, explaining a time traveling experience to Elizabethan England and then writing a letter to Shakespeare comparing his theatre to ours, allows students to write humorously and imaginatively. In a unique response to this assignment, a freshman wrote his fictional letter to Shakespeare

Dear Mr. Shakespeare:

[. . .] On the subject of actors, I could not help but notice that every role was played by [a male]. While this did slightly unnerve me, I understand why. Unlike in my times, women seem to be held to stricter rules; that is to say, I do not think they are even supposed to talk to other men, so flaunting them around on a stage may be just too much for someone's heart to handle. [. . .] In our day, women play their parts, and they are not tied down to such strict rules. Men and women both move throughout the stage, under cover of darkness and lights that we have learned to manipulate.

—Austin Nguyen, 9th grade

To Mr. Austin Nguyen:

Am I to understand that you have transcended time to speak matters with me? [. . .] Let it be known that my first thought, upon reading your letter, was one of confusion. It did not get better as I continued my attempt to make sense of it—confusion turned to puzzlement to outright bewilderment—but 'tis well, 'tis well, for it turned out alright in the end, after the initial shock. Though our grammars greatly differ, we share enough that I could understand you after going through your letter word by word. [. . .] I fail to grasp your use of the word "electronically," and, at first, "time machine," though I pieced it together after reading your letter—which admittedly was very strange, in both content and style. [. . .] Truly, it seems miraculous. A row of lights? Dimmed or moved, all at the press of a button. Buttons! The future has repurposed buttons to create light! I cannot conceive of how such a thing could be done, or why buttons would be chosen to produce such a phenomenon—though I am sure there is a good reason. Many males unnerve you, you said. Perhaps times have changed there as well. I am inclined to believe that women are not as good as men at acting—there are exceptions, of course, but the talents of women lie in other things, such as cooking, caring for children, and sewing. Might it be possible that women have improved their own abilities over time? Or possibly—just possibly—all of us men have prejudged women as inferior this entire time, and thus discouraged them from developing any talents they had? [. . .] Your letter was very enlightening, my dear friend. You have left me with much to think about and much to hope for.

I wish you the very best,

William Shakespeare

—Andy Nguyen, 11th grade

Engaging with the Romeo and Juliet *Text: Help from a Children's Book*

Stephen Krashen emphasizes the importance of *amplifying* rather than *simplifying* material for ELL students. Actually, all students need multiple exposures to content in order to facilitate learning. Using a multigenre approach to introduce the reading of Shakespeare's play, I first employ a children's prose version of the play; the 1998 Margaret Early illustrated book provides visual reinforcement and previews the play in a non-threatening way. I read it aloud, emphasizing affectionate attention to detail. Having already introduced the character and plot elements, I now employ a cloze activity. With a cloze activity, I pause occasionally for the class as a whole to call out terms I have omitted such as "apothecary" or "wherefore," thus reinforcing the pronunciation of the play's challenging vocabulary.

Because this is a choral response, individual student anxiety is lessened as they acquire the Elizabethan language.

Amplification from Charles and Mary Lamb: Romeo and Juliet *in Prose*

Subsequent to Early's children's version, we read the Charles and Mary Lamb (1995) late 19th century prose version of the play. This activity typically takes about two hours of class time between reading aloud and stopping to check for understanding. The Lamb version of *Romeo and Juliet* is not a "dumbed-down" narrative, but an eloquently written prose version containing highly complex sentence structures and incorporating Shakespeare's actual language throughout. The Lamb rendition lets students—especially ELLs—"get their feet wet" before approaching the more complex Shakespearean text.

Student Letter to Character from Romeo and Juliet

Once we have completed the classroom reading of *Romeo and Juliet*, the students write letters to any character in the play they wish; I encourage them to "tell that character off." This activity teaches characterization and theme in a less intimidating mode. One memorable line from a former student read, "Dear Friar, You are an idiot!. . . ." At a later time, students can restructure these letters to produce formal essays about characterization in the play. Student anxiety is reduced when they realize that with their letters to the characters, they have made significant headway into producing the formal essay.

Letter to Franco Zeffirelli

Students then view the 1968 Franco Zeffirelli film *Romeo and Juliet*, after which they write Zeffirelli a letter evaluating his interpretation. Beforehand, the class brainstorms directorial film choices, and this is a good time to introduce the terminology that accompanies formal writing about film and its conventions. Although new academic language is being introduced, with the expectation that students will employ it in their letters, the letter-writing genre facilitates authentic student voice.

Letter to Baz Luhrmann

After discussing what is meant by reinterpreting a piece of literature, the class watches the Baz Luhrmann 1996 film *Romeo + Juliet*. Students then write a letter to Luhrmann with a more concretely structured beginning or "sentence starter." The students begin their letter to him with, "Dear Mr. Luhrmann, I have just seen Franco Zeffirelli's version of *Romeo and Juliet* as well as yours and I think. . . ." This allows students the freedom to form an opinion of both films while encouraging them to cite evidence from each. In effect, they are writing the beginnings of a formal essay while once again employing more passionate prose as they start writing in a less intimidating genre.

Shakespeare in Love—*Employing the Genre of Film Academically*

A bonus activity is John Madden's 1998 film *Shakespeare in Love*. The film cannot be shown in its entirety in a middle or high school classroom because it is R-rated, but the final scenes contain no objectionable material. They depict a 16th century Globe Theatre production of *Romeo and Juliet* with the various theatrical elements of that time such as males portraying female characters, red ribbons being used to represent blood, a prologue to establish setting in place of scenery, and the groundlings as audience. The film's conclusion also portrays the idea of theater patronage through the appearance of Elizabeth I and her spoken requests of Shakespeare, including one to write a play for the Twelfth Night holiday.

Romeo and Juliet *via the Musical* West Side Story— *Employing Two Genres with Film and Musical*

I next introduce the 1961 musical film *West Side Story,* directed by Jerome Robbins and Robert Wise, which is based on *Romeo and Juliet*. Although this is a fairly conventional application of film in a *Romeo and Juliet* unit, for many students it provides another mode of accessibility. I use the musical to review theatrical conventions, now introducing those conventions of musical theatre/film with which students are not yet familiar. As students watch the film, we identify ways in which *West Side Story* parallels *Romeo and Juliet* regarding the conventions being used in the film in general and the musical in particular.

Analytical Essay—Romeo and Juliet/West Side Story— *A "Stress Free" Culminating Activity*

The formal essay assignment varies depending on the students' language development level. If they are in a class geared specifically to ELLs, I model a complete essay with them, discussing the character parallels between *Romeo and Juliet* and *West Side Story*. The students later complete their own multi-paragraph essay in which they compare the plots and themes of both stories.

What follows is a model of a classroom-constructed essay that students wrote with me about how the characters in *West Side Story* serve similar functions as the ones in *Romeo and Juliet*. (The full six-paragraph essay was written on the whiteboard in my classroom over three days with students participating and copying in longhand in order to have their own unique classroom model. I have only included the introductory, first body, and concluding paragraphs here, with the play and movie titles underlined rather than italicized, to reflect the fact that the essay was written in class on the board, not word processed.)

A Sample Multi-Paragraph Essay Composed by the Class: *R&J/West Side Story*

Introductory Paragraph

Does William Shakespeare's tragedy Romeo and Juliet *have anything to say to the modern world? Of course it does, and this is evident in the musical based on the play called* West Side Story. *Although Shakespeare's play is set in Verona in the 1300s, and the musical is set in New York in the 1950s, they share themes about love, hate and violence. In Shakespeare's play, the protagonists Romeo and Juliet are struggling to find a way to be together despite the rivalry between their parents, and in Leonard Bernstein's musical, Tony and Maria also struggle because of hatred between two gangs. Because the two stories have similar themes, the characters in* West Side Story *are based on the ones in* Romeo and Juliet.

First Body Paragraph

The characters Romeo and Juliet are represented by Tony and Maria in the musical. Both of these pairs of lovers are not supposed to be together according to the rival groups in the stories. In Romeo and Juliet's case, the Capulets and Montagues have been feuding for years, and in Tony and Maria's case, the Anglo gang called the Jets has an ongoing feud with the Puerto Rican gang, the Sharks. Also, both couples fall in love "at first sight" at an event where music and dance are involved. Another similarity between the couples is that their love overpowers other people's objections. Further, both are willing to make sacrifices to be together. Because both sets of lovers are so similar in character, it is easy to imagine the truths of their stories. [. . .]

Concluding Paragraph

After viewing both Romeo and Juliet *and* West Side Story *or reading Shakespeare's play, it becomes obvious that the original story still has much to say to a modern audience. Because of the similarities between the roles of the characters in each of the stories, the modern audience can easily relate to Shakespeare's tale. Many of the central themes in both stories are about the senselessness of violence. For example, violence only leads to more violence, even if the original violent act seems small. Also, when we see the pain and loss of the survivors of both stories, we understand that feuding about anything is not worth the loss of loved ones. Additionally, the stories examine the danger of excessive pride and boastfulness, which can have dangerous consequences. Both* Romeo and Juliet *and* West Side Story *have doomed, tragic love stories in them, and this love is ironically the only emotion that reconciles the rival groups. Thus, perhaps one of the stories' most powerful themes is about the healing nature of love.*

Having students respond to this quite challenging text through a wide variety of different types of writing, and well as re-experiencing the text itself through film interpretations and musical adaptations, has made this Elizabethan play far more accessible, especially to my English Language Learners. This multi-model/multigenre approach has also engaged my students with the story in ways that more conventional approaches often fail to do..

References and Resources

American Memory Project. The Library of Congress. http://memory.loc.gov/ammem/index.html

Anderson, Laurie Halse. *Fever 1793*. New York: Simon & Schuster Children's Publishing, 2002.

Bishop, Elizabeth. *The Fish*. bcs.bedfordstmartins.com/ virtualit/poetry/fish_elements.html

Burke, Jim. *Reading Reminders*. Portsmouth, NH: Heinemann, 2000.

Cannucciari, Clara. "Great Depression Cooking with Clara." Online Cooking Classes.

Depression Era Cooking and Recipes at http://www.squidoo.com/depression-era-cooking

Dunbar, Paul. "We Wear the Mask." *The Complete Poems of Paul Laurence Dunbar*. Paul Laurence Dunbar. New York: Dodd, Mead, and Co., 1913.

Early, Margaret, editor and illustrator. *Romeo and Juliet*. Hachette Livre Australia: Lothian Books, an imprint of New Ed edition, February 1, 1998.

Edson, Russell. "Dinner Time." In *Sudden Fiction*. Salt Lake City, UT: Gibbs M. Smith, 1986.

The Folger Shakespeare Library. http://www.folger.edu/

Foster, Bee. "Redefining Text." digitalis.nwp.org

Jolley, Susan Arpajian. "Integrating Poetry and *To Kill a Mockingbird*." *English Journal,* 92.2 (November 2002): 34–40.

Kaufman, Bel. "Sunday in the Park." In *Sudden Fiction*. Salt Lake City, UT: Gibbs M. Smith, 1986.

Lamb, Charles and Mary. *Tales From Shakespeure*. New York: Puffin, 1995.

Lasky, Kathryn. *Beyond the Burning Time*. New York: Scholastic, 1994.

Lee, Harper. *To Kill a Mockingbird*. New York: Warner, Inc., 1960.

Luhrmann, Baz, Director. *Romeo +Juliet*. 1996.

Mack, Nancy. "The Ins, Outs, and In-Betweens of Multigenre Writing." *English Journal,* 92.2 (November 2002): 91–101.

Madden, John, Director. *Shakespeare in Love.* 1998.

Marzano, Robert J. *Classroom Instruction That Works: Research-Based Strategies for Increasing Student Achievement*. Alexandria, VA: Association for Supervision & Curriculum Development, 2001.

McKay, Claude. "If We Must Die." Poets.org– http://www.poets.org/viewmedia.php/prmMID/15250

Meeropol, Abel. "Strange Fruit." http://www.metascholar.org/MOSC/essays/meeropol.htm

Murphy, Jim. *An American Plague*. New York: Houghton Mifflin, 2003.

National Governors Association Center for Best Practices, Council of Chief State School Officers. *Common Core State Standards*. National Governors Association Center for Best Practices, Council of Chief State School Officers: Washington, DC, 2010.

The National Writing Project. http://www.nwp.org/

Newkirk, Thomas. *Holding On to Good Ideas in a Time of Bad Ones*. Portsmouth, NH: Heinemann, 2009.

Nin, Anaïs. *The Diary of Anais Nin*, Volume 3. Orlando, FL: Mariner Books, 1971.

Robbins, Jerome, and Robert Wise, Directors. *West Side Story.* 1961.

Romano, Tom. *Blending Genre, Altering Style*. Portsmouth, NH: Boynton/Cook, 2002.

Shapard, R., and J. Thomas, ed. *Sudden Fiction*. Salt Lake City, UT: Gibbs M. Smith, 1986.

Shakespeare, William. *Romeo and Juliet.*

Steinbeck, John. *Of Mice and Men*. New York: Penguin, 1993 edition.

Zeffirelli, Franco, Director. *Romeo and Juliet.* 1968.

8

Empowering English Language Learners: Moving Toward Competency as Speakers, Readers, and Writers

by Marie Milner

In her contributions to Chapters 4, 5, and 7, Marie Milner has shared a range of writing strategies that can be used successfully with all student writers. In this chapter, Marie highlights in greater depth the more daunting challenges English language learners face in the complex literacy of writing.

Introduction

Fear is the single most powerful obstacle to learning. Nowhere is this more apparent than in the English language learner. I have seen students embrace not only learning in general, but writing in particular when I've "lowered the affective filter" for my ELL students. In their work on language acquisition, Jim Cummins (1996) and Stephen Krashen (1982) describe the affective filter as the way in which stressful environments prevent students, particularly second language learners, from acquiring new skills and abilities. Testing situations create the highest anxiety. By definition, a test environment is stressful and increases the *affective filter*.

Developing writers do best in environments where they feel supported, engaged, validated, and respected. Because of this, I've created a "no testing environment" in my classes with English language learners. I teach in a school with a high percentage of English learners, along with a significant number of native speakers who are also considered "at risk for failure" because they read at about the fourth or fifth grade level. Both of these groups of students come into my classes with high anxiety levels. To help address my students' feelings of apprehension, I provide them with an enriched language environment where material is presented to them in multiple ways. I call this my "forget fast food—serve them a banquet" curriculum. ELLs bring so many unique and varied experiences to the classroom that it is insulting to teach them as if they are small children. Instead, they need multiple opportunities to build their language skills.

Academic Language Instruction: The Lessons of Robin Scarcella and Kate Kinsella

Both Robin Scarcella (2003) of the University of California at Irvine and Kate Kinsella (2009) of San Francisco State University have written and spoken extensively about the necessity of providing access to academic language for ELL students. Without it, they do not have access to the power they need to be successful. With these women as role models, I have learned to provide a framework within which my ELL students can more fearlessly access academic language.

Whether they are in mainstreamed or ESL classes, ELLs benefit through strategies that fit into three broad categories:

- Engagement in activities that lower the affective filter
- Exposure to extensive modeling
- Learning language conventions (grammar) through compelling content

Part I: Lowering the Affective Filter: Updating a Conventional Mythology Unit for ELLs

Classical mythology, which is often an opening unit in regular ninth grade English classes, is also one I use for my ELL classes, where students cover the grade level curriculum along with other special instruction. In teaching classical Western mythology, teachers can engage immigrant students by using parallel myths from their own cultures. The notion of the universality of human experience is a complex one, but I've found that my mythology unit helps my ELLs access this difficult concept.

For example, in reading Laurence Yep's *Child of the Owl* (1977), which contains an elaborate Chinese myth within Yep's larger story, my Vietnamese students see much of their own culture reflected because of the profound influence 1,000 years of Chinese rule continues to have on Vietnamese culture.

Since I teach my mythology unit at the beginning of the school year, we are well into the unit when Halloween rolls around. I make use of this quintessentially San Francisco Bay Area holiday by reviewing Halloween traditions and creating a word bank with terms describing Halloween costumes, practices, and treats. Students write a humorous story describing a Halloween party on Mt. Olympus, building on their knowledge of the Greco-Roman gods' and goddesses' amazing transformational powers, magical tools, and conflicted family relationships. These stories are read aloud for practice in speaking and listening comprehension.

Here is an excerpt from one of my ELL students' "Halloween on Mt. Olympus" story:

> *Artemis races across the sky, putting the [shining] moon up. Apollo leads his chariot and horses into his stables and changed into conductor clothes, ready to fill the halls of Olympus with music. Poseidon followed, rushing in like a tsunami, he appeared in a mermaid costume. [Hephaestus] marched into the room, clunking, in his Spock costume. Behind him followed his two assistants dressed as Star Trek look-alikes."*

—Nguyen Hoang, ninth grade

The stress level for ELL students naturally increases when they are asked to read in front of their peers, so I lower their anxiety level by reading their stories for them with energy and enthusiasm. I then ask students to comment on how well the students have incorporated their understanding of myth into their stories. The rule for this read-aloud activity, which I state clearly and reinforce frequently, is that the student audience may only comment positively on how well a given student's story has demonstrated a comprehension of mythology. As Stephen Krashen (1981) emphasizes, if a teacher wants an ELL to write authentically and engagingly about any topic, there are gentle ways of promoting Standard English usage while still validating and encouraging student voice. Thus, as I read the student stories aloud, I edit the non-Standard English in them. Because of this strategy, student writers hear the Standard English form while still having their creativity acknowledged. The students learn that I will not highlight their errors in written English, and that with each successive story-writing assignment they will be given another opportunity to "show off," rather than feel uncomfortable with their developing skills.

I tell my students that they have accumulated a vast knowledge of classical mythology by this point in the semester and that these stories are a chance not only to show off their knowledge, but also to make us laugh!

Before each read-aloud, I remind the classroom audience that they are already widely read mythology scholars. Now is their opportunity to show off by recognizing the allusions to mythology in their peers' stories. For example, consider a student story containing the line "Aphrodite come dressed as a which because she usually so beautiful," which I would have read as "Aphrodite came dressed as a witch because she is usually so beautiful." At the end of the read-aloud, a fellow "scholar of mythology" in the classroom might remark that "Jose remembered that Aphrodite is the goddess of beauty as well as love, so it is ironic that she would come as a witch." I acknowledge both the student scholar and the writer for his or her extensive mythological expertise.

On these Halloween/Mt. Olympus days everybody wins. The students are afforded a chance to be validated and enjoy writing creatively. They review the content of mythology in a non-threatening way, and their creative and humorous intelligence is rewarded. I can also model reading aloud with passionate emphasis, validating and supporting other peoples' talents and efforts, and utilize Standard English conventions with my at-the-moment read-aloud revisions of my students' narratives.

As December approaches, the class brainstorms regarding the various holidays that are celebrated in different cultures at this time, and I give students a broader choice to write a story imagining the gods and goddesses of Mt. Olympus celebrating any holiday they choose. Since we will have completed another work of literature at that point, perhaps *Romeo and Juliet*, I ask the students to imagine a holiday story in which the Greek and Roman gods and goddesses have invited a couple of characters from that work of literature to attend their holiday party.

My students' stories become more sophisticated as the unit proceeds. The students strive to impress and outdo one another with how well they can blend their understanding of the content and purposes of myth with the world in which they live. They often use contemporary humor in their stories, and I encourage them to do so, validating their use of topical allusions.

These stories, in which different cultures and traditions are intermingled, may be adapted to any unit. For example, I've asked my students to write about how Casey Young, the protagonist in *Child of the Owl*, would react as a new student in our high school. This narrative assignment encourages student voice, lowers the affective filter, and my reading of these stories frees students from the dread of being called upon to read their own stories aloud.

Adding Orality to the Mix: The Mythology Talk-Show Panel

Almost everybody likes to play "dress up," and English language learners are no exception. A number of years ago, I began asking my mainstreamed ELL students to participate in a panel of gods and goddesses. I wanted to help them become engaged in their study of classical mythology while also practicing their oral language skills.

A couple of weeks into our mythology unit, I explain that we will present a panel of gods and goddesses in another teacher's classroom, but that we will take several weeks to prepare. I lay out our task. While I am to become their "talk show host," they are to become experts on one particular mythological figure. In this visit from "Mt. Olympus" to "Earth," I will be interviewing them in character. Since the interview will not be scripted or rehearsed, they need not worry about forgetting their lines. We will have many practice interviews beforehand, so they will feel confident on the day of their visit. Kate Kinsella's notion of sentence starters is applicable here. Students practice responding to my impromptu questions with sentence starters such as, "My powers are many because I can . . ." or "I know I am the most important of the Greek gods because. . . ."

The students help each other build costumes and prop banks. What has always impressed me is how little encouragment it takes from me for students to bring props in for one another in preparation for these mythology talk shows. My classroom soon becomes filled with aluminum foil-covered tridents, shields, crowns, and daggers.

My students begin the process of choosing a mythological character with a quick-write: *If you could be any Greek or Roman mythological character, who would you be and why?* We start the oral practice sessions slowly in order to build student confidence. Over a few classroom meetings, two or three students at a time sit together in front of the class, while the other students and I take turns asking questions. A sample dialogue might run as follows:

Teacher: Zeus, where are your brothers today?
Student: Hades is at home in the Underworld, and I think Poseidon is still in his home. Why?
Teacher: I may need Poseidon's help if I'm going to sail today.
Student: Oh, he's in a bad mood. I think he lost his trident!
Teacher: Do you get along with your brother?
Student: I suppose so, but I know I am the most important of the Greek gods because after all, I am the King of the Gods and Lord of the Skies. What could be more important?

Most students easily slip into character, and the stress seems to slide off their shoulders. For my end of the bargain, I generally ask one of the teachers with a class of predominately ELL students if we may present our mythology talk show to his or her class.

I've never had a negative experience with this activity. If a particular student does not attend class on performance day, all is not lost because there are no scripted roles or rehearsed dialogues. The students in the classrooms we visit have been consistently attentive and supportive of my students. The fact that they are all English language learners seems to lower everyone's stress level, including mine!

A day or so after the completion of the mythological panel classroom visit, the students reflect on their experiences. When they do so, most students state how easily they overcame their initial anxieties once the interviews were underway. I also write a letter to the students, complimenting them on their performances and acknowledging the courage it took for many of them to speak before an audience of their peers when their own command of spoken English is still developing.

Students follow up this activity with a letter of recommendation, akin to those I write for students applying to college, for the character they have just finished role-playing. An excerpted letter from an ELL student follows.

Dear Mr. Pawlikowski:

I am writing this letter to inform you that I think my student, Poseidon C. Oshin, would be a great fit at the University of California, San Diego. In particular, I would recommend Poseidon for the marine biology program. He has always shown a love for learning about sea creatures and is very knowledgeable about them. I definitely noticed this while he was in my class, which is an AP Biology course. Whenever the class would write essays, Poseidon would surprise us with things even I didn't know.

Sincerely,

—Robert Zalog, ninth grade student

The theatrical aspects of this assignment, with its focus on developing confidence in oral presentations on one's chosen character, thoroughly engage students and subsequently elicit passionate and authentic writing.

Part II: Modeling Multi-Paragraph Essays with ELL Students

Robin Scarcella argues that ELLs are often not given enough basic academic language to prepare them for working at a college or university level. She believes that the language acquisition strategies espoused by Stephen Krashen and Jim Cummins must be balanced with rigorous exposure to academic language and conventions. Having witnessed the frustrations and obstacles ELLs encounter when academic language is essentially dismissed in favor of "fun" activities meant to lower student anxiety, I could not agree more.

ELLs are expected to write formally and academically, and they are frequently expected to generate such writing "on demand," even as they struggle to acquire preliminary English language skills. Expository or informational writing is the genre most often required at the college level, and is the skill most frequently evaluated on national assessments. Additionally, the Common Core State Standards (CCSS) place an increased emphasis on expository and informational writing. Knowing the fears English language learners harbor regarding such writing assignments, I try to demystify this genre for them by extensive modeling. Far from robbing their writing of passion, modeling strong academic writing for ELLs provides them with the security afforded by any scaffolded material. When the conventions of academic writing are revealed to them, they begin to develop their own strong writing voices.

In my regular English classes, I always model an entire, full-length formal essay toward the beginning of the school year. However, with my ELL classes, I model essays periodically throughout the entire academic year. My ELL students generally write shorter papers than students in my regular English classes, so it takes a few class sessions for us to write a multi-paragraph essay.

The students understand that on the third day of this essay-writing unit, they will be asked to write their own multi-paragraph essay. Student anxiety level is lessened, however, because they know they can use the essay we wrote together as a model, and the topic of their essay will be closely related to it. For example, if we have written together during a mythology unit about which *goddesses* we find to be the most powerful, the students might later write about which *gods* they find most powerful. As the students' English language skills develop over the course of the year, they take on more complex and varied topics. My long-term goal is for students to be able to develop their own topics. In what follows, I describe an essay writing activity that is highly adaptable to a wide range of classroom situations.

Todd Rafalovich

Marie Milner

Beginning with a very broad topic such as "gods and goddesses," we narrow it down to something like "goddesses who would be powerful in today's world." We review the basic structure of a multi-paragraph essay, as I write a skeleton version of one on the board. The model is not limited to the conventional five-paragraph essay "formula," although the structure I use shows students that an essay contains certain components and conventions. I resist following any one scripted or formulaic writing program because I don't want to deaden my students' prose or restrict their ideas.

We use a variety of pre-writing activities such as mapping or clustering to demystify the writing process. Sometimes we complete a traditional outline together. We then review the conventional elements of an essay introduction such as an attention-grabbing opener or "hook," background or contextual information, and a clear thesis, assertion, or claim.

I also explain that the purpose of body paragraphs is to contain supporting evidence for the writer's thesis, while commenting on the significance of that evidence, and the function of concluding paragraphs is generally to restate a paper's thesis while summarizing and commenting on some of its central ideas. I reiterate the importance of ending the essay with a powerful closing statement. The concluding paragraph is one that often challenges fluent English speakers, so powerful models are especially critical for the ELL student. For them, the fatigue that accompanies their struggle to be expressive in a second or subsequent language may partly explain why their essays lose steam when they reach their conclusions.

To start, the class offers a variety of opening "hooks" or "grabbers" until the students collectively choose one they prefer. At the beginning of the year, this step is especially intimidating, so students benefit from explicit models. Some of these might include provocative questions, startling statements, anecdotes, or relevant quotations.

Developing a strong opener with students is not sufficient, however. They need explicit instruction in how to incorporate the opener into the rest of the introductory paragraph, so that they don't merely have an out-of-place attention grabber. I show them how to blend their grabber with the upcoming background information. For example, we might collectively compose, following a hook that classical Greek and Roman myths have had a profound impact on much of Western culture, something about the origins of myth in general. Students then copy the opening sentence and the rest of the opening paragraph from the board, or from the document camera.

The class then reviews the content that needs to go into the background portion of an essay's introduction. With an essay about the Greek and Roman goddesses, students learn to focus on the era in which these stories were created and by whom and for what purpose. As we compose our essay, students offer ideas, phrases, and whole sentences, and I model how to construct them using "Standard" English language conventions.

Together we review the purpose of a well-written thesis statement and then convert our essay topic into one. In writing about the powerful Greek and Roman goddesses we might develop a thesis that states, "Sometimes the Greek and Roman gods are deemed the most powerful, but the goddesses wield an incredible amount of power as well."

Moving on to body paragraphs, students learn to construct focused topic sentences while providing strong evidence for their thesis statement. We revisit the conventional structure of a body paragraph, which includes contextualizing or introducing evidence, such as why Aphrodite is such a powerful entity because of her role as goddess of love and beauty. I enjoy playing the "Why?" or "So what?" role with students as we practice providing meaningful commentary. As we continue to compose, I review the following literacy skills: using appropriate academic language, sentence variety, punctuation for clarity, and transitions that help readers follow the flow of the writer's thoughts. Additionally, I model the value of reading back through their initial paragraphs in order to ascertain "flow" and do early revision, drawing attention to those revisions that will improve the coherence of the text.

In the concluding paragraph, my ELL students' essays always decline in power; therefore, when I model essays with them, we spend a great deal of time on this paragraph, reiterating its importance and discussing ways to impress our readers with our *grand finale.* As we compose a concluding paragraph together, students are reminded to somehow refer to their hook or grabber and then restate the thesis statement. If the students are writing about a specific piece of literature, they can easily conclude their essay with a discussion of the work's themes, but with the essay about goddesses they can also easily anticipate their readers' needs with comments that answer general questions or deflect criticism. For example, we might write about why freshmen in a typical English class would be reading and writing about Greek mythological characters 3,000 years after their creation.

When we have completed this "class essay," which students have copied as it has developed on the dry erase board or projection screen, we proofread it together. I read aloud, stopping at specific points to see if students can identify the steps we took and the choices we made as we composed. I might point out a transitional sentence and ask students to identify it as such or ask them to restate the important contextual components in our introductory paragraph. I might also review the importance of the topic sentence in a body paragraph, emphasizing the role it plays in focusing the reader's attention. I reiterate the importance of providing thoughtful commentary rather than simple summary in body paragraphs and emphasize the necessity of a powerful conclusion. I also emphasize the need to proofread one's work aloud in order to "hear" errors. I collect the model essays once we have completed them, and award nominal points for student completion and participation.

Why a Handwritten Copy? Why Model at All?

Since students will have physically written the essay in class as we composed it, they will now have a copy of it in their own handwriting to use later as a model for their individual papers. Recent neurological studies suggest that having students physically copy the modeled essay helps hard-wire the language structures and patterns into their brains. I've witnessed this to a significant degree in my own classroom; I often see a marked improvement in the next written essay my students submit after copying down a modeled essay.

This modeling strategy allows students to internalize the various language patterns and structures that are being modeled. The clear advantage of having the teacher model the essay, by writing it longhand using a document camera or typing it using an LCD projector, is that students and teachers can revise and edit the essay as they compose. This process allows the teacher to emphasize the importance of revision and editing to the overall writing process, and instills in students the writing habits that will make them more likely to be successful in completing their writing assignments as they move from high school to college.

Part III: Refining Language Conventions (Grammar)
Through Compelling Content

Mythology has built-in appeal; however, most students fail to dance a little jig of happiness when the subject of grammar is broached. I'd wager the average teacher of grammar units does not dance one, either. A number of years ago, however, I inadvertently discovered a highly motivating way to teach ELLs how to improve their writing with sentence variety (i.e., compound and complex sentences). While I generally stand on the shoulders of giants in my liberal borrowing from the best practices of the best teachers with whom I've worked, this particular unit—using primatology (the scientific study of primates) to teach sentence variety—is unique to my classroom.

I love literature with all my heart, but I also have a profound passion for primatology, having once imagined myself heir to such respected primatologists as Jane Goodall, Dian Fossey, and Francine "Penny" Patterson. Because I bring this excitement to the grammar unit, I have had great success with it.

Although most English teachers might not share my enthusiasm for primates, the unit is adaptable to other areas of teacher and student fascination. Once teachers determine an area of high interest to themselves and their students, the unit can proceed from there. Since the Common Core emphasizes writing across the curriculum, this unit could also be team-taught by a language arts teacher and a teacher from another subject area.

Why Primates? A Rationale

About 20 years ago, I was teaching a summer school Language Arts class comprised of English language learners who were trying to pass a state-mandated writing exam. These summer school students had some English abilities, having been in the United States for at least a few years, but the great number of mechanical errors they made in their writing made it unlikely that they would pass the test. Chief among those errors were run-on sentences and sentence fragments.

Having long believed that a whole language approach to grammar is best, I told the students that I could help them improve their writing by teaching them "sentence variety." This approach is less punitive than informing students that they must *fix* their run-on sentences by learning about compound sentences or *solve* their sentence fragment *problem* by studying complex sentences.

Late on a Friday afternoon, as class was winding down during one of the early weeks of summer school, I casually broached the topic of Koko, a lowland gorilla who had been taught American Sign Language. Having studied sign language along with primatology, I continued to be intrigued by the study and wanted, just for fun, to share some news of Koko with my students. Soon I found a classroom full of engaged students. The room had that electrified air recognizable to anyone who loves teaching. The more I discussed Koko, the faster the questions flew at me. Then the questions grew in sophistication. Was Koko a monkey or an ape? How could a gorilla learn sign language? What exactly is sign language?

I then had one of those teaching epiphanies. I realized I could employ the students' newfound fascination with Koko to review the grammar we had begun working on in class. I went to the chalkboard and wrote, "Koko is an ape, for she has no tail." I also wrote "Gorillas are not violent by nature, for they are vegetarian," since I knew that information always stuns and intrigues students. We also utilized a variety of resources, including Koko's official website (http://www.koko.org) and Nigel Cole's 1982 movie, *A Conversation with Koko*, for additional information to write about.

Over the next several years, I earned the reputation of "gorilla lady" at my high school, filling my classroom with primate-themed gifts from students who had obviously enjoyed this unit. What follows is this unit's basic structure, which generally takes six weeks to complete.

First, my students take a pre-quiz about general primate topics. This activity generates a great many dismayed stares. A sample question to pique their interest might be, "What animal besides a human being can use sign language?" Another might be, "What does a gorilla eat, and for how many hours a day does he eat?" (Seven hours of chomping on mostly grass and leaves!)

We subsequently discuss the answers to the quiz questions, and I whet the students' appetites with primate pictures from my vast collection. Student engagement is evident with statements such as "Oh, I wondered why you had so many gorilla and monkey toys in your classroom." Once the excitement has been generated, I tell the students that we are going to be learning more about primates as we practice some sentence variety. No one has ever protested, and I feel this is a direct result of using a topic with broad student and teacher interest.

We begin by watching the National Geographic documentary *Gorilla* issued in 1998. Each class watches the entire film, quietly attentive to the animal science information being presented in the documentary. I pause the film periodically to comment and clarify. Students' eyes are riveted on the screen, as they whisper knowing comments to each other such as, "That's just like Koko in the other movie!"

The students have several days to complete this writing assignment. I have them underline all of the *coordinating conjunctions* in their paper, so that I can tell if they are grasping sentence coordination or just randomly underlining words such as *for* as a preposition, or *and* when used in a list. Since some of the students are at first puzzled by how to *respond* to a film, we brainstorm ideas in the form of questions. "Did you learn anything from this film?" "Did any one part really capture your imagination?" "Would other people in your life enjoy the film?" "What would your science teacher say if she knew you had watched this film in your English class?"

To validate ELL student learning and to give them practice using academic language, I have each student share aloud what he or she learned from or enjoyed about the film. This brief oral practice offers early preparation for upcoming group presentations in class about a particular primate topic. This student talk also facilitates subsequent writing about primates.

Complex Sentences—More Primate Excitement!

Eventually, I introduce complex sentences, building on my students' schema of compound sentences and examining the similarities and differences between the two grammatical structures. I use the same strategies I did when teaching compound sentences, but with some variations in instruction and assignments. Two students might compose complex sentences together, writing their sentences on the board so the class can review them aloud. To keep the emphasis on content and grammar in context, we always evaluate these sentences first with respect to their scientific accuracy. I might say, "Hmmm. Tuan's sentence says, 'Chimpanzees are not monkeys because they have no tails.' Is that true? Are chimps, in fact, apes?" Once the students have acknowledged that, indeed, chimpanzees are apes rather than monkeys, I will proceed to examine the accuracy of the grammar in the sentence.

As the unit progresses, and the students' knowledge of primates increases, the writing topics become more complex and the students have more choice in their assignments. At some point the students start employing compound, complex, and compound-complex sentences to discuss such topics as the similarities and differences among primates, as well as the similarities between humans and other primates.

An Oral Presentation—Science, Grammar, and "Chat" in the English Class

To facilitate my ELLs' oral language skills, I assign a presentation based on the primatology they have been studying. For this presentation, students are expected to do independent research as well as review what the class has learned together. I generally have the students present with a partner or on a panel, lowering my students' anxieties about oral presentations. In order to further lower their anxieties, my students use a visual aid in the form of a student-created poster and refer to its pictures or text when they feel the need. This visual aid also proves valuable in facilitating the learning of the classroom audience.

Once the students have given their presentations, they write about their experience doing so. I also ask the audience members to write about what new information they acquired from each of the presentations. In doing so, I continue to ask students to underline the coordinating and subordinating conjunctions in their writing to reinforce their acquired knowledge and allow me to ascertain their developing grasp of sentence variety.

In this unit's final assignment, students reflect on the value of having learned some language conventions in conjunction with an animal science unit. Students may quick-write in class and then pair-share before going home to formally complete this assignment.

At the end of the school year, as a culminating activity, I have my students reflect on their growth throughout the year. I am always touched by how frequently students write about the primatology/sentence variety unit. If I've played my monkey and ape cards right, that final paper is also filled with sophisticated sentence variety, and there is rarely a run-on sentence or inappropriate fragment in sight. I do, of course, always enjoy those *appropriate* sentence fragments such as, "Gotta love that Koko!"

Some Reflection—Fearless (Almost) ELL Strategies

Learning another language is always challenging, but it should never be threatening. Learning to write well in any language is also a challenge, but it should be something that students look forward to rather than dread. In my classrooms, I strive to lower the students' anxiety level with various strategies so that writing and speaking will become something that empowers them. Over the past 20 years, the assignments and activities I've described in this chapter have gone a long way toward my goal of engendering passionate writing from my beloved ELLs.

References and Resources

Cole, Nigel, Director. *A Conversation with Koko.* 1982.

Cummins, Jim. *Negotiating identities: Education for empowerment in a diverse society.* Los Angeles, CA: California Association for Bilingual Education, 1996.

Kinsella, Kate. http://www.sccoe.k12.ca.us/depts/ell/kinsella.asp

Koko. http://www.koko.org

Krashen, Stephen. "The Fundamental Pedagogical Principle in Second Language Teaching." *Studia Linguistica,* 1981.

Krashen, Stephen. *Principles and Practice in Second Language Acquisition.* Oxford, Oxfordshire: Pergamon Press, 1982.

National Geographic. Gorilla. VHS, 1998.

Scarcella, Robin C. *Accelerating Academic English: A Focus on the English Learner.* Berkeley, CA: Regents of the University of California, 2003.

Yep, Laurence. *Child of the Owl.* New York: Harper Collins Publishers, 1977.

9

Practical Guidelines for Portfolios: Promoting Qualitative Assessment in a Test-Prep Climate

by Suzanne Murphy, Amy Thompson, and Kathleen González

Introduction

Throughout this book, the teacher-authors have reiterated that the best student writing is engaging, authentic, and comprehensive—longer than the short-answer type essay required for standardized tests or benchmark exams. They have advocated for writing-infused curricula, shared assignments, and student samples to support the kinds of writing that build students' stamina for writing. When students do substantive writing, they validate writing as a process; portfolios provide the opportunity for students to get much deserved feedback and to reflect on their progress. While the concept of portfolio keeping has been well established, in this era of assessment, many teachers find their time and energy diverted instead to test preparation.

Sadly, teachers have begun putting aside this powerful tool for student reflection and documentation of growth just when the Common Core State Standards (CCSS) call for learning to spiral upwards through grade levels. In *Pathways to the Common Core*, Lucy Calkins, Mary Ehrenworth, and Christopher Lehman (2012) write, "[T]eachers need to study student work, taking cues from instances when student writing improves and instances when it does not" (157).

Further, the CCSS explicitly call for student writing to cross the subject areas and for content area teachers to engage students in writing consistently to demonstrate learning. Even more important, student writers need to engage in the three writing types: narrative, persuasive, and informational. Portfolios afford students opportunities to apply writing skills and the writing process in all three types of writing as well as in a variety of subject areas.

This chapter highlights the ways portfolios can and do specifically answer the demands of assessment, providing qualitative, substantive, and essential evidence of the ways students can learn the comprehensive literacy of writing. Because of the validity portfolios give to the consistency of students' writing using the stages of the writing process and providing opportunities for reflection, they provide essential daily nutrients to promote a passion for writing. In Part I of this chapter, Suzanne Murphy and Amy Thompson describe the ways they use portfolios in middle school, including for student-led conferences. In Part II, Kathleen González offers a detailed guide to the portfolio process in high school, with particular emphasis on helping students become active participants in their own learning.

Part I: The Case for Portfolio Practice with Middle School Students
by Suzanne Murphy and Amy Thompson

In this era of assessment, we want our students to write often and to move beyond writing only for tests. We want them to reflect on their growth and be able to see that building their writing stamina is valuable. Donald Graves, author of *Writing: Teachers and Children at Work* (1983), has commented that students must return or revisit their writing for it to be worth doing. Portfolios can be a collection site for writing in process, affording students access to material for further revision, new directions, or other stages in the writing process.

In middle school, students write widely and variously; therefore, middle school is the appropriate time and place to initiate the portfolio process. The biggest challenge is the sheer mass of paper that can accumulate. What is the best way to organize it—by subject area? Grading period? Does every draft for a writing piece or project need to be in the portfolio? What about assignments that may not easily fit into a typical file folder? While electronic files can help to store student work, the writing process needs documentation in drafts reflecting the actual revisions and editing. The "hard copy" that contains teacher or peer feedback and actual changes in revision plays a critical role in helping students practice and master writing skills.

The number of guides for setting up portfolios attests to the validity of this method for tracking writing progress. A quick Google search on "portfolios and middle school students" yields over three million sites; however, many of these sites were created prior to the era of assessment. While educational research consistently supports portfolio keeping, and students consistently understand their value as well, learning how to manage portfolio keeping can pose a real challenge.

Four Ways Suzanne Murphy Uses Portfolios

I offer the following four ways that teachers can use portfolio keeping in their classrooms

- For students' works in progress
- As evidence for student-led conferences

- As material for parent communication
- As a reflection on students' own learning

Since my students produce a variety of writing—from drafts of theme essays, character sketches, and poetry to shorter works like word study paragraphs and literature responses—they simply do not have the room to store all the different "texts" they need to have at hand in the daily writing workshop. I provide easily accessible portfolio "bins" for students to keep works-in-progress, evidence for student-led conferences, parent communication, and reflective pieces. These portfolio bins or storage crates contain alphabetically labeled hanging folders housing assessed pieces as well as a manila file folder (identified as the "working file") holding all writing at some stage of the process. Students use a Writing Record (see Table 9.1) to keep track of anything they put into their portfolio. When we have a writing conference, students bring the working file with in-process pieces as well as the record of individual writing goals. The portfolios are open (for parents and teachers in other subject areas) and are available to assist in IEP and ILP meetings.

TABLE 9.1 *Student Writing Record*

Name:			Grade:	
No.	**Name**	**Genre**	**Date Completed**	**Writing Goal**

Although the purpose of the collection is primarily to document writing progress, students also include artwork, writing from across the curriculum, and material from non-academic activities (such as a service learning experience) in the hanging file folder. For projects too large to fit into the hanging file, students create a photo study of their work. Since the original intent of a portfolio is to create a portable collection of work, students can use their imagination to document larger pieces.

Because the workshop process takes place exclusively within the classroom, students use their portfolios to store all writing. Post-assessment writing does go home for students to format for larger audiences. This step allows students to practice word processing skills and to prepare selections to post in class newsletters or on hallway bulletin boards for public viewing.

Student-Led Conferences

At our school during November, students make a presentation to their parents and teacher in a student-led conference. During this time, they show evidence of what they have learned in their subject areas to that point and write realistic and measurable goals for the remainder of the year. The portfolio plays an important part in the students' preparation for the conferences because they draw the concrete evidence to support their assessment of their learning from their portfolios, as well as information to help them focus on their goals.

Table 9.2 shows the form that students use to get organized for the conference. The actual worksheet is printed in landscape orientation on 8 × 11.5 paper.

An additional way that students use their portfolios to consider their academic progress is by choosing a piece to share with their parents, guardians, or a responsible adult. Students can choose any piece, any genre—in any stage of writing—and write a short reflection about it. The reflection can include why they wrote it, what they learned from the writing (including content and writing skills), and what prompted them to choose the particular piece. Students then take the writing and reflection home to a parent or significant adult who reads the piece and writes a response. This process, occurring periodically throughout the year, is designed to encourage students to share what they write with an audience outside the school walls, and it does a better job than mid-term progress reports of showing parents what their students are doing in class. The Parent Response Forms, along with the student writing and reflection, are put in the portfolio. See Tables 9.3 and 9.4 for examples.

TABLE 9.2 *Getting Organized for Your Conference*

Directions: As a successful student, think about the strategies, processes, activities, and interesting things you have learned this quarter. List your ideas on the following planner and highlight the three to four in each subject area that are most important to you. Use this planner to share with your parents what you've learned this quarter and to write your education goals for this year.		
Math	**Reading/Writing**	**P.E.**
Social Studies	**Science**	**Spanish**

TABLE 9.3   *Student Reflection on a Writing Selection*

Student Name: _____

Name of Writing Piece: _____

Assessed _____ Draft _____

My writing purpose

_____

_____

_____

What I did well

_____

_____

_____

My writing goal for the next writing piece

_____

_____

_____

_____

Date: _____

TABLE 9.4   *Parent Response Form*

Student Name: _____

Name of Writing Piece: _____

Writing Genre: _____

What did you enjoy most about this writing piece?

_____

_____

_____

_____

What do you think the writer should work on in the next writing experience?

_____

_____

_____

_____

Date: _____

Parent Name and Signature: _____

Digital Portfolios

If the classroom technology allows, students can store their work on CD/DVD or flash-drives. Electronic portfolios can hold media as well as written text within a small physical space; students can also collect iMovies, videos, and photographs in e-portfolios.

Another advantage of technology is the possibilities it presents for the writing process itself. When a student submits an electronic copy for teacher feedback, the teacher can highlight areas for revision or editing on the screen. This helps make student-teacher writing conferences more collaborative.

By the end of the year, students generally have a large collection of work to review as they reflect on their learning and how they have met grade level expectations. Using a graphic organizer and a copy of the Common Core State Standards for their grade level, students write reflections in their own words about how they've achieved each standard. When they complete the organizer, students search their portfolios for evidence that demonstrates their learning in each standard. Through this process, students discover their successes in writing and the breadth and depth of their writing growth, ultimately describing these successes in a summary for the portfolio.

Using Portfolios for Student-Led Conferences— Amy Thompson

> *The portfolio was good because it gave me a good idea of what I've accomplished this year. Also, practicing the portfolio presentation gave me a good idea of how to arrange portfolios. What you should put in them, and what to expect from them. The portfolio is a good thing to keep because it can show your progress in one school year, and it can encourage you to keep doing better.*
>
> —Sara M., eighth grade

Sara's experience reviewing and organizing her portfolio is one of the reasons I find the student-led conference so valuable. Student-led conferences are a way to have students take responsibility for their own learning. They organize and arrange their work in portfolios, write goals for the rest of the year and in anticipation of moving on to high school, and present these to their parents during Open House. Isabel's experience shows how valuable this process is, and even indicates how the portfolio has changed her parents' perceptions of her.

> *Sharing anything with my parents isn't as easy for me as it sounds. I get scared and I never do share and they don't even care because I had to force my mom to go to Open House. Thanks to the goals sheet my mom now knows that I really want to get into college so I can prove that I'm not stupid like they call me.*

When I began teaching middle school, I noticed that many parents consider Open House a wonderful time for a mini-teacher conference regarding their child. Although I knew better, I got sucked into speaking with the most insistent parents and failed to touch base with others. In an effort to find a way for more parents to connect more with their child's learning and academic performance, I went to the California League of Middle

Schools Conference (CLMS) and learned about student-led conferences. Carol Smith's article, "Assessing and Reporting Progress Through Student-Led Portfolio Conferences," on the National Middle School Association's website and the book, *A School-Wide Approach to Student-Led Conferences* (Kinney, Munroe, and Sessions, 2000) provide a fuller description of these conferences.

The first year that I held student-led conferences, students shared work only from the courses I taught in social studies and language arts. The following year I asked my math and science teammates to contribute. Ultimately, we added P.E. evaluations. A sample of the Physical Education Student/Teacher Evaluation Form (Table 9.5) shows how it can

TABLE 9.5 *Physical Education Student/Teacher Evaluation*

Level of cooperation with other students:						
Student	1	2	3	4	5	6
Teacher	1	2	3	4	5	6
Effort (participating to the best of one's ability):						
Student	1	2	3	4	5	6
Teacher	1	2	3	4	5	6
Absences made up:						
Student	1	2	3	4	5	6
Teacher	1	2	3	4	5	6
Level of honesty and fair play (sportsmanship):						
Student	1	2	3	4	5	6
Teacher	1	2	3	4	5	6
On time to class and on assigned attendance number:						
Student	1	2	3	4	5	6
Teacher	1	2	3	4	5	6
Transitions between activities:						
Student	1	2	3	4	5	6
Teacher	1	2	3	4	5	6
Listening skills/Following directions:						
Student	1	2	3	4	5	6
Teacher	1	2	3	4	5	6
Golden Rule: **Do I treat others the way I would like to be treated?**						
Student	1	2	3	4	5	6
Teacher	1	2	3	4	5	6

Name: _____   Date: _____

PE Period: _____   PE Teacher: _____

Core Teacher: _____

be used in the student-led conference and offers a good example of portfolio entries from across the disciplines.

At our school, every student has a "portfolio" made up of at least two file folders. One is designated for language arts and kept in the language arts classroom; the other is for mathematics and is kept in the students' math class. District assessments follow students from year to year, so assessments from sixth and seventh grade language arts and mathematics are also in their portfolios. In my eighth grade language arts and social studies core, I select at least one assignment for students to put in their portfolios as we end each unit. Students are also asked to select at least one assignment to include. I suggest that they either select assignments they worked hard on and are proud of or something they did very poorly on that they know they will improve on in the future. This simple act of reflection makes a difference for students. Instead of asking, "How will this help me?" students ask, "Is this going in my portfolio?"

I make an exception during the first social studies unit of the year. After the first unit is completed, I have students file the entire unit so that they can use any part of it as a comparison later in the year. I also file "kudos" [awards] if students have earned special recognition for an assignment or behavior.

During the week before Open House, I talk with the science and math teachers to get their list of required assignments for the student-led conferences. Then in class, students take their portfolios and look over everything they have accumulated. They talk and share as they rediscover work that they had forgotten. They are consistently amazed at the growth they have already made, as Spencer's comments indicate:

> *I have gotten a lot better academically. I also like to see how much I have improved over my three years I really like reviewing my portfolio because I get to see what I did badly, and what I did well. Looking at the writing assessments I have taken I have definitely improved on my work since sixth grade. I have expanded my vocabulary and also showed that I can use thesis statements.*

—Spencer M.

Todd Rafalovich

Amy Thompson

Once students have had a few minutes to look through their portfolios from my class, I pass out a table of contents sheet (see Table 9.6). I fill out the required parts on a transparency so that students can copy these onto their table of contents page. The first year that multiple teachers used student-led conferences, each teacher required one portfolio piece from each unit taught since the beginning of the year. However, in time we learned that a more manageable number is a total of two to three pieces per subject. Generally, each subject has two required teacher-selected submissions and one piece of the student's choosing. The organizing, culling, and selecting of pieces from language arts and social studies classes take one 50-minute class period.

In my social studies class, I usually require one set of notes from a social studies unit from the beginning of the year and one recent set, showing how students have improved in their organization and note-taking abilities. I also require a test or culminating project. Initially, I wanted parents to see the content students had learned; however, I've realized that showcasing work from a variety of learning modalities is more valuable for students and parents. I select notes, essay tests, individual projects, timelines, and graphs so that students and parents can see which

TABLE 9.6 *Table of Contents*

Student-Led Conferences: Union Middle School
Name _____
• Dear Parent Letter
• Language Arts
_____
_____
• Social Studies
_____
_____
• Science
_____
_____
• Math
_____
_____
• Science
_____
• P.E.
• Goals for Success
• Parent/Guardian Homework

types of assignments most challenging. From language arts, I require students to include one of the district's quarterly on-demand writing assessments as well as drafts and a final piece that has gone through the writing process. In addition, students are encouraged to select at least one other piece from each subject area to include in their portfolio.

I tell the students that they will be sharing this portfolio with their parents during Open House and that this conference presentation is a requirement. Students fill out a self-evaluation for their physical education classes. The physical education teachers then put their evaluations alongside the students'—this evaluation (Table 9.5) is a required part of the conference.

For homework, students use a handout to help them write a letter to their parents, describing honestly and specifically their progress so far. Table 9.7 provides the outline students complete.

During the next class period, students add work from their math and science portfolios. We also talk about the order in which they would like to share the contents with their parents. I suggest that students start and end with their strongest classes. This is a graded presentation, and they need to present their work in the most professional manner possible, using clear communication skills.

Next, I demonstrate how to make a formal introduction. I tell students that although I have met many of their parents, I don't usually remember their names, and I don't want to embarrass myself by calling them by an incorrect name. I write the introduction on the board so that students can practice it and know where to look for it on the night of the Open House. The script for the introductions follows:

_____, I'd like you to meet my social studies/language arts teacher Mrs. Thompson. Mrs. Thompson, I'd like you to meet my_____, Mr./Mrs. _____.

Students select a partner to role-play their parent as they do a "dry run" of the student-led conference. The practice usually takes one 50-minute class period. The following day, the entire class goes outside, and each lines up with a "parent." As each pair comes the classroom door, the "students" introduce me to their "parents." invite their "parents" to a desk, get out their portfolios, and start practicing their conferences. As the first students finish their presentations, they line up again and switch roles.

Inevitably, one student feigns outrage at some piece of work and starts to "yell" at his or her "student." I excuse myself from the doorway, calmly walk to the "concerned parent," and say, "I so appreciate you being here for your son or daughter's presentation. I'm not sure if you know it, but students are receiving a grade for how well they do on this presentation. He or she has worked hard to be able to explain this to you and get the best grade he or she can. If you still have questions at the end of the presentation, I'd be happy to schedule a conference with you both." This never fails to get everyone's attention during practice, and someone will always ask if I will really do that during Open House; I assure them that I will.

The other inevitable question is, "What if my parents can't come to Open House?" The student-led conference is a class requirement. If their parents can't attend, I will have "stunt parents" available. To do this, I ask my family, board members, and even high school students to be ready during Open House. Students who don't show up themselves are surprised to be called to the office during class time the following day to present their portfolios to the principal, vice-principal, or even the counselor.

TABLE 9.7 *Goal Setting*

Name _____

My strengths are:
- •
- •
- •

I need to work on:
- •
- •
- •

First Goal _____

_____

To achieve this goal, I will

1. _____

2. _____

Second Goal _____

_____

To achieve this goal, I will

1. _____

2. _____

Third Goal _____

_____

To achieve this goal, I will

1. _____

2. _____

People who can help me attain these goals are:

Distractions that may get in the way of accomplishing these goals are:

As a rule, students may not take their portfolios home; however, I make exceptions and allow students who can't attend Open House to take their portfolio home, present it to their parents, and return it the next day.

Students are often anxious about their conference because it is more stressful than being in front of the class. However, the anxiety is quickly replaced by confidence as they share what they have learned and ways they can improve. All our preparation helps students present their academic work in a way that is empowering.

The student-led conference is a great exercise in formal presentations for students, and everyone who does the presentation receives the same number of points. The part I focus on is the letter that they have written to me, which is the last piece in the portfolios.

A letter to parents shows how they, too, can become involved in writing as they support their children by responding to the student-led conferences. Students love the idea that their parents have a homework assignment.

Parents are appreciative of a more personal Open House experience. They are shown not only what their students have done, but also how well they do on a variety of academic tasks. They better understand how their child uses time in school, and they become a part of the goal setting for how to help students improve their skills.

The middle school portfolio can be shaped into whatever form serves the unique requirements of any classroom. Whether it contains showcase materials for formal presentations, in-process work for writing workshop, or demonstrations of growth across the curriculum areas, it should be, as my student Sara so aptly puts it, *"a good thing to keep because it can show your progress."*

Part II: The Portfolio Process in High School: Empowering Student Participation in Learning
by Kathleen González

You can always reflect on the past and life in general, but you hardly ever get the chance to make any changes. Constructing a portfolio in English made it possible for me to go back and make those necessary changes in my writing. My portfolio is a reminder to me of what I can accomplish and what I need to do to get better. I can see my mistakes in organization or punctuation, but at the same time, remember that I had good voice and grammar in the essay.

—Ashleigh, ninth grade

Having a portfolio of my work throughout the year was a good experience for me. The one thing I saw the most improvement on was my wording and vocabulary. Another thing that improved was quoting and analyzing quotes.

—Alicia, ninth grade

It was a way for me to look at how I'd written, as well as display any skills I have in writing to colleges, or if my future career involved writing, I have a great variety of examples to provide. From making a portfolio, I've learned that if you didn't have a place to put all of your writing together, it wouldn't be as easy to know how you need to improve or what you need to improve on.

—Audrianna, ninth grade

Portfolios are a great thing to look at towards the end of the year to ponder how I've changed as a person. Nostalgia isn't always a bad thing! It's also fun to laugh at yourself sometimes for making silly grammar mistakes or to laugh at how you worded certain things. That's when you really realize how much you've improved.

—Joanna, ninth grade

Why Use Portfolios

I had gone into a portfolio program reluctantly wondering how to fit yet another requirement into an already packed curriculum. Yet now I'm an advocate, a presenter on this topic, dare I say a devotee? The main reasons for this are students' comments like those noted above and the excitement that is evident as my students present their showcase portfolios at year's end. I see how proud they are of themselves, as am I, and we both see the results of all we've done throughout the year. When students can see their growth on a matrix, see that they've met goals, or can show others their best writing, it boosts their morale and self-esteem.

Dr. Wayne Jacobson, Assessment Coordinator at the University of Iowa, uses portfolios with students and faculty for development, support, and assessment. In his article "Teaching Through Portfolios" (2011), Jacobson states, "Portfolios help us teach students to recognize that they need to be active participants in their learning, not simply passive recipients of knowledge distributed by faculty members" (7). Portfolios are so much more than a storage folder; they are a tool for self-reflection and a source of proof for students' growth and goals attainment. In this way, portfolios also document the quality of students' work, not merely the quantity of knowledge gained.

Furthermore, the Common Core State Standards (CCSS) for writing state that students should "Write routinely over extended time frames (time for research, reflection, and revision) and shorter time frames (a single sitting or a day or two) for a range of tasks, purposes, and audiences" (Common Core State Standards Initiative, 41). What better way to achieve this standard than to keep writing in a portfolio where it can be accessed, reviewed, revised, and shared with wider audiences?

Once teachers decide that portfolios do indeed have value and are worth trying, the challenge is trying to fit them into their stuffed curriculum. Fortunately, portfolios take little time away from other activities; they offer a cohesive and meaningful part of an existing curriculum by adding a level of depth and critical thinking, and they take very little time to grade. Nonetheless, many teachers hesitate to use portfolios because they don't know how to manage the setup, the bulk of folders, or the class time needed for related activities. The following description gives the specifics of the process for using portfolios with ninth graders; however, the process can be adapted for any grade level.

Basics for Beginning the Portfolio Process

Basic portfolio setup takes about 15 minutes of class time. Within the first week or two of school, students bring in a pocketed folder that stays in the classroom and can hold 15 to 20 pieces of writing. I watch for "Back to School" sales and buy a stack of these folders to sell cheaply to students, or keep some "gently used" ones to hand out to students who can't afford their own. Students write their names on address labels, which are affixed to the top right corner of the folder so that when all folders are placed in the file cabinet the students' names all face the same way. These details help streamline the process of taking out or accessing portfolios. Also, it's important that all their writing "lives" in the classroom so that they still have it by year's end for their showcase portfolios. This requirement reinforces the students' organization skills and responsibility for saving one's work. Prior to using portfolios, I watched a student throw away an essay I'd spent 20 minutes grading into the trash because he was "done" with it, and felt a little stabbed in the gut. By having students keep their work, it provides a record of students' growth that adds value to their finished writing.

Also at the beginning of the year, students receive the requirement sheets, which provide a kind of "map" for where the portfolio is going. The portfolio is meant to hold all writing of a paragraph or more—for example, essays, short stories, poems, research papers, and speeches, along with their rough drafts and rubrics to record both writing growth and achievement. Additionally, any major tests, presentation rubrics, and even PowerPoint presentations are included since they document students' language arts skills. Since I use the Socratic Seminar as a discussion technique, students also store their feedback sheets in their portfolios to show their growth in discussion skills.

Table 9.8 details portfolio requirements. The sample provided fits *my* classroom; however, student portfolios should be meaningful to the content of your classroom. For

Todd Rafalovich

Kathleen González

TABLE 9.8 *Portfolio Requirements*

Student Name: _____   Grade Level: _____

Course: _____   Teacher: _____   Year: _____

Rationale:

The following portfolio guidelines are suggested for three specific reasons:

• To train you how to self-assess your own written work.
• To train you how to self-regulate your own learning process.
• To document your growth in specific skills.

Required Content:

_____   **Letter of Introduction** (personally introduces you to the reader).

_____   **Goal Setting Document** (includes a minimum of five specific goals written by you designating what you expect to learn throughout the year. Goals should be linked to ESLRs (Expected School-Wide Learning Results) and reflect your motivation for learning).

_____   **Reflection on Goals** (minimum of two pieces, written mid-year and year-end, that reflect progress, critique accomplishments, and target areas for improvement).

_____   **Writing and Rubrics** (minimum of three different types of evidence).

• May include essays or research papers from any subject area that are autobiographical, interpretive, persuasive, reflective, argumentative, comparative, descriptive, analytical, or controversial.
• May also include outlines of speeches, oral presentations or debates, short stories or poetry, community service writings, or journal entries.

_____   **Technology Piece** (your work representing the use of technology).

• May include examples of Internet research, presentation software, interactive video, DVD production, clip art, or computer-generated design.

_____   Standards Matrix

_____   Two Socratic Seminar check sheets

_____   Reading Survey and Learning Styles Inventory

Optional Content:

_____   **Evidence of Speaking** (may include speech outlines, audio and/or video cassette tapes, and/or note cards).

_____   **Student's Choice**

• Poetry
• Multimedia projects
• Prose
• Presentation rubrics
• Journal entries
• Visual assignments like the *Romeo and Juliet* picture quilt

instance, the "Writing and Rubrics" section can be tailored to match the genres of writing that you teach.

The "Technology Use" piece may be any text that students have created for English class that shows their skill using technology: PowerPoint presentations, clip art illustrations, or use of the Internet for research. These options allow for differentiation. The reading surveys and learning style inventory assignments I give at the beginning of the year help me get to know the students and help them get to know themselves better. Furthermore, in their portfolios, students include writing specific to state, district, and school assessments.

Students also keep a Standards Matrix in their portfolios. My department uses a Standards Matrix that lists the "power standards" we emphasize. At the completion of each unit, students look over the Standards Matrix and check off the growth they have attained on each skill, indicating the approval level: "I can do this with help," "I can do this on my own," or "I can teach this to others." By the end of the year, they will have marked virtually all the skills and also listed documentation (such as a test, essay, rubric, etc.) showing their skill level. This Standards Matrix, which is not graded, provides a practical tool for students to track progress toward their goals. Table 9.9 shows a portion of the Standards Matrix for ninth and tenth grade English in California.

TABLE 9.9   *Standards Matrix*

		I can do this with help.	I can do this on my own.	I can teach this to others.	Documentation
Writing	Legibility				
	Format—paragraph, indenting				
	Attention grabber				
	Introduction				
	Thesis/controlling idea				
	Preview points				
	Appropriate organizing structure				
	Support/analysis				
	Conclusion paragraph				
	Topic & concluding statements				
	Quotations & cited sources				

The Value of Portfolios for Goal Setting

Within the first two weeks of school, students write their goals for English class for the year. These can be based on the school's outcomes/goals or state standards. My school uses ESLRs—Expected School-Wide Learning Results—upon which our curriculum is based. Having consistent goals and using portfolios within a department creates continuity among courses and teachers. This continuity in turn leads to a stronger English department and a more transparent experience for students moving from course to course. When teachers create clearer goals and outcomes, this backward mapping guides their own curriculum development, teaching, and assessment. Students write a goal for each area. Table 9.10 provides the assignment sheet.

When students write their initial goal statements, we go through each school goal one-by-one, discuss its meaning, and come up with examples. Their goals must be measurable, with an explanation of why the student chose the goal; this writing activity promotes precise and critical thinking. For instance, if Ricky writes, "I will get better at writing

TABLE 9.10 *Beginning of the Year Portfolio Goal Statement*

Objective: Set goals to work toward, so that at year's end you can see if you have met your goals. This list will also help you connect your learning to our school's Expected School-Wide Learning Results (ESLRs).

Directions:

- Take out binder paper. Put a proper heading on your paper and title it "Portfolio Goal Statement."
- On your paper, list the five ESLRs with space (about four to five lines) between them.
- Write a goal for each ESLR and tell why it is your goal. Make sure each goal is measurable so you'll know if you met it.
- Turn in your paper to the teacher to get points.
- When you get this paper back, keep it in your portfolio so you can look at it again in January and June. Don't lose it!

Examples:

- Responsible Decision Maker: I will write all my assignments on my calendar and check it when I get home because I don't want to forget my homework like I did last year, OR I will do my own work and won't copy off classmates so I can learn the material myself.
- Essential Social Skills: I will learn to organize my groups when we have a project so we can get our work done, OR I will listen quietly during directions to respect the teacher and get the information.
- Essential Academic Skills: I will stop writing run-on sentences so people will understand what I have to say, OR by the end of the year I will write an essay that gets a 3 on the rubric so I can show improvement.
- Critical Thinking Skills: I will speak at least twice during class discussions so I can learn to analyze literature, OR I will talk with my mom about how each book I read relates to my life so I can make learning more meaningful.
- School and the Real World: When I present in front of the class, I will speak loudly and clearly because it's something I'll have to do in college or on the job, OR I will read the newspaper three times a week so I can learn more about the world.

essays," how will he know if he's better than he was before? A goal that is measurable, clear, and documentable might state: "I will write essays that are organized into proper paragraphs" or "I will write an essay that completely addresses the prompt," or "I will learn to use examples and quotations properly to support my ideas."

One candid ninth grader wrote a goal about being a responsible decision maker. At the beginning of the year she wrote, "I will buy a planner to write all of my assignments and test dates in. I will also check this planner every day." Her goal is very specific and measurable; later she can easily determine if she met this goal. At the beginning of the second semester, she wrote: "I did not meet this goal. I will meet it in the second semester by buying a planner as soon as possible." As her end of the year final reflection shows, she ultimately met her goal: "I did meet this goal during the second semester because I bought a planner and began to write down all of my assignments. I think that this was a very good decision because it really helped me stay organized and not forget to complete any of my assignments. My goal for next year is to not only buy a new planner but to stay committed to it all year."

Beyond goal setting related to decision-making and social aspects, portfolios specifically facilitate improvement of student writing. Because all writing assignments are kept in a centralized location, it's easy for students to refer to them. When I assign a new essay, I have students look at their last essay and determine what they need to work on, then set this as a goal for the new assignment. Similarly, when I hand back papers graded with a rubric, students take out previous papers and compare their growth from one rubric to the next. As Dr. Jacobson points out, "Through portfolios, students become partners in documenting, assessing, and improving their own learning" (7), cultivating their autonomy while also developing their skills at self-evaluation and critical thinking.

As Standard XIII from the National Board for Professional Teaching Standards for English Language Arts (2003) states, "Teachers recognize that the collection of work samples in a portfolio provides insight into students' skill, approaches to assignments, preparedness, organization, development, and comprehension" (66). The National Board sets the standard for teaching practice in America; thus, their portfolio advocacy reinforces the essential value of portfolios as a teaching tool. Writing isn't just done and forgotten; the portfolio provides the opportunity for the writing process to be recursive and growth-oriented, part of a comprehensive literacy plan.

During the Year

Obviously students will go to their portfolios as they continue to store their work there; however, they will also refer to previous work to reflect on it. Table 9.11 provides a mid-year goal reflection assignment. Students are more likely to meet their goals if they write them down and reflect on them periodically in multiple ways (paragraph writing, checking off a matrix, listing, choosing showcase work, describing goals to others, etc.). Here again is the value of writing about their writing: students retain learning longer if they remember what they've learned, recall it, and reflect on it, a metacognitive activity where they learn about their own learning. The Semester Portfolio Goals Reflection can be an in-class or homework assignment.

In order to keep portfolios alive and relevant during the year, students can self-assess on the Standards Matrix at the end of each unit of study. This only takes them

TABLE 9.11 *Semester Portfolio Goals Reflection*

Objective: Since we are halfway through the school year, it's a good time to reflect on your growth and your goals. This will help you stay focused on what you need to accomplish.

Directions:

- From your portfolio, take out your "Portfolio Goal Statement" from the beginning of the year. Re-read it.
- On a fresh sheet of binder paper, put a heading and the title "Semester Goals Reflection."
- Copy each ESLR, with space between.
- Tell how you have met each of your goals.

  OR

  How you plan to meet them in the second semester.

- Be as specific as possible.
- You may change your goal at this point. You may also set a new goal if you have already met this one. Be sure to tell how you will meet the new goal.
- Staple the two pages together, with the Reflection on top, and turn it in.

5 to 10 minutes. Students also store other evaluative forms, such as presentation or reading rubrics, Socratic Seminar check sheets, major exams, or other papers that document their ability to perform skills. Since all pieces of writing of a paragraph or more—including essays, research papers, creative stories, poems, or informal journal-type writing—are kept in the portfolio, every time I hand back a graded assignment, I also hand out the student portfolios so that those papers are saved.

The portfolio helps students focus on their writing as a continual growth process, not merely an occasional or isolated activity. A few times each year, students go through both their portfolios and their journals, choosing something they want to revise and take through the writing process. Table 9.12 provides the assignment. This process promotes student

TABLE 9.12 *Portfolio Revision Assignment*

1. Choose something in your journal or portfolio that you want to revise. It should be an essay assignment rather than a poem or quiz. Consider this paper a rough draft.
2. Revise the essay to follow formal essay structure. This includes:

   - An introduction, body, and conclusion.
   - A thesis statement that previews your main points.
   - More details or explanations. Be sure your ideas are clear and logical.
   - A creative title.
   - Correct mechanics.

3. Read this draft to a partner to check for clarity. Your partner should fill out a rubric to give you feedback. Have the partner sign the rough draft.
4. Write out a final clean draft of this essay. Write on the front side only and include a proper heading.
5. Turn in the rough draft, rubric, and new final draft (on top).

   Points possible: _____

   Due date: _____

choice and a sense of ownership and is differentiated since each student works on the skill that most needs improvement. The revision assignment takes students through the steps of the writing process more often so they'll internalize these and get more practice with peer editing. These papers are graded on how much revision the student did. Students are excited about reviewing their previous writing, and their responses are more interesting to read because students put more time and effort into revisions they find personally valuable and meaningful. Table 9.13 provides a sample feedback form.

End of the Year

A few weeks before the end of the year, students begin preparing a showcase portfolio, which is a large part of their final "exam" (see Table 9.14). At this point, the portfolio shifts from being a storage space to being a showcase. As Table 9.13 illustrates, students include their best work as delineated on the requirements sheet (Table 9.8). Then they perform the most important steps: evaluating their work and growth, analyzing what they've learned, choosing their best pieces, and explaining both the process and product to others. Students also complete the Standards Matrix one last time to assess their growth and make sure they have documented all their skills.

The true value of the portfolio now comes to the fore as students engage in the metacognitive activity of reflecting on their own learning. As Jean Florman, Director of

TABLE 9.13 *Portfolio Piece Feedback Form*

Name of Writer: _____ Name of Evaluator: _____

Title or Piece of Writing: _____

Please check off some strengths of this piece:

_____ neat work	_____ creative
_____ very entertaining	_____ good visuals/cover
_____ good organization	_____ good vocabulary
_____ intelligent ideas	_____ shows a lot of work
_____ few/no errors	_____ supports ideas with examples

Now please check off some suggestions for improvement:

_____ work could be neater	_____ add a cover or pictures
_____ needs more details/adjectives	_____ make it longer/develop ideas more
_____ organize it better	_____ use a bigger vocabulary
_____ needs more proofreading	_____ add more examples

Additional comments:

_____ _____

Signature   Title (parent, coach, etc.)

TABLE 9.14 *End of the Year Showcase Portfolio—Final Assignment*

1. Write a "Letter of Introduction" addressed to "Dear Reader" so your portfolio reader will know a little bit about you. Describe yourself as a writer and reader—your strengths, weaknesses, and goals. This goes at the front of your portfolio.
2. Write a year-end "Reflection on Goals" piece based on your ESLRs from earlier this year. Look at the "Goal Statement" and "Semester Goals Reflection" to tell how you met (or didn't meet) each goal and why. This goes after your Letter of Introduction.
3. Now find the "Portfolio Requirements" handout to use as a check sheet. Include this page after the "Reflection on Goals."
4. Empty everything from your portfolio. Put back in each thing listed on the Requirements sheet. Keep all rough drafts and rubrics with the original pieces.

   • For each piece of your writing that you include, write a sentence or two telling why you picked it. Title this "Rationale" and place it after the "Portfolio Requirements."
   • You may include more than the required things if you want others to see that work in the future.

5. At this time, you may wish to buy a new folder and decorate it to really show your best work. You may also wish to do "extras" to go beyond the basic requirements. See the Evaluation Form for ideas of "extras."
6. Have a parent and a peer evaluate your portfolio on the Evaluation Forms. Include these completed forms in the back of your portfolio.
7. On the day of the final, you'll sit with me and show me all your hard work! I will ask you a few questions and grade your portfolio at that time.

Points possible: 100 points

---

the University of Iowa Center for Teaching, points out in "Tales from Real Life" (2011), "Decision making and reflection hone students' cognitive thinking skills, and the framework of the learning portfolio brings to light the full scope of their learning" (5). Whereas a final class project or test could measure students' memorization capabilities or mastery of grammar rules—focusing on the lower order skills of remembering and understanding—the portfolio focuses on their abilities to analyze and evaluate, skills that are two and three steps higher in Bloom's taxonomy. Students won't develop this ability unless they are given an opportunity and guidance to practice it, and the portfolio is the perfect venue. It puts them in the driver's seat for their own learning, developing skills beyond what one teacher or subject area might teach them that they can use far into their futures.

Table 9.15 is the teacher's Evaluation Form. This lists the requirements as well as the ways in which students can go beyond the requirements and earn an A grade. The "extras" are also where students personalize their portfolios and shine as individuals—for example, a photographer can add her own photos on divider pages between her writings; a computer-proficient student can create a DVD; the verbal learner has the opportunity to talk to the teacher about his growth—as portfolios can be adapted to different levels of proficiency and different learning styles.

Step 4, the Rationale, is a short but valuable element of the portfolio that leads students to reflect on each piece of writing they are including. Having them write the Rationale explaining what they learned and how putting together their showcase portfolio demonstrates their learning causes students to reflect in a deliberate and focused way. "In portfolios the artifacts do not speak for themselves," Jacobson points out. "The answer to the question, 'What did you learn?', is found in a student's description of what an artifact represents" (6). This step, along with the final teacher meeting, provides the greatest opportunity for reflective learning.

The portfolio activities and requirements are open-ended enough that students can address them at a variety of levels. By their very nature, portfolios allow for differentiation that promotes student success at individual levels, and the assignment is easily adaptable to language learners, gifted students, and students with various special needs. For instance, a developing writer might show proficiency by simply having enough writing samples organized in one place, whereas a proficient writer might revise the chosen samples to show fresh improvement. In fact, a student with a learning disability wrote in her final portfolio reflection, "I proved to myself that I could do this even with learning disabilities." Depending on the resources available to students, you may even choose to do an electronic portfolio, where all work is stored on a server or DVD. This makes it possible for students to store larger projects, as well as those in varied electronic formats. The work stored electronically takes up virtually no classroom space; however, it may be more difficult to include all peer response pieces or rough draft work. See the articles by Chen and Light (2010) or by Labissiere and Reynolds (2011) in the References and Resources section for more information about electronic portfolios.

On the day portfolios are due, I sit with each student as she or he leads me through her or his portfolio page by page, showing each text that documents her or his abilities and meets the requirements. I check off requirements using the Teacher Portfolio Evaluation Form (Table 9.15) and write a couple of comments, grading the assignment on the spot. I always end with two to three questions for the student, typically asking:

- Which assignment are you most proud of and why?
- On which writing skill did you improve the most and which text shows that?
- Which goals did you meet or not meet and why?
- What is your best piece of writing and what makes it so good?
- What are your writing goals for next year and why?

These questions not only represent my students' reflections on their growth processes, but they're my chance to connect with my students one last time.

While I meet with individual students, the other students are paired with a classmate to review each other's portfolios and complete similar evaluation forms. Alternatively, students can write comments on sticky notes and place them in each other's portfolios. This is also a "milk and cookies" day as we celebrate the publication of their portfolios by enjoying milk or juice and cookies while discussing portfolios. Thus, we create an air of accomplishment and satisfaction within a room of collaboration and autonomy. The final exam period is two hours, so as I meet one-on-one, students are also working on the rest of the exam.

You can change the title of this Evaluation Form so it can also be used with parents. Before students bring their finished portfolios to class, they must have a parent or other adult in their life respond to their portfolio. This serves two purposes: one, to have someone else review the work to ensure that it has met the requirements in time to fix any

TABLE 9.15 *Teacher Portfolio Evaluation Form*

Writer's Name: _____

_____ Parent evaluation

_____ Classmate evaluation

Requirements Met (check off):

_____ Letter of Introduction		_____ Rationale piece	
_____ Goal Setting Document		_____ Standards Matrix	
_____ Mid-Year Reflection		_____ Two Socratic Seminar check sheets	
_____ End-of-Year Reflection		_____ Standardized test scores	
_____ Three pieces of writing (essays, stories, etc.)		_____ Reading Survey	
		_____ Learning Styles Inventory	
_____ One piece showing technology use			

Extras:

_____ Title page	_____ Extra writing evidence	
_____ Table of contents	_____ Many pieces are typed	
_____ Dedication	_____ Pictures, graphics, decorations	
_____ Shows extra revision	_____ Tabbed sections, dividers	
_____ New folder/binder	_____ Other: _____	

The best thing about the portfolio was:

The part that could be improved was:

Final Grade (100 Points): _____

deficiencies; and two, to garner immediate feedback from a real audience about whom the student cares. Although I meet with each student, it's invaluable for students to see that teachers are not the only audience for their writing. Since their showcase portfolio is part of their final, I won't have the opportunity to write more detailed notes or feedback to the student, though that five minutes of personalized feedback may be more valuable than 15 minutes of written comments.

Let me be clear—portfolio grading is done! Since I've seen virtually all this work already during the year, grading each one takes little time; the only new parts are the letter of introduction and the personal reflection. My meetings with each student take a maximum of five minutes.

When I assign the showcase portfolio as part of the final exam, students often express excitement and relief when they begin the process—their final is about them! What they often don't realize is that they are engaging their minds at deep levels of analysis and evaluation. They are participating fully in their learning process rather than being merely recipients of learning, and this type of learning actually stays with them longer than memorizing lists or merely demonstrating comprehension. Students have gone beyond "observation and recall of information" to "seeing patterns" and making connections, which are higher order thinking skills. Besides, there's a certain thrill when students see that fat portfolio full of writing and realize that they did indeed produce it all.

As my excerpts at the beginning of Part II show, students find great value in the portfolio process. In fact, I recently received this email from Jason, a former student: "Today I was going through and cleaning my house when I stumbled upon the English portfolio I did for your class. Reading the pieces I had written over 10 years ago brought back many memories from your seventh period class." Jason is on track to become a university professor, and he says later in his message that "I want you to know that a lot of my values regarding teaching are drawn from my experiences in classes like yours, where the teacher genuinely loves her students." Students develop these types of feelings not only because a teacher is caring, but also because what they have written has become personally meaningful.

References and Resources

Bloom, Benjamin S. "Bloom's Taxonomy." *Taxonomy of Educational Objectives.* Boston: Allyn & Bacon, 1984.

Calkins, Lucy, Mary Ehrenworth, and Christopher Lehman. *Pathways to the Common Core: Accelerating Achievement.* Portsmouth, NH: Heinemann, 2012.

Chen, Helen C., and Tracy Penny Light. *Electronic Portfolios and Student Success: Effectiveness, Efficiency, and Learning.* Washington, DC: American Association of Colleges and Universities, 2010.

Common Core State Standards Initiative. http://www.corestandards.org

Florman, Jean. "Tales From Real Life." *Thriving in Academe,* 28.5 (June 2011). http://www.nea.org/assets/docs/June2011AdvOnline.pdf

Graves, Donald. *Writing: Teachers and Children at Work.* Portsmouth, NH: Heinemann, 1983.

Jacobson, Wayne. "Teaching Through Portfolios." *Thriving in Academe,* 28.5 (June 2011). http://www.nea.org/assets/docs/June2011AdvOnline.pdf

Kinney, Patti, Mary Beth Munroe, and Pam Sessions. *A School-Wide Approach to Student-Led Conference: A Practitioner's Guide.* National Middle School Association, 2000.

Labissiere, Y., and C. Reynolds. "Using Electronic Portfolios as a Pedagogical Practice to Enhance Student Learning." *Inventio,* 2.6 (January 12, 2011).

Ledbetter, Mary Ellen. *Writing Portfolio Activities Kit: Ready-to-Use Management Techniques and Writing Activities for Grades 7–12.* New York: The Center for Applied Research in Education, 1998.

Locke, Edwin A., and Gary P. Latham. "New Directions in Goal-Setting Theory." Yahoo. August 23, 2011. http://home.ubalt.edu/tmitch/642/Articles%20syllabus/Locke%20et%20al%20New%20dir%20goal%20setting%2006.pdf. Online.

Lovell, Jonathan H., and Bonnie S. Sunstein, eds. *The Portfolio Standard: How Students Can Show Us What They Know and Are Able to Do.* Portsmouth, NH: Heinemann, 2000.

Murray, Donald M. *A Writer Teaches Writing,* 2nd edition. Stamford, CT: Wadsworth, 2003.

National Board for Professional Teaching Standards. *Adolescent and Young Adulthood English Language Arts Standards,* 2nd edition. Washington, DC: National Board for Professional Teaching Standards, 2003.

Schrock, Kathy. "Kathy Schrock's Guide for Educators." http://school.discoveryeducation.com/schrockguide/assess.html

Smith, Carol. "Assessing and Reporting Progress Through Student-Led Portfolio Conferences." http://www.nmsa.org/Publications/WebExclusive/Portfolio/tabid/650/Default.aspx

Underwood, Terry. *The Portfolio Project: A Study of Assessment, Instruction, and Middle School Reform.* Urbana, IL: National Council of Teachers of English, 1999.

Williams, Rachel Marie-Crane. "Tales From Real Life." *Thriving in Academe*, 28.5 (June 2011). http://www.nea.org/he

Yancey, Kathleen Blake, ed. *Portfolios in the Writing Classroom: An Introduction.* Urbana, IL: National Council of Teachers of English, 1992.

10

Keeping Heart: Dealing with the Realities of the Paper Load While Providing Authentic Response

by Kathleen González and Maria Clinton

Introduction

Among the teachers who have had some role in writing this book, we are unanimous in our feeling about grading. It's overwhelming! And while many of our colleagues in other subjects have easier methods of assessment, including Scantron sheets for multiple-choice answers, English language arts teachers rarely have it so easy. Additionally, in the face of larger class sizes, even the more seasoned teachers who have developed stratagems for managing the paper load, such as staggering due dates, find themselves worn down by the sheer numbers of papers demanding response.

Further, we understand that students DO need to write and their writing deserves response. We frequently tell students that just as they practice daily to improve their skills as soccer players or musicians, they need to write daily to build their writing muscles. Because they will become better writers as they write (and read) more often, the conundrum arises: How can we maintain a passion for writing and continue to evoke and support this passion in our students' writing? How can we as teachers of writing keep up with the paper load while providing meaningful feedback?

In Part I of this chapter, Kathleen González shares a range of techniques to help teachers deal with the reality of the paper load. In Part II, Maria Clinton addresses how Common Core Standards-based grading can provide authentic assessment while lessening the number of assignments to grade.

Part I: TimeBusters!—Techniques for Saving Time When Grading
by Kathleen González

Okay, I'll say it: I resent grading. It cuts into my home life and personal time. As budgets get cut and class sizes grow, my paper load expands until I've started tallying: "Really? Thirty-five hours for this one research assignment?" I've said many times over the years that if it weren't for grading papers I could teach forever.

On the other hand, I'm not about to stop assigning essays, projects, and homework just to relieve myself of the paper load. I believe strongly that writing frequently makes people better writers, just as reading a lot makes them better readers. Reading students' writing is also one of the primary ways teachers get to know their students and connect with them on a personal level. Commenting on my students' papers gives me a few moments to have precious one-on-one silent conversations with them. So how can I assess my students' writing without feeling angry or overwhelmed?

Over the years, I've picked up a number of tips to save time in all aspects of grading, from essays to reading quizzes, to projects and journals. Most importantly, I've been able to achieve this without losing rigor and while still focusing on higher order thinking skills. In addition, since I can return papers more quickly using these tips, I don't have to cut back on assigning writing.

Let's Start with Essays and Rubrics

It's all about the rubric. Get a good rubric that works for you and highlights your students' skill levels. Although I could provide you with half a dozen rubrics, my years working with my English department colleagues has shown that a good rubric is pretty specific and personal to your goals, student population, and style. For example, you could select a rubric that's aligned with Common Core State Standards or required high-stakes tests in your state or district; that way, you're concurrently preparing your students for the kind of testing situation they'll face. Furthermore, you can build your own rubric at the Rubistar site (http://www.rubistar.4teachers.org), search for existing ones online (try Kathy Schrock's webpage cited in this chapter's References and Resources), or search other school and district websites. For a lengthy discussion on the pros and cons of using rubrics, you can also visit the National Council of Teachers of English website (http://www.ncte.org/) and search "rubric."

Before students write their papers, you should spend some time going over the rubric with them so they know what your expectations are and how to read your feedback. I don't spend too much time on this at first with my own students—we scan the general rubric format and focus on three or four key skills per essay. Once you're comfortable with using the rubric, you'll start flying through them. To personalize the grading more, I usually write one positive and one "needs improvement" comment on each paper as well. It's when I hand BACK the papers that we take more time to review the rubric's categories and levels of proficiency. I also have students, in pairs, share something they did well and something that needs improving. This assures that they read my feedback, and it also gives me the opportunity to clarify, for the class as a whole, any rubric items that might be confusing. Finally, I make a clear distinction between the rubric score and the grade; I use the rubric to provide formative feedback to the student, highlighting individual bullet points in each section. My final grades, however, are based on how well students have met the requirements of the assignment.

For errors in grammar or conventions, I don't play the role of "copy editor" for my students' papers. Instead, I put an X in the margin beside the error. When I hand papers back, I make students find their own errors. If they can't find them, they ask a neighbor. If the neighbor can't help, that's where I'll come, somewhat begrudgingly, to the rescue. My guiding principle here is that I don't need practice finding and correcting errors—they do!

Rubrics are great because students can use them to check their growth during the year. Simply have students take out all their essays and compare one rubric to the next. You can ask them verbally or on paper to tell you which skills they improved upon or which skills they need to work on next time—a process that encourages them to become more reflective writers.

Number Your Comments

Sometimes you need something besides a rubric. It may happen that using the rubric is just too time consuming, or you're unable to make copies because the copier is down, or you forgot to bring your rubrics with you to the coffee shop where you grade your students' essays. Or maybe, like me, you are tired to death of writing the same comment 150 times. You know that empty feeling you get when you see a student drop the essay you just spent time responding to into the trash? Well, you don't have to feel that way again.

The trick is to number your comments. Figure out what feedback you repeat to students over and over again, and make a numbered list. You will often come up with complementary phrases such as "Great title"/"Title needs work" "Strong attention grabber"/"Attention grabber could be improved." Limit your list to around 20 items. As you grade papers, write the appropriate number in the margin. I usually average about five numbers per paper. Again, by the fifth paper or so, you start memorizing your list and picking up speed. Written comments to students can now be limited to remarking on their logic or thought process rather than their mechanics or organization. While it's important to write comments or give specific feedback to students in case they choose to revise a piece later, the practice of providing numbered comments plus limited written response honors the time they took to write their papers by giving them feedback that is more thorough and informative than just a letter grade.

When you hand papers back, put the list of comments on the overhead projector and have students copy the comments that correspond to your numbering system! This assures that they actually read your comments, and you can move around the room, clarifying comments or talking to your students one-to-one while they are copying.

One other point: Grade only for specific skills rather than for everything. Perhaps with one essay you'll focus on basic essay structure and not worry about the quality of ideas, or vice versa. For most emerging writers, having teachers make broadly inclusive comments on their papers is daunting and depressing. Don't do it. Another option: Have the student write you a note requesting that you look at a specific skill, such as the introduction or her use of complete sentences. Focus on that one skill. That time will also connect you to the student on a personal level.

Journals

If you want your students to do a lot of writing but you don't want to actually read it all, use journals. I assign in-class journal writing two or three times a week. Some topics are extra skills practice, like writing only the introductory paragraph for an essay; most of the time, however, I give topics such as "Would you rather have strength, wisdom, or beauty?" (mythology unit) or "Write the plot summary of a love story involving a dance, a potion, and a dagger" *(Romeo and Juliet)* To get full credit, students must write a full page. Mechanics don't count; the goal is fluency and getting past writer's block, so we brainstorm where necessary.

I used to read and comment on a few journal entries per student. When I saw that they didn't read what I wrote, however, I stopped. Now, I simply give a plus (full credit), check (partial credit), or minus (itty bitty credit) and total these for their journal score for that grading period. In this manner, I can grade a class set of 30 journals in 30 to 40 minutes. Once every grading period, I have students choose something from their journals to develop further. These assignments I read. Since the students are working on topics they care about, they do higher quality work; consequently, their essays are more satisfying to read. It's fun to see students poring through past journal prompts exclaiming, "I remember writing this!" or "This is awful! I'm going to work on it." Alternatively, I have students choose a piece to show to an adult in their lives. The adult completes a simple feedback form, the student revises the piece, and the adult's feedback responses are attached to the piece when the student turns it in. Of course, these assignments are graded on completion rather than skill level, but it gives students yet another audience and opportunity to grow as writers.

Reading Quizzes

Reading is the best way to improve student writing. On the one hand, we need to push our students to read a lot; on the other hand, we need to provide them with recreational/free choice as well as assigned readings. How do we accomplish that without creating more papers to grade? I believe in providing students with multiple ways they can show they did their reading.

Todd Rafalovich

Kathleen Gonzales

For longer books like *To Kill a Mockingbird* or *The Odyssey*, I generally assign a chapter a night for homework and quiz them daily. I use what I call Card Questions, an idea adapted from a former colleague (see Table 10.1). Questions should check for comprehension and simple recall. The beauty of the process is that you can use these simple questions to move on to a class discussion of deeper issues.

You won't be able to call on every student every day; therefore, each day you should reshuffle the deck. This way, students won't know whether or not they'll be called on. Over the years, this technique has quite accurately shown me who's reading and who's not without taking up a lot of time for quizzes. It also becomes a game that students look forward to; they even seem to forget they're taking a quiz.

If you have a student who has already read the book or is a stellar reader, give him or her the privilege of asking the questions alongside you. You can still control the deck and

TABLE 10.1 *Card Questions Quizzing Technique*

1. Have students write their names on 3 × 5 cards. They can decorate the front if they want. The teacher keeps these cards.
2. Write out 7 to 10 questions for each chapter of the novel you're reading. This takes time up front but saves you time in the future. (You can also have students write these, find questions online, or share the work with a colleague.) These should be general, factual questions. Also include some extra tough ones (put a star next to these).
3. Each day, quiz students on the previous night's reading.

   Procedure:
   a. Shuffle the cards every day.
   b. The student whose name is on the top card gets the first question. If s/he answers correctly, write a plus on the back of the card.
   c. If s/he can't answer it, write a minus.
   d. If s/he can't answer it but can prove s/he read the chapter by giving a related answer, write a check on the card.
   e. Treat your extra hard questions as bonuses. Have students volunteer to answer these questions. Call on the student whose hand is raised first. Reward a plus, check, or minus. That card then goes to the bottom of the stack.
4. Go through all the questions for that chapter.
5. When you finish reading the book, score like this:
   a. Eliminate one of the minus grades the student received.
   b. Total the number of plusses.
   c. Add the total plusses and divide by the total of the minuses and plusses, ignoring the checks.
   d. This gives you a percentage. I usually divide this in half and make the quiz grade worth 50 points.

Sample card:

+ + + + − − + − + + − + + +

Throw out one minus. Ignore the checks.
(10 plusses) divided by (10 plusses + 3 minuses) = 10 divided by 13 = 76.9%. This is 38 points or a C.

write down the points earned, even as students strive to earn the privilege of asking the questions. A few other tips: About halfway through the book, hand students their cards so they can calculate their current grades; this often helps wake up the ones who aren't keeping up with reading, since their grade is so visible. Also, tell students at this point that cards with more minuses "weigh less." This is when I stop shuffling randomly, telling my students that the "less weighty" cards have mysteriously "floated" to the top of the stack. Ha!

Another in-class quiz technique I use is asking one question that students answer in a short paragraph. I use this for short books that have more emotional content, like *Night* (Wiesel, 1972) or *House on Mango Street* (Cisneros, 1984). For each chapter or section of the book, I ask one question at the beginning of the class and students respond on binder paper in a "fat" paragraph (five to seven sentences). The key is to prove they read the material. I skim the paragraphs quickly and look for key ideas or events; in this way, I can grade a whole class of 35 quizzes quite quickly. Quizzes are generally 10 points each, although you should tailor the points to match your system. These questions generally lead to great discussions. Table 10.2 gives sample questions.

TABLE 10.2 *Quiz Questions for House on Mango Street by Sandra Cisneros*

Quiz #1: pp. 3–22

- What does Esperanza think of her family? Her friends? What kinds of things does she say about them? What interactions does she have?

Quiz #2: pp. 23–52

- Describe the most interesting character in this section (besides Esperanza). What did he/she do? Why was he/she interesting?

Quiz #3: pp. 53–80

- Many things upset Esperanza or make her sad. Describe one or more of these people or events. OR—Describe a section that made <u>you</u> upset or sad.

Quiz #4: pp. 81–110

- A lot of women are mentioned in this section. How are they treated? How do they live their lives? How does Esperanza interact with them?

Quiz Questions for *Night* by Elie Wiesel

Ch. 1: Was there anything you didn't understand?

Ch. 2: What reactions did you have to particular characters?

Ch. 3: What caused your strongest feeling in the story?

Ch. 4: What events seemed strange or interesting?

Ch. 5: What important events happened in this chapter? What big decision(s) did Elie and his father face?

Ch. 6: Describe the deaths of particular characters in this chapter.

Ch. 7: What events seemed strange? Disturbing? Interesting?

Ch. 8–9: Write today's quiz in the form of a letter to Elie. Tell him how you feel about the events in this chapter. Remember to include details to prove you read the material.

If your goal is to have students read books of their own choice, here are some other projects to try. I use the Postcard Book Report (see Table 10.3) when students read a novel or biography/autobiography with a coming of age theme, as well as for science fiction. However, the assignment can be tweaked to fit most any genre, even short stories. Students can earn extra credit for mailing the postcard; I also offer extra extra credit for the card that comes from farthest away. Some students will complete a book early, create the postcard, mail it to a relative in say, Vietnam, and have it mailed back to me. I put two grades on it—25 points for the front side artwork, and 25 points for the writing on the back—and total it up. I can grade a set of 30 postcards in half an hour.

I've used this next project (shown in Table 10.4) with paired texts, such as *Romeo and Juliet/West Side Story* or *The Odyssey/The Human Comedy*.

For the Life Graph (Table 10.5), students create a chart listing at least 30 events from the book in chronological order. Each event is valued as positive, negative, or neutral to the protagonist's life. Students usually add all sorts of creative decorations, themes, and backgrounds. They enjoy creating posters, and these look great on the walls. I also allow students to create PowerPoint slideshows; this not only shows pretty clearly who has read the book and who hasn't, but also differentiates the lesson enough to let various learning styles shine. I grade these projects by using a rubric, so each one takes only a few minutes. It's not necessary to read every event a student lists; eyeballing the first and last ones and checking for quotations is enough to ensure that the student comprehended and connected with the book.

TABLE 10.3 *Postcard Book Report—Coming of Age*

You will be given a 5 × 8 card. First, you are to create two pictures on the <u>lined</u> side of the card. One-half of the card must depict the main character surrounded by family members or close friends. The other half of the card should represent the main character involved in the climactic moment of the novel—the turning point or event where s/he comes of age. <u>Make sure that none of the lines on the card are visible when you have finished your decorations</u>, which may be done with felt pens, crayons, colored paper, pictures cut from magazines (but not one large picture), and so on. Include the <u>title</u> of the novel.

Next, divide the blank side of the card in half, just like a regular postcard. On the right half write the following address:

Ms. Kathy Gonzalez
Everytown High School
1234 Main Street
Cityville, CA 95123

For five points extra credit, mail the card to me! Place a stamp in the upper right corner. (If you mail it, keep a copy just in case.)

On the left side of the card, write a note to me from any character in the book. In the note, have the character describe any conflicts s/he is having with others, family, or the community. Finally, have the character reflect on the ways s/he is growing up. Make the comments of your note authentic; that is, any place names, plot details, references to other characters, and so on, must be genuine according to the content of the novel. Then sign your real name beneath the character's name you've borrowed.

This assignment is worth 50 points: 25 points for the picture side and 25 for the written side (mechanics count, of course). Due: _____

TABLE 10.4 *The Human Comedy Project*

Directions: Fold an 8 ½ × 11 blank white paper into three sections.

Put the book title at the top and your name at the bottom.

1. In section 1, list similarities to *The Odyssey*.
2. In section 2, illustrate your favorite scene in color (drawing, graphics, magazine cut-outs, construction paper, etc.).
3. In section 3, make a character chart for your favorite character (looks, personality, thoughts, and actions) plus a picture of that character (same choices as #2 above).

Points Possible: 60 points—20 for each section.

Due Date: _____

Since much of the project consists of pictures or lists, these take very little time to grade. Even so, they allow students to show that they comprehended the texts, can synthesize the information, and are able to compare and contrast elements of both stories. As I grade, I put a number between 1 and 20 as the points earned for that third of the project, then total those scores up for the final grade. I can grade a whole class of these in about 20 minutes. If you aren't convinced that the student read the book based on his or her drawings and writing, you can do a brief oral quiz as well.

One final technique to get students reading more is a monthly reading calendar, an idea suggested by another colleague. The complete assignment sheet is in Table 10.6. Basically, students keep track of how many minutes they read each month. They earn points based on this and can also earn extra credit. Although they max out at 20 points extra credit, to encourage more reading I mail home postcards to the top two to three readers in each class and also let them choose a prize (pencils, stickers, doodads) from a box I keep in my classroom. Students (and parents) love receiving these nominal rewards. As we go through the year, I increase the required number of minutes by about 100 every two months. I occasionally call home to verify that students did the reading, and I send out the information to parents at back-to-school night, by email, and at parent meetings. Most parents are thrilled to support their students' reading in this simple fashion, and scoring a set of calendars takes about 10 minutes.

Projects—and Outside Readers

Speaking of parents, let's turn our attention from reading to projects. First of all, let someone else grade them! I'm exaggerating, of course, but students should have other audiences besides teachers to read or view their work. Furthermore, if other audiences are reading these projects, it takes the pressure off their teachers to write extensive comments.

During a poetry unit, for example, students create an anthology or collection of poems that fits certain requirements (rhyming and non-rhyming poems, poems about nature or love, personal poems, and so on). Even though I highlight comments on a rubric, these projects can take a while to grade because I like to write a few personal comments

TABLE 10.5 *Life Graph Assignment*

Directions: After reading the book, make a list of the major events in the protagonist's life in chronological order. Then label each one as positive, neutral, or negative. Place these on a timeline and label each one. To create a stellar project and get an A, do the items suggested in the A–B column of the rubric. (50 points)

Due Date: _____

Grading Rubric for Life Graph

A–B

- More than 20 events, listed in chronological order
- Sentences with each event, some details
- Quotations from the book; approximate dates of events
- Events <u>creatively</u> labeled as positive/negative/neutral
- Color ink, felt pen, or computer
- Larger format, poster, PowerPoint
- Very attractive: glitter, borders, pictures, graphics, etc.
- Creative title (not just the book title)

B–C

- Complete timeline for whole book: minimum of 20 events
- Chronological order
- Words/phrases for each event
- Events labeled as positive/negative/neutral
- Black ink (not pencil) or computer
- 8 ½″ × 22″ size (like two sheets of paper)
- Legible, neat
- Title of book

D–F

- Incomplete chart; fewer than 20 events; out of order
- Doesn't represent the whole book
- Incomplete description for each event
- Events <u>not</u> labeled as positive/negative/neutral
- Pencil; stray marks
- Small; binder paper
- Illegible, messy
- Missing title

on each one. Before the project is due, therefore, I require students to have a parent complete an evaluation form to check that the requirements have been met and also to provide immediate feedback. If the parent is not available or doesn't speak English, students can turn to a teacher, coach, minister, relative, or neighbor. On the day the project is due, have students trade and respond to each other's anthologies while holding a "milk and cookies" day. Students love to check out each other's projects, so make it a celebration. Now that

TABLE 10.6 *Reading Calendar*

Reading a lot of material, and doing so often, is the easiest and fastest way to improve your reading skills, increase your comprehension of all subjects, and build your vocabulary painlessly. The more you read, the smarter you become—it's as simple as that.

Instead of book reports, this monthly Reading Calendar will be your reading assignment for class. Here's how it works:

1. Read 20 minutes a day, five days a week, for a total of 400 minutes in a month. This amount will increase during the year.
2. Each day, fill in the number of minutes read and have it initialed. <u>Anyone</u> can initial this box, but your parents must agree to trust you and verify that you actually did the reading.
3. At the end of the month, total your number of minutes read on the calendar. Your parent/guardian <u>must</u> sign this calendar before you turn it in. Your calendar will not be accepted without a total and signature. As usual, you may turn in your paper up to two days late with a dropped grade each day.
4. You may read <u>anything</u>—newspapers, magazines, textbooks, novels, short stories, nonfiction books, even comic books with real text. Reading assignments for class also count.
5. What doesn't count? Memorizing lists, studying for tests, comics, looking at pictures, television, movies, personal letters, email, or surfing the web.
6. The assignment is worth 50 points a month.

361–400 min.	= 45–50 pts.	= A
321–360 min.	= 40–44 pts.	= B
281–320 min.	= 35–39 pts.	= C
241–280 min.	= 30–34 pts.	= D
below 240 min.	= 29/less pts.	= F

7. You may also earn extra credit. This is an easy way to boost your grades—simply read more.

   **5 points extra credit for every 100 minutes over the requirement. Max out at 20 points extra credit.

8. Each month, the student in each class period who reads the most minutes wins a prize (stickers, pens, toys, etc.).
9. Cheating: Forging your parent's signature is an automatic zero and may also get you a referral. I may compare the signature to your original course outline or call your parents to confirm that they saw you do the reading. Actually, there's little reason to cheat—reading for 20 minutes a day is easy and painless to accomplish!

students have had two responses to their projects, they aren't as anxious that I provide extensive feedback.

Participation Points

Finally, we come to Participation Points. Over time, I have eliminated lots of things I used to assign 10 or 20 points to. Instead, I give these assignments plus/check/minus credit. I keep these scores on a separate page in my grade book and total them up as a "participation grade" every three to six weeks. Formerly, for example, students would routinely perform poorly on their grammar homework. I would spend hours grading it, most students would earn low grades, and we all felt crummy about it. Now we do grammar practice aloud together, and they receive full/partial/itty bitty credit for completing it. If they need further practice, I assign some as homework; they again get credit for completion, and we review the answers together aloud in class.

Besides grammar, I now use Participation Points for things like bringing books to class, reading during SSR or aloud in whole class readings, and making a contribution to a Socratic Seminar. This year I even took the bold step of not grading their five rough draft poems during our poetry unit; instead, students chose two poems to revise, and I read and evaluated these. I didn't hear a single complaint. You can use participation grading for questionnaires, annotations of texts, grammar practice, note taking, board work you review together, short group presentations, and even in-class study guides. Each year it seems I find something new to grade as Participation Points. The good news is that it doesn't affect the quality of my instruction.

This leads to my final thoughts. To be effective teachers, we need to be happy people. If we're pleased with ourselves, we connect to students more easily and are kinder, gentler individuals. After all, how can we be happy if we're always angry or resentful? Don't feel guilty or selfish, therefore, if you spend less time grading papers or writing "Great idea!" for the ten-thousandth time. Instead, take up dancing, play the flute, pet your cat, take a bath. Both you and your students will be happy you did.

Part II: Standards-Based Grading
by Maria Clinton

Having taught for over 20 years, I often begin my school year by mentioning to the kids, "I'm pretty old, but. . . ." The context of this comment usually has something to do with technology, as in, "I'm pretty old, but I think we should text in correct, standard English." The students laugh, and continue writing "idk" on their quizzes when they don't know an answer. However, having taught for almost half my life causes me to look at the changes taking place in education through a different lens.

When I was in my teacher preparation program and when I was a new teacher, there was no talk of standards. For my first several years, my school and/or department decided what should be taught at each level. Yes, my district happened to have a proficiency exam that all seniors had to pass in order to graduate, but teachers had an amazing level of freedom in deciding the rigor of their own expectations and assignments. While this independence felt invigorating on some level, as a new teacher I received very little guidance about whether I was too thorough or rigorous, or not thorough and rigorous enough. This caused me a great deal of anxiety. How could I know that I was doing a good job? If students failed, was it because I was grading too harshly, or because my instruction was lacking in some way?

Yet when most states in the nation began implementing the Common Core State Standards, I approached them with the same skeptical attitude as many of my peers. After all, what did federal-level bureaucrats know about education? How could they tell me what I should be teaching? Once my school began implementing these standards, however, I found them to be very valuable. As someone who was now a department chair, working with new and pre-service teachers, I saw that the Common Core State Standards gave these new professionals a concrete place to start in planning units and evaluating their students' work.

Now that 46 states have adopted the Common Core State Standards in English, we are beginning to see more movement toward using these standards as a basis for grading. Standards-based grading has already been utilized at the elementary level for many years. My school as a whole is very slowly moving in this direction. Like many teachers, I origi-nally believed that standards-based grading would be too confusing to put on a report card for parents. After reading a great deal, talking with colleagues who have adopted the practice, and participating in in-service programs provided by my district, I believe that standards-based grading, if implemented correctly and explained carefully, has the poten-tial to help us manage our paper loads and deliver truly meaningful feedback to students and their families.

Two years ago, the teachers on my sophomore team decided to implement a form of standards-based grading for our English classes. While the process was hardly a smooth one, the structure allowed us to actually evaluate students on what they had learned. This in turn allowed us to evaluate the effectiveness of our lessons. Somewhat to our surprise, it also significantly cut down on our paper load.

Our structure was simple. During the second semester, we decided to have students write either an in-class essay or response paper every other Friday. The topic would focus on the standards we had been covering during those two weeks of class time. The students were allowed to use any in-class or homework assignment they had completed in the previous two weeks to help them with the essay. With this arrangement, we did not need to collect these assignments as they were completed. Instead, we told the stu-dents that completing these assignments would be very helpful to them once they were assigned their end-of-second-week response papers. For examples of a response paper and one of the preparatory assignments for Hermann Heese's *Siddhartha* (1922), see Tables 10.7 and 10.8.

Not surprisingly, prior to writing the first response paper many students had chosen not to do the homework, simply because we weren't collecting it. What they discovered, however, was that they were completely unprepared for their essay assignment, and they saw other students poring through their completed homework for ideas and information. The next in-class essay was different. Most of my students completed at least some of their assignments during the two-week period and were able to use these completed assignments in writing their essays. Over the semester, the number of students completing their home-work assignments increased, with a predictable increase in the quality of students' response papers. An added bonus was that I didn't have to grade their daily homework in time for stu-dents to write their response papers. I simply graded their "final products"—their response papers. Assessing these papers allowed me to evaluate what content they had learned during the two weeks and how they were progressing toward the standards we had selected in read-ing and writing from the Common Core Standards.

TABLE 10.7 *Siddhartha*

Response Paper 1:

Prompt: Discuss and analyze the setting, mono-myth, and archetypes in part 1 of the novel, and explain how the hero changes.

You Can and Should Use:

- Handout with character list and themes
- Reading guide (mono-myth chart)
- Archetype chart

Advanced papers will also include one or more words from our vocabulary list.

GRADING SCALE:

10—ADVANCED—Advanced writing is persuasive and analytical. The writer offers convincing insights supported by detailed evidence. Advanced writers also demonstrate above grade level mastery of elements of composition such as content, organization, conventions, and style. The writing is insightful and shows effective, consistent control over language.

8—PROFICIENT—Proficient writing is reasonable. Though they are somewhat less precise in their analysis than advanced writers, these writers demonstrate their ability to express their ideas clearly and support their claims with evidence. Proficient writers demonstrate grade level appropriate skill in elements of composition such as content, organization, conventions, and style.

7—PARTIALLY PROFICIENT—Partially proficient writing is plausible, but superficial. These writers often rely on paraphrasing or summarizing rather than analysis. If there is some analysis, it's more implicit and the reader has to make inferences to exact meaning. Partially proficient writers demonstrate some skill in the elements of composition (content, organization, conventions, and style), but there are some surface errors that interfere with the meaning of the piece.

6—DEVELOPING—Developing writing is partial and/or unconvincing. These writers often paraphrase or summarize rather than analyze. If they make an attempt at analysis, the analysis might be slight or misconstrued. The writing may also demonstrate a lack of control over the conventions of composition (content, organization, conventions, and style) and their writing is often marred by errors.

0–5—INSUFFICIENT—Insufficient writing is incomplete and/or incomprehensible. This writing shows some attempt to respond to the prompt, but the writer's assertions are supported with little to no clarity, organization, or support. This writing might be a complete misreading, unacceptably brief, or simply incoherent.

In addition, my students learned some valuable lessons. Students made efforts to improve their organization so they could easily locate their assignments. Students who didn't do homework assignments because they thought they were "stupid" or "pointless" started to do them because we made sure that it was clearly connected to their response paper topics. We emphasized the connections when we explained the homework, and we also put the standard right on the assignment when we typed it up.

This year, we have begun standards-based grading with our freshman curriculum. While our focus has not necessarily been on lightening our paper load, I have found that

TABLE 10.8 *Siddhartha Archetype Analysis*

Archetypes are universal symbols, motifs, or themes that may be found among many different cultures. They recur in the myths of people worldwide. These symbols carry similar meanings for a large portion, if not all, of mankind.

Find three examples of each of the following archetypes from part 1 of *Siddhartha*. Suggest the symbolic meaning, as it might apply to *Siddhartha*, of each archetype.

Archetype	Quote From Text (including page number)	Possible Symbolic Meaning
River		
Tree		
Child		

Ashley Kidder

Maria Clinton

this often happens when I concentrate on grading only the work that demonstrates my students' progress toward achieving the standards.

A recent assignment consisted of students looking over four short writing assignments they had done. As a class, we examined student samples of proficient and non-proficient work. By comparing the samples, the students discovered a major difference between the two was a lack of specific examples in the non-proficient writing. This is exactly what I had been trying to teach them. Their assignment then became to choose one of their own pieces to expand and revise.

Some might argue that, by using the rubric based on the Common Core State Standards, we are "teaching to the test." I don't believe that is true. After collaboratively examining many rubrics, my colleagues and I found that they all value and emphasize the same writing skills that we do as professional educators. The Common Core Standards for writing are simple to read and follow, which is a benefit for our weaker readers and writers. Of course, we are under pressure to improve our test scores, but this is something I rarely mention in class. Our classroom emphasis is on becoming better writers, because, as the standards remind us, these are skills that will be needed for both college and our students' future careers.

Using CCSS-based rubrics, I also find I am purposefully not collecting or grading parts of assignments that aren't specifically related to the reading and writing skills I am addressing. For example, I had students do an "Open Mind" diagram of Melinda, the protagonist of Laurie Halse Anderson's *Speak* (2001). On the first side of the paper, the students had to fill in the outline of Melinda's head with words, images, and quotes that demonstrate what is in Melinda's mind. On the back of the paper, the students had to write a few paragraphs explaining the words, symbols, and quotes they had chosen to put in Melinda's mind. An example of the assignment appears in Table 10.9.

Some of the students spent a great deal of time drawing Melinda's head, giving her hair, eyes, lipstick, and so on. However, they neglected to write their paragraphs with care. On the other hand, some students were very thoughtful when they completed this "Open Mind" assignment. They included words, symbols, and quotes that provided material for their writing. When I graded the assignment, all I graded was the writing. Filling in Melinda's "Open Mind" was a form of pre-writing, just like my sophomores' homework assignments prepared them for their response papers. There was no reason for me to spend

TABLE 10.9   *Open Mind*

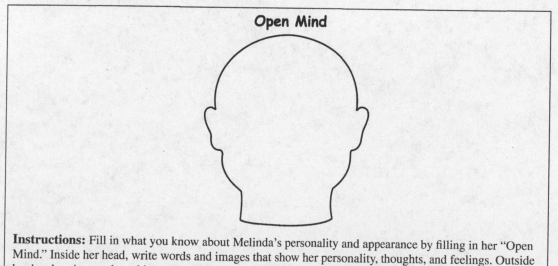

Instructions: Fill in what you know about Melinda's personality and appearance by filling in her "Open Mind." Inside her head, write words and images that show her personality, thoughts, and feelings. Outside her head, write words and images that show her appearance. Use at least two quotes from the novel.

my time grading these "pre-writings." Instead, my time was spent, much more effectively, giving feedback on their writing.

While I am no expert on standards-based grading, I believe that if we structure it correctly, we will only be grading work that relates directly to the standards. At the high school level, I believe that this could help us manage our paper loads much more effectively, allowing us to focus our valuable time on what the students are actually supposed to be learning, rather than scoring class sets of assignments that might be engaging to the students, but have tenuous connections to the actual skills we wish our students to learn.

References and Resources

Anderson, Laurie Halse. *Speak*. New York: Penguin, 2001.

Brown, Clarence, Director. *The Human Comedy*. 1943.

Cisneros, Sandra. *The House on Mango Street*. New York: Vintage, 1984.

Hesse, Hermann. *Siddhartha*. New York: New Directions, 1922.

Homer. *Odyssey*. Translated by Robert Fagles. New York: Penguin Classics, 2006.

Lee, Harper. *To Kill a Mockingbird*. New York: Warner, Inc., 1960.

National Council of Teachers of English. "Rubrics." http://www.ncte.org

Partin, Ronald L. *Classroom Teacher's Survival Guide: Practical Strategies, Management Techniques, and Reproducibles for New and Experienced Teachers*. West Nyack, New York: The Center for Applied Research in Education, 1995.

Robbins, Jerome, and Robert Wise, Directors. *West Side Story*. 1961.

"Rubistar." http://rubistar.4teachers.org/

Schrock, Kathy. "Teacher Helpers: Assessment & Rubric Information." *Kathy Schrock's Guide for Educators*. http://school.discoveryeducation.com/schrockguide/assess.html

Shakespeare, William. *Romeo and Juliet*.

Wiesel, Elie. *Night*. New York: Hill and Wang, 1972.

Index